The Best Test Prepar

MW00666815

AP
Calculus BC Exam

David R. Arterburn, Ph.D.
Associate Professor of Mathematics
New Mexico Tech, Socorro, New Mexico

J.R. Hubbard, Ph.D.
Associate Professor of Mathematics & Computer Science
University of Richmond, Richmond, Virginia

Michael A. Perl
Director of Computer Science Learning Center
Brookhaven College, Farmers Branch, Texas

Research & Education Association
Visit our website at
www.rea.com

Research & Education Association
61 Ethel Road West
Piscataway, New Jersey 08854
E-mail: info@rea.com

The Best Test Preparation for the
AP CALCULUS BC EXAM

Printed in the United States of America

Library of Congress Control Number 2006924440

International Standard Book Number 0-87891-647-4

C06

CONTENTS

PREFACE

This book gives you the tools to prepare effectively for the Advanced Placement Examination in Calculus BC. These tools include a concise subject review and six full-length practice tests. Our review succinctly covers areas considered most relevant to this exam. Each REA practice test contains every type of question you can expect to encounter when you sit for the AP exam. **(Readers should note, however, that the number and types of questions, as well as the length of time allotted for the actual AP exam, can vary slightly from one test administration to another.)** Following each of our tests is an answer key complete with detailed explanations designed to clarify the material for you. By completing all six tests and studying our explanatory material, you will put yourself in a position to master the AP Calculus BC exam.

ABOUT THE TEST

The AP Calculus BC Examination is offered each May at participating schools and multi-school centers throughout the world.

The Advanced Placement Program is designed to allow high school students to pursue college-level studies while attending high school. The participating colleges, in turn, grant credit and/or advanced placement to students who do well on the examinations.

The Advanced Placement Calculus BC course is designed to represent college-level mathematics, and is considerably more extensive than Calculus AB. The full-year course covers the calculus of functions, including such topics as sequences, series, and differential equations, in addition to the topics covered in Calculus AB. The course is intended for students who have a thorough knowledge of analytic geometry and elementary functions, as well as college-preparatory algebra, geometry, and trigonometry. The exam is divided into two sections:

Section I. **Multiple-choice:** Composed of 45 multiple-choice questions, designed to measure the student's abilities in a wide range of mathematical topics. These questions vary in difficulty and complexity. This section consists of two parts. Part A comprises 28 questions, for which a calculator may not be used. Part B contains 17 questions, some of which may require the use of a graphing calculator. One hour and forty-five minutes is allotted for Section I.

Section II. **Free-response:** Designed to demonstrate the student's reasoning aptitude, Section II is composed of six questions—three in Part A (portions of which *require* a graphing calculator) and three in Part B (in which calculator use is *not* permitted). This section involves a more extensive application of calculus and other mathematical principles as compared to the Section I questions. Forty-five minutes is allotted for each part of this section.

USE OF CALCULATORS

The use of graphing calculators is allowed on certain portions of the exam and students are expected to bring their calculators to the exam. Students should be familiar with all the functions of their graphing calculator and adept at using them.

A graphing calculator appropriate for use during the exam should have the capability to:

- plot the graph of a function
- find the zeros of functions
- numerically calculate the derivative of a function
- numerically calculate the value of a definite integral

For a list of acceptable calculators approved for use on the exam and more information regarding the use of calculators, please visit the College Board website.

The practice tests in this book provide calculator-related questions with explanations that include the steps that should be carried out with a calculator. These steps are illustrated after the word *calculator,* where the keystrokes that should be used are listed.

The practice tests in this book incorporate Section II free-response solutions that approximate the content breakdown you will encounter on the AP exam. The overall timing and formatting of the practice tests in this book mirror the actual test; examinees should note, however, that this section is split into two parts on the AP exam. Furthermore, prospective examinees should pay attention to restrictions on calculator use. For details, consult current official College Board materials in print or on the Web at *http://apcentral.collegeboard.com.*

ABOUT THE REVIEW SECTION

This book contains review material that students will find useful as a study aid while preparing for the AP Calculus BC Examination. This review provides information that will most likely appear on the actual test. Included in this section are the following topics:

Elementary Functions — This chapter describes the Properties of Functions, the Properties of Particular Functions, and Limits.

Differential Calculus — This chapter deals with Derivatives and Application of the Derivative.

Integral Calculus — This chapter explains Anti-Derivatives, Applications of Anti-Derivatives, The Law of Exponential Change, Techniques of Integration, The Definite Integral, and Applications of the Integral.

Sequences and Series — This chapter describes the Sequences of Real Numbers and Functions; Convergence, Series of Real Numbers, Series of Functions, and Power Series

Elementary Differential Equations — This chapter deals with First Order, Variable Separable Equations.

SCORING THE TEST

SCORING THE MULTIPLE-CHOICE SECTION

For the multiple-choice section, use this formula to calculate your raw score:

_____ – (_____ × 1/4) = _____ 17

number right — number wrong* — raw score (round to nearest whole #)

* DO NOT INCLUDE UNANSWERED QUESTIONS

SCORING THE FREE-RESPONSE SECTION

For the free-response section, use this formula to calculate your raw score:

_____ + _____ + _____ + _____ + _____ + _____ = _____

problems one through six — raw score

The score for each problem should reflect how completely the question was answered, that is, the solution that was produced and the steps taken. You should gauge at what point a mistake was made, and determine whether any use of calculus or mathematics was incorrect. Each problem is given a score of between 0 and 9 points. More points should be given for correct answers that include all work in the answer explanation, and fewer points should be given for incorrect answers and necessary work that was not written down. It might help to have a teacher or an impartial person knowledgeable in calculus decide on the points to be awarded.

THE COMPOSITE SCORE

To obtain your composite score, use the following method:

1.200 × _____ = _____ (weighted multiple-choice score)

multiple-choice raw score — round to the nearest whole number

NOW ADD:

__________ + __________ = __________

weighted multiple-choice raw score — free-response raw score — composite score

Compare your score with this table to approximate your grade:

AP GRADE	COMPOSITE SCORE
5	78 - 102
4	64 - 77
3	45 - 63
2	30 - 44
1	0 - 29

The overall scores are interpreted as follows: 5-extremely well qualified; 4-well qualified; 3-qualified; 2-possibly qualified; and 1-no recommendation. Most colleges will grant students who earn a 3 or above either college credit or advanced placement. Check with your school guidance office about specific school requirements.

AP Calculus BC

Course Review

CHAPTER 1

ELEMENTARY FUNCTIONS: Algebraic, Exponential, Logarithmic, and Trigonometric

A. PROPERTIES OF FUNCTIONS

Definition: A function is a correspondence between two sets, the domain and the range, such that for each value in the domain there corresponds exactly one value in the range.

A function has three distinct features:

a) the set x which is the domain,

b) the set y which is the co-domain or range,

c) a functional rule, f, that assigns only one element $y \in Y$ to each $x \in X$. We write $y = f(x)$ to denote the functional value y at x.

Consider Figure 1. The "machine" f transforms the domain X, element by element, into the co-domain Y.

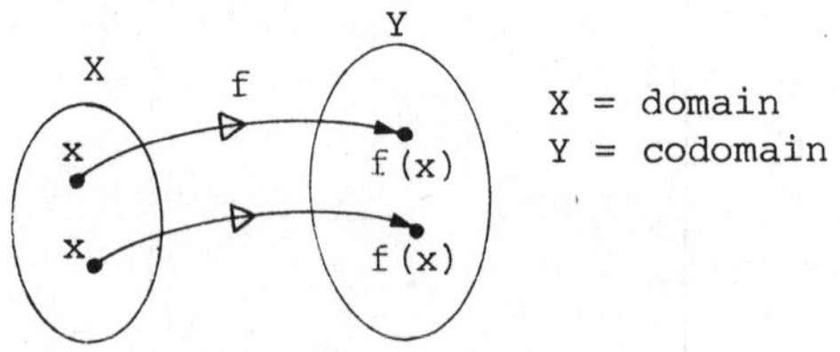

FIGURE 1

■ PARAMETRIC EQUATIONS

If we have an equation $y = f(x)$, and the explicit functional form contains an arbitrary constant called a parameter, then it is called a parametric equation. A function with a parameter represents not one but a family of curves.

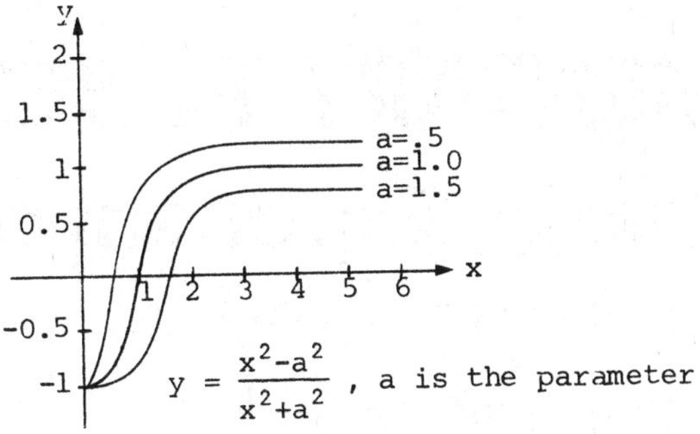

FIGURE 2

Often the equation for a curve is given as two functions of a parameter t, such as

$$X = x(t) \text{ and } Y = y(t).$$

Corresponding values of x and y are calculated by solving for t and substituting.

■ VECTORS

A vector (AB) is denoted $\overrightarrow{AB}$, where B represents the head and A represents the tail. This is illustrated in Figure 3.

The length of a line segment is the magnitude of a vector. If the magnitude and direction of two vectors are the same, then they are equal.

Vectors which can be translated from one position to another without any change in their magnitude or direction are called free vectors.

The unit vector is a vector with a length (magnitude) of one.

The zero vector has a magnitude of zero.

The unit vector, $\vec{i}$, is a vector with magnitude of one in the direction of the x–axis.

The unit vector $\vec{j}$ is a vector with magnitude of one in the direction of the y–axis.

When two vectors are added together, the resultant force of the two vectors produce the same effect as the two combined forces. This is illustrated in Figure 4.

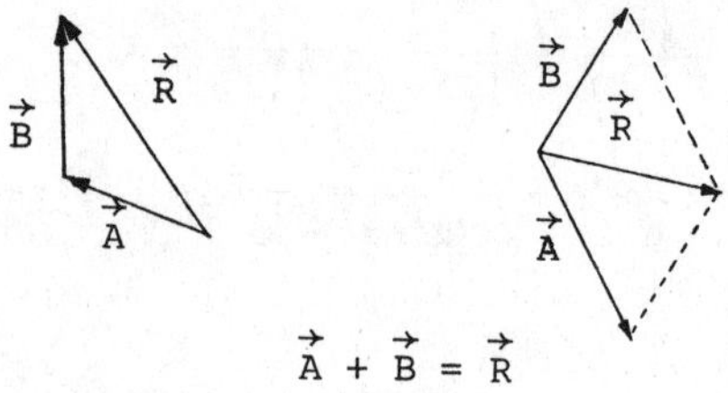

FIGURE 4

In these diagrams, the vector $\vec{R}$ is called the resultant vector.

■ COMBINATION OF FUNCTIONS

Let f and g represent functions, then

a) the sum $(f + g)(x) = f(x) + g(x)$,

b) the difference $(f - g)(x) = f(x) - g(x)$,

c) the product $(fg)(x) = f(x)\, g(x)$,

d) the quotient $\left(\frac{f}{g}\right)(x) = \frac{f(x)}{g(x)}, g(x) \neq 0$,

e) the composite function $(g \circ f)(x) = g(f(x))$ where $f(x)$ must be in the domain of g.

■ GRAPHS OF A FUNCTION

If (x, y) is a point or ordered pair on the coordinate plane R then x is the first coordinate and y is the second coordinate.

To locate an ordered pair on the coordinate plane simply measure the distance of x units along the x-axis, then measure vertically (parallel to the y-axis) y units.

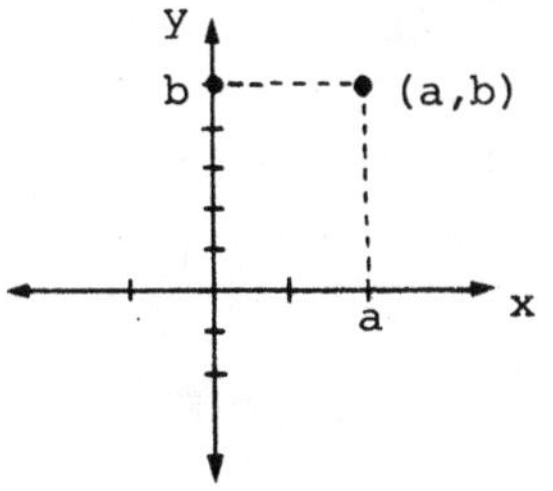

FIGURE 5

This graph illustrates the origin, the x–intercept and the y–intercept.

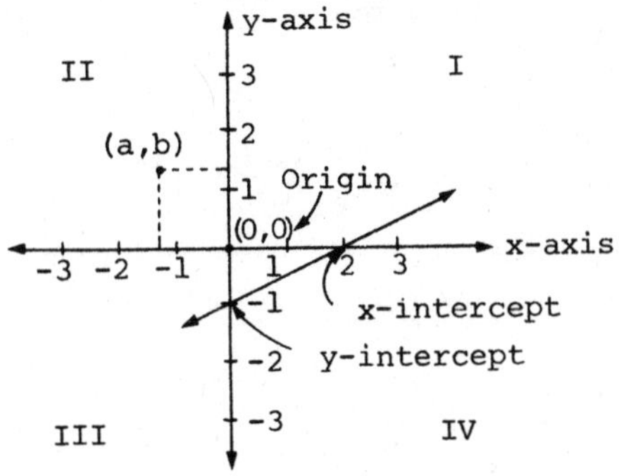

I, II, III, IV are called quadrants in the COORDINATE PLANE.
(*a, b*) is an ordered pair with *x*–coordinate *a* and *y*–coordinate *b*.

FIGURE 6–Cartesian Coordinate System

The following three graphs illustrate symmetry.

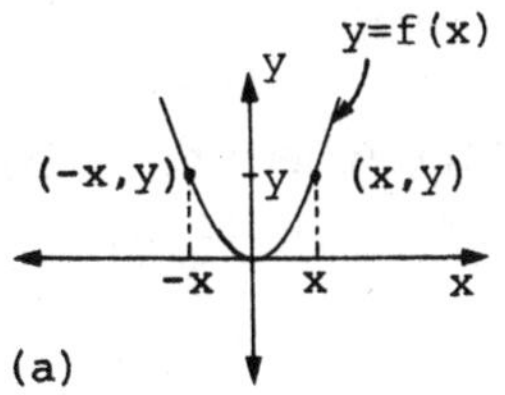

Symmetric about the *y*–axis

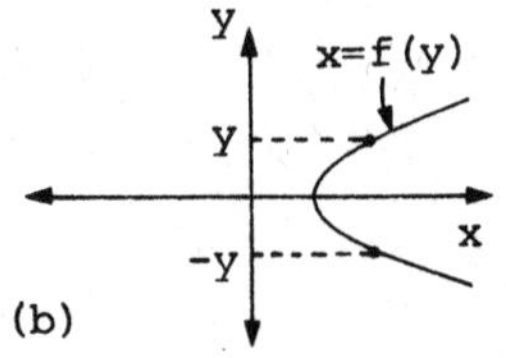

Symmetric about the *x*–axis
Note: This is not a function of *x*.

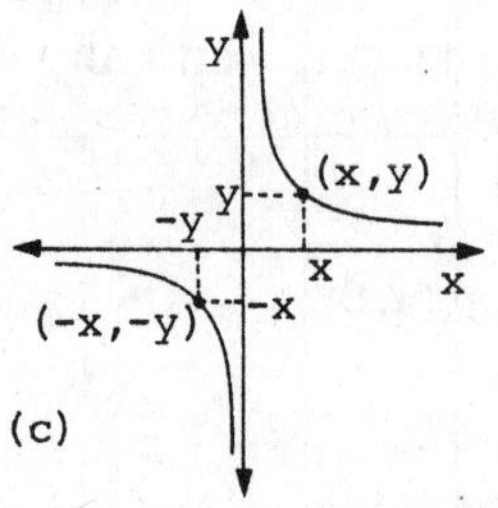

Symmetric about the origin.

FIGURE 7

Another important part of a graph is the asymptote. An asymptote is a line which will never be touched by the curve as it tends toward infinity.

A vertical asymptote is a vertical line $x = a$, such that the functional value $|f(x)|$ grows indefinitely large as x approaches the fixed value a.

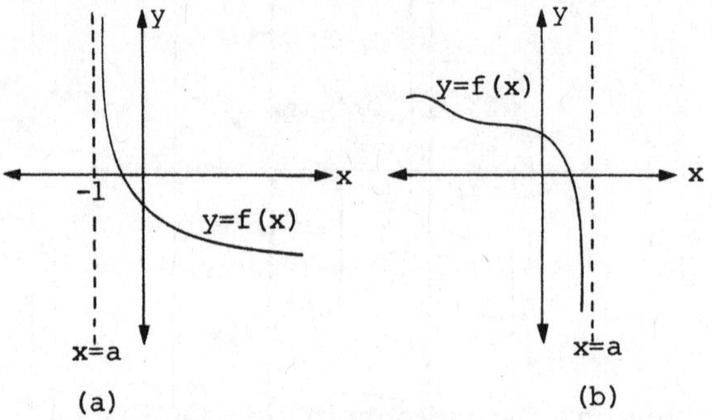

x = *a* is a vertical asymptote for this function

FIGURE 8

The following steps encapsulate the procedure for drawing a graph:

a) Determine the domain and range of the function.

b) Find the intercepts of the graph and plot them.

c) Determine the symmetries of the graph.

d) Locate the vertical asymptotes and plot a few points on the graph near each asymptote.

e) Plot additional points as needed.

■ POLAR COORDINATES

Polar coordinates is a method of representing points in a plane by the use of ordered pairs.

The polar coordinate system consists of an origin (pole), a polar axis and a ray of specific angle.

The polar axis is a line that originates at the origin and extends indefinitely in any given direction.

The position of any point in the plane is determined by its distance from the origin and by the angle that the line makes with the polar axis.

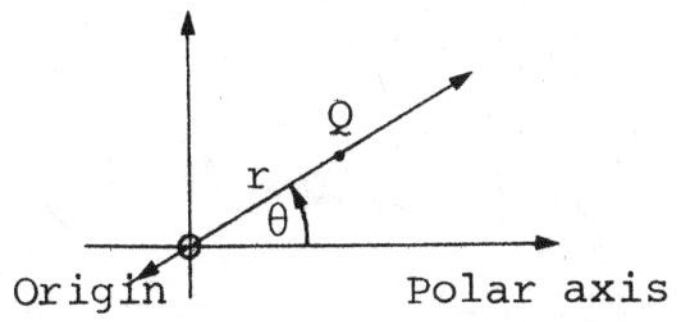

FIGURE 9

The coordinates of the polar coordinate system are (r, θ).

The angle (θ) is positive it if is generated by a counterclockwise rotation of the polar axis, and is negative if it is generated by a clockwise rotation.

The graph of an equation in polar coordinates is a set of all points, each of which has at least one pair of polar coordinates, (r, θ), which satisfies the given equation.

To plot a graph:

1. Construct a table of values of θ and r.
2. Plot these points.
3. Sketch the curve.

■ INVERSE OF A FUNCTION

Assuming that f is a one-to-one function with domain X and range Y, then a function g having domain Y and range X is called the inverse function of f if:

$$f(g(y)) = y \text{ for every } y \in Y \text{ and}$$

$$g(f(x)) = x \text{ for every } x \in X.$$

The inverse of the function f is denoted f^{-1}.

To find the inverse function f^{-1}, you must solve the equation $y = f(x)$ for x in terms of y.

Be careful: This solution must be a function.

■ EVEN AND ODD FUNCTIONS

A function is even if $f(-x) = f(x)$ or

$$f(x) + f(-x) = 2f(x).$$

A function is said to be odd if $f(-x) = -f(x)$ or $f(x) + f(-x) = 0$.

■ ABSOLUTE VALUE

Definition: The absolute value of a real number x is defined as

$$|x| = \begin{cases} x & \text{if } x \geq 0 \\ -x & \text{if } x < 0 \end{cases}$$

For real numbers a and b:

a) $|a| = |-a|$

b) $|ab| = |a| \cdot |b|$

c) $-|a| \leq a \leq |a|$

d) $ab \leq |a||b|$

e) $|a + b|^2 = (a + b)^2$

■ PERIODICITY

A function f with domain X is periodic if there exists a positive real number p such that $f(x + p) = f(x)$ for all $x \in X$.

The smallest number p with this property is called the period of f.

Over any interval of length p, the behavior of a periodic function can be completely described.

■ ZEROES OF A FUNCTION

To locate an ordered pair on the coordinate plane simply measure the distance of x units along the x-axis, then measure vertically (parallel to the y–axis) y units.

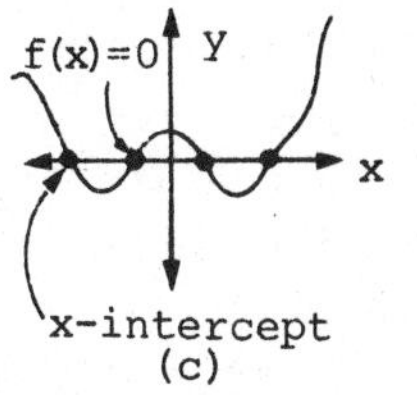

Zeroes of a function
FIGURE 10

B. PROPERTIES OF PARTICULAR FUNCTIONS

In order to graph a trigonometric function, it is necessary to identify the amplitude and the period of the function.

For example, to graph a function of the form

$$y = a \sin (bx + c)$$

$$a = \text{amplitude} \quad \text{and} \quad {}^{2\pi}/_{b} = \text{period.}$$

Let us graph the function $y = 2 \sin(2x + {}^{\pi}/_{4})$. Amplitude = 2, period = ${}^{2\pi}/_{2} = \pi$, phase $\measuredangle = {}^{\pi}/_{8}$.

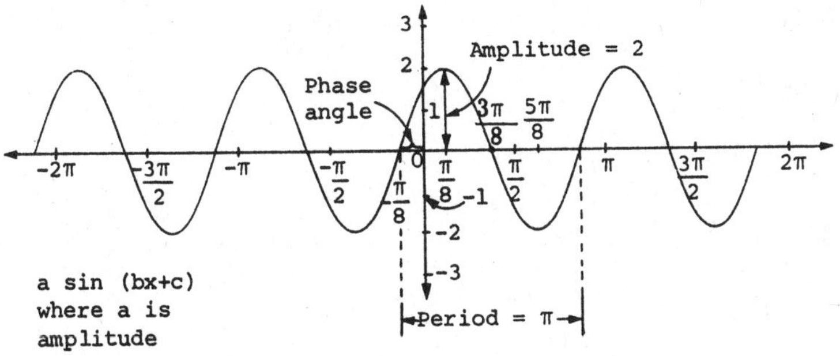

FIGURE 11

The following graphs represent the functions $y = \sin x$ and $y = \cos x$. The amplitude of each is one, while the period of each is 2π.

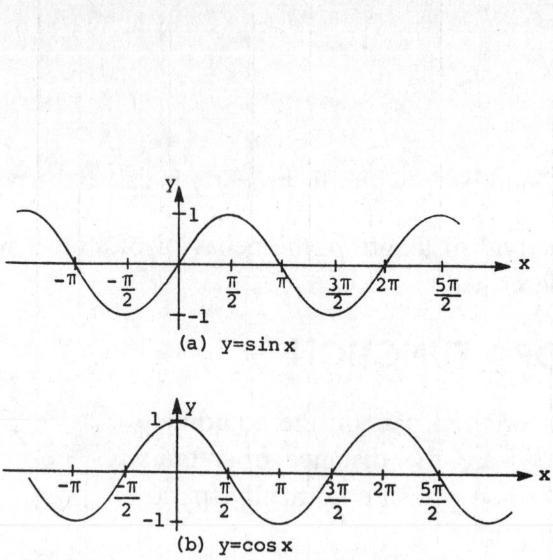

FIGURE 12

■ IDENTITIES AND FORMULAS FOR TRIGONOMETRIC FUNCTIONS

Provided the denominators are not zero, the following relationships exist:

$$\sin t = \frac{1}{\csc t} \qquad \tan t = \frac{\sin t}{\cos t}$$

$$\cos t = \frac{1}{\sec t} \qquad \cot t = \frac{\cos t}{\sin t}$$

$$\tan t = \frac{1}{\cot t}$$

If *PQR* is an angle *t* and *P* has coordinates (*x*, *y*) on the unit circle, then by joining *PR* we get angle *PRQ* = 90° and then we can define all the trigonometric functions in the following way:

sine of *t*, sin t = y

cosine of *t*, cos *t* = x

tangent of *t*, $\tan t = {}^{y}/_{x}$, $x \neq 0$

cotangent of *t*, $\tan t = {}^{x}/_{y}$, $y \neq 0$

secant of *t*, $\sec t = {}^{1}/_{x}$, $x \neq 0$

cosecant of *t*, $\csc t = {}^{1}/_{y}$, $y \neq 0$.

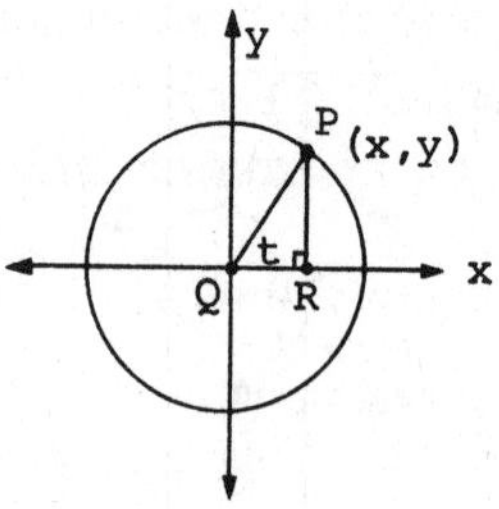

FIGURE 13

$$\cos^2 x + \sin^2 x = 1$$

Therefore,

$$\sec^2 = 1 + \tan^2\theta, \quad \csc^2\theta = 1 + \cot^2\theta$$

$$\sin(A + B) = \sin A \cos B + \cos A \sin B$$

$$\sin(A - B) = \sin A \cos B - \cos A \sin B$$

$$\cos(A + B) = \cos A \cos B - \sin A \sin B$$

$$\cos(A - B) = \cos A \cos B + \sin A \sin B$$

$$\sin^2\theta = \frac{1 - \cos 2\theta}{2}$$

$$\cos^2\theta = \frac{1 + \cos 2\theta}{2}$$

Sine law: $$\frac{a}{\sin\theta} = \frac{b}{\sin\phi} = \frac{c}{\sin\psi}$$

Cosine law: $$a^2 = b^2 + c^2 - 2bc\cos\theta$$

$$b^2 = c^2 + a^2 - 2ca\cos\phi$$

$$c^2 = a^2 + b^2 - 2ab\cos\psi$$

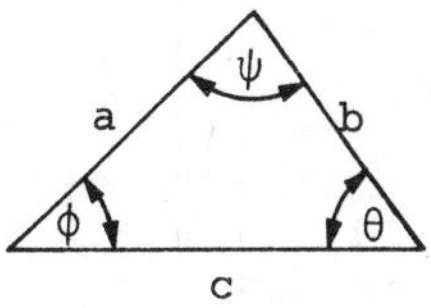

FIGURE 14

■ EXPONENTIAL AND LOGARITHMIC FUNCTIONS

If f is a nonconstant function that is continuous and satisfies the functional equation $f(x + y) = f(x) \cdot f(y)$, then $f(x) = a^x$ for some constant a. That is, f is an exponential function.

Consider the exponential function a^x, $a > 0$ and the logarithmic function $\log_a x$, $a > 0$. Then a^x is defined for all $x \in R$, and $\log_a x$ is defined only for positive $x \in$ R.

These functions are inverses of each other,

$$_a\log_a x = x; \log_a(a^y) = y.$$

Let a^x, $a > 0$ be an exponential function. Then for any real numbers x and y

a) $a^x \cdot a^y = a^{x+y}$

b) $(a^x)^y = a^{xy}$

Let $\log_a x$, $a > 0$ be a logarithmic function. Then for any positive real numbers x and y

a) $\log_a(xy) = \log_a(x) + \log_a(y)$

b) $\log_a(x^y) = y \log_a(x)$

C. LIMITS

Definition:

$$\lim_{t \to c} F(t) = L$$

[read, the limit of $F(t)$ as t approaches c is the number L] if: Given any radius $\varepsilon > 0$ about L, there exists a radius $\delta > 0$ about c such that for all t

$$0 < |t - c| < \delta \text{ implies } |F(t) - L| < \varepsilon$$

The following are important properties of limits: Consider

$$\lim_{x \to a} f(x) = L \text{ and } \lim_{x \to a} g(x) = K, \text{ then}$$

A) Uniqueness – If $\lim_{x \to a} f(x)$ exists then it is unique.

B) $\lim_{x \to a} [f(x) + g(x)] = \lim_{x \to a} f(x) + \lim_{x \to a} g(x) = L + K$

C) $\lim_{x \to a} [f(x) - g(x)] = \lim_{x \to a} f(x) - \lim_{x \to a} g(x) = L - K$

D) $\lim_{x \to a} [f(x) \cdot g(x)] = \lim_{x \to a} f(x) \cdot \lim_{x \to a} g(x) = L \cdot K$

E) $\lim_{x \to a} \dfrac{f(x)}{g(x)} = \dfrac{\lim_{x \to a} f(x)}{\lim_{x \to a} g(x)} = \dfrac{L}{K}$ provided $K \neq 0$

■ SPECIAL LIMITS

A) $\lim_{x \to 0} \frac{\sin x}{x} = 1,$

B) $\lim_{n \to \infty} \left(1 + \frac{1}{n}\right)^n = e,$

Some nonexistent limits which are frequently encountered are:

A) $\lim_{x \to 0} \frac{1}{x^2}$, as x approaches zero, x^2 gets very small and also becomes zero therefore $^1/_0$ is undefined and the limit does not exist.

B) $\lim_{x \to 0} \frac{|x|}{x}$ does not exist.

■ CONTINUITY

A function f is continuous at a point a if

$$\lim_{x \to a} f(x) = f(a).$$

This implies that three conditions are satisfied:

A) $f(a)$ exists, that is, f is defined at a.

B) $\lim_{x \to a} f(x)$ exists, and

C) the two numbers are equal.

To test continuity at a point $x = a$ we test whether

$$\lim_{x \to a^+} M(x) = \lim_{x \to a^-} M(x) = M(a)$$

■ THEOREMS ON CONTINUITY

A) A function defined in a closed interval $[a, b]$ is continuous in $[a, b]$ if and only if it is continuous in the open interval (a, b), as well as continuous from the right at "a" and from the left at "b."

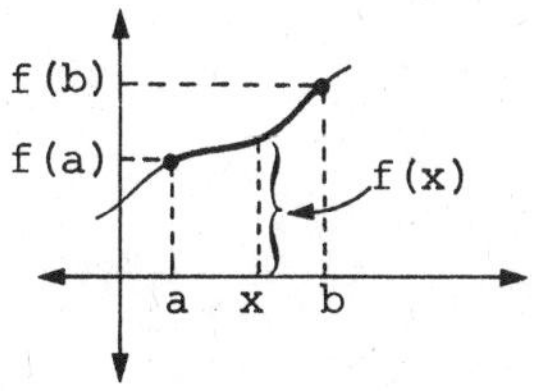

FIGURE 15

B) If f and g are continuous functions at a,

then so are the functions $f + g, f - g, fg$ and f/g where $g(a) \neq 0$.

C) If $\lim_{x \to a} g(x) = b$ and f is continuous at b,

$$\lim_{x \to a} f(g(x)) = f(b) = f[\lim_{x \to a} g(x)].$$

D) If g is continuous at a and f is continuous at $b = g(a)$, then

$$\lim_{x \to a} f(g(x)) = f[\lim_{x \to a} g(x)] = f(g(a)).$$

E) Intermediate Value Theorem. If f is continuous on a closed interval $[a, b]$ and if $f(a) \neq f(b)$, then f takes on every value between $f(a)$ and $f(b)$ in the interval $[a, b]$.

CHAPTER 2

DIFFERENTIAL CALCULUS

A. THE DERIVATIVE

■ THE DEFINITION AND Δ-METHOD

The derivative of a function expresses its rate of change with respect to an independent variable. The derivative is also the slope of the tangent line to the curve.

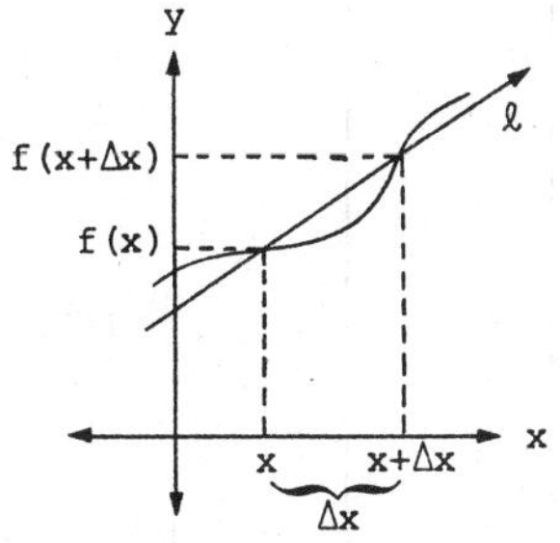

FIGURE 16

Consider the graph of the function f in Figure 16. Choosing a point x and a point $x + \Delta x$ (where Δx denotes a small distance on the x–axis) we can obtain both $f(x)$ and $f(x + \Delta x)$. Drawing a tangent line, l, of the curve through the points $f(x)$ and $f(x + \Delta x)$, we can measure the rate of change of this line. As we let the distance, Δx, approach zero, then

$$\lim_{\Delta x \to 0} \frac{f(x + \Delta x) - f(x)}{\Delta x}$$

becomes the instantaneous rate of change of the function or the derivative.

We denote the derivative of the function f to be f'. So we have

$$f'(x) = \lim_{\Delta x \to 0} \frac{f(x+\Delta x) - f(x)}{\Delta x}$$

If $y = f(x)$, some common notations for the derivative are

$$y' = f'(x)$$

$$\frac{dy}{dx} = f'(x)$$

$$D_x y = f'(x) \text{ or } Df = f'$$

■ RULES FOR FINDING DERIVATIVES

General Rule:

A) If f is a constant function, $f(x) = c$, then $f'(x) = 0$.

B) If $f(x) = x$, then $f'(x) = 1$.

C) If f is differentiable, then $(cf(x))' = cf'(x)$

D) Power Rule:

If $f(x) = x^n$, $n \in Z$, then

$f'(x) = nx^{n-1}$; if $n <= 0$ then x^n is not defined at $x = 0$.

E) If f and g are differentiable on the interval (a, b) then:

a) $(f + g)'(x) = f'(x) + g'(x)$

b) Product Rule:

$(fg)'(x) = f(x)g'(x) + g(x)f'(x)$

Example:

Find $f'(x)$ if $f(x) = (x^3 + 1)(2x^2 + 8x - 5)$.

$$\begin{aligned} f'(x) &= (x^3+1)(4x+8) + (2x^2+8x-5)(3x^2) \\ &= 4x^4 + 8x^3 + 4x + 8 + 6x^4 + 24x^3 - 15x^2 \\ &= 10x^4 + 32x^3 - 15x^2 + 4x + 8 \end{aligned}$$

c) Quotient Rule:

$$\left(\frac{f'}{g}\right)(x) = \frac{g(x)f'(x) - f(x)g'(x)}{[g(x)]^2}$$

Example:

Find $f'(x)$ if $f(x) = \dfrac{3x^2 - x + 2}{4x^2 + 5}$

$$f'(x) = \frac{-(3x^2 - x + 2)(8x) + (4x^2 + 5)\ (6x - 1)}{(4x^2 + 5)^2}$$

$$= \frac{-(24x^3 - 8x^2 + 16x) + (24x^3 - 4x^2 + 30x - 5)}{(4x^2 + 5)^2}$$

$$= \frac{4x^2 + 14x - 5}{(4x^2 + 5)^2}$$

F) If $f(x) = x^{m/n}$, then

$$f'(x) = \frac{m}{n}\, x^{\frac{m}{n} - 1}$$

where $m, n \in Z$ and $n \neq 0$.

G) Polynomials. If $f(x) = (a_0 + a_1x + a_2x^2 + \ldots + a_nx^n)$ then

$$f'(x) = a_1 + 2a_2x + 3a_3x^2 + \ldots + na_nx^{n-1}.$$

This employs the power rule and rules concerning constants.

■ THE CHAIN RULE

Chain Rule: Let $f(u)$ be a composite function, where $u = g(x)$. Then $f'(u) = f'(u)\ g'(x)$ or if $y = f(u)$ and $u = g(x)$ then $D_xy = (D_uy)(D_xu) = f'(u)g'(x)$.

Example:

Find the derivative of: $y = (2x^3 - 5x^2 + 4)^5$.

$$D_x = \frac{d}{dx}.$$

This problem can be solved by simply applying the theorem for $d(u^n)$.

However, to illustrate the use of the chain rule, make the following substitutions:

$$y = u^5 \quad \text{where } u = 2x^3 - 5x^2 + 4$$

Therefore, from the chain rule,

$$D_x y = D_u y \cdot D_x u = 5u^4 (6x^2 - 10x)$$
$$= 5(2x^3 - 5x^2 + 4)^4 (6x^2 - 10x).$$

■ IMPLICIT DIFFERENTIATION

An implicit function of x and y is a function in which one of the variables is not directly expressed in terms of the other. If these variables are not easily or practically separable, we can still differentiate the expression.

Apply the normal rules of differentiation such as the product rule, the power rule, etc. Remember also the chain rule which states

$$\frac{du}{dx} \times \frac{dx}{dt} = \frac{du}{dt}.$$

Once the rules have been properly applied we will be left with, as in the example of x and y, some factors of $\frac{dy}{dx}$.

We can then algebraically solve for the derivative $\frac{dy}{dx}$ and obtain the desired result.

Example:

Find y' in terms of x and y, using implicit differentiation, where

$$y' = \frac{dy}{dx},$$

in the expression:

$$y^3 + 3xy + x^3 - 5 = 0.$$

The derivative of y^3 is $3y^2y'$. The term $3xy$ must be treated as a product. The derivative of $3xy$ is $3xy' + 3y$. The derivative of x^3 is $3x^2$. The derivative of -5 is 0. Therefore,

$$3y^2y' + 3xy' + 3y + 3x^2 = 0.$$

We can now solve for y':

$$y' = -\frac{y + x^2}{y^2 + x}.$$

■ TRIGONOMETRIC DIFFERENTIATION

The three most basic trigonometric derivatives are:

$$\frac{d}{dx}(\sin x) = \cos x,$$

$$\frac{d}{dx}(\cos x) = -\sin x,$$

$$\frac{d}{dx}(\tan x) = \sec^2 x.$$

Given any trigonometric function, it can be differentiated by applying these basics in combination with the general rules for differentiating algebraic expressions.

The following will be most useful if committed to memory:

$D_x \sin u = \cos u \, D_x u$

$D_x \cos u = -\sin u \, D_x u$

$D_x \tan u = \sec^2 u \, D_x u$

$D_x \sec u = \tan u \sec u \, D_x u$

$D_x \cot u = -\csc^2 u \, D_x u$

$D_x \csc u = -\csc u \cot u \, D_x u$

■ INVERSE TRIGONOMETRIC DIFFERENTIATION

Inverse trigonometric functions may be sometimes handled by inverting the expression and applying rules for the direct trigonometric functions.

For example: $y = \sin^{-1} x$

$$D_x y = D_x \sin^{-1} x = \frac{1}{\cos y} = \frac{1}{\sqrt{1 - x^2}}, \quad |x| < 1.$$

Here are the derivatives for the inverse trigonometric functions which can be found in a manner similar to the above function:

$$D_x \sin^{-1} u = \frac{1}{\sqrt{1-u^2}} D_x u , \qquad |u| < 1$$

$$D_x \cos^{-1} u = \frac{-1}{\sqrt{1-u^2}} D_x u , \quad |u| < 1$$

$$D_x \tan^{-1} u = \frac{1}{1+u^2} D_x u , \qquad \text{where } u = f(x) \text{ differentiable}$$

$$D_x \sec^{-1} u = \frac{1}{|u|\sqrt{u^2-1}} D_x u , \quad u = f(x),\ |f(x)| > 1$$

$$D_x \cot^{-1} u = \frac{-1}{1+u^2} D_x u , \qquad u = f(x) \text{ differentiable}$$

$$D_x \csc^{-1} u = \frac{-1}{|u|\sqrt{u^2-1}} D_x u , \quad u = f(x),\ |f(x)| > 1$$

■ HIGH ORDER DERIVATIVES

The derivative of any function is also a legitimate function which we can differentiate. The second derivative can be obtained by:

$$\frac{d}{dx}\left[\frac{d}{dx} u\right] = \frac{d^2}{dx^2} u = u'' = D^2 u ,$$

where $u = g(x)$ is differentiable.

The general formula for higher orders and the nth derivative of u is,

$$\underbrace{\frac{d}{dx}\frac{d}{dx}\cdots\frac{d}{dx}}_{n \text{ times}} u = \frac{d^{(n)}}{dx^n} u = u^{(n)} = D_x^{(n)} u .$$

The rules for first order derivatives apply at each stage of higher order differentiation (e.g., sums, products, chain rule).

A function which satisfies the condition that its nth derivative is zero, is the general polynomial

$$p_{n-1}(x) = a_{n-1} x^{n-1} + a_{n-2} x^{n-2} + \ldots + a_0 .$$

■ DERIVATIVES OF VECTOR FUNCTIONS

A) Continuity

Let $f(x)$ be a function defined for all values of x near $t = t_0$ as well as at $t = t_0$. Then the function $f(x)$ is said to be continuous at t_0 if

$$\lim_{t \to t_0} f(t) = f(t_0)$$

or, equivalently,

$$\lim_{t \to t_0} f(t) = f(t_0)$$

if and only if for all $\varepsilon > 0$, there exists a $\delta > 0$, such that $|f(t) - f(t_0)| < \varepsilon$, if $|t - t_0| < \delta$.

B) Derivative

The derivative of the vector valued function $V(t)$ with respect to $t \in R$ is defined as the limit

$$\frac{dV(t)}{dt} = \lim_{\Delta t \to 0} \frac{V(t + \Delta t) - V(t)}{\Delta t}.$$

If a vector is expressed in terms of its components along the fixed coordinate axes,

$$V = V_1(t)i + V_2(t)j + V_3(t)k,$$

there follows

$$\frac{dV}{dt} = \frac{dV_1}{dt} i + \frac{dV_2}{dt} j + \frac{dV_3}{dt} k.$$

For the derivative of a product involving two or more vectors the following formulae are used:

$$\frac{d}{dt}(A \cdot B) = A \cdot \frac{dB}{dt} + \frac{dA}{dt} \cdot B$$

$$\frac{d}{dt}(A \times B) = A \times \frac{dB}{dt} + \frac{dA}{dt} \times B$$

$$\frac{d}{dt}(A \cdot B \times C) = \frac{dA}{dt} \cdot (B \times C) + A \cdot \left(\frac{dB}{dt} \times C\right) + A \cdot \left(B \times \frac{dC}{dt}\right).$$

■ PARAMETRIC FORMULA FOR $^{dy}/_{dx}$

According to the chain rule,

$$\frac{dy}{dt} = \frac{dy}{dx} \cdot \frac{dx}{dt}.$$

Since $\frac{dx}{dt} \neq 0$, we can divide through by $\frac{dx}{dt}$ to solve for $\frac{dy}{dx}$. We then obtain the equation

$$\frac{dy}{dx} = \frac{dy}{dt} \div \frac{dx}{dt}.$$

Example:

Find $\frac{dy}{dt}$ from

$$y = x^3 - 3x^2 + 5x - 4,$$

where $x = t^2 + t$.

From these equations, we find

$$\frac{dy}{dx} = 3x^2 - 6x + 5$$

$$= 3(t^2 + t)^2 - 6(t^2 + t) + 5,$$

$$\frac{dx}{dt} = 2t + 1.$$

Since

$$\frac{dy}{dt} = \frac{dy}{dx} \frac{dx}{dt}$$

from the chain rule,

$$\frac{dy}{dt} = [3(t^2 + t)^2 - 6(t^2 + t) + 5]\,(2t + 1).$$

We can also first substitute the value of x in terms of t into the equation for y. We then have:

$$y = (t^2 + t)^3 - 3(t^2 + t)^2 + 5(t^2 + t) - 4.$$

When we differentiate this with respect to t, we obtain:

$$\frac{dy}{dt} = 3(t^2 + t)^2\,(2t + 1) - 6(t^2 + t)(2t + 1) + 5(2t + 1)$$

$$= [3(t^2 + t)^2 - 6(t^2 + t) + 5]\,(2t + 1),$$

which agrees with the previous answer.

The first method using the chain rule, however, often results in the simpler solution when dealing with problems involving parametric equations.

■ EXPONENTIAL AND LOGARITHMIC DIFFERENTIATION

The exponential function e^x has the simplest of all derivatives. Its derivative is itself.

$$\frac{d}{dx}e^x = e^x \text{ and } \frac{d}{dx}e^u = e^u\frac{du}{dx}$$

Since the natural logarithmic function is the inverse of $y = e^x$ and $\ln e = 1$, it follows that

$$\frac{d}{dx}\ln y = \frac{1}{y}\frac{dy}{dx} \text{ and } \frac{d}{dx}\ln u = \frac{1}{u}\frac{du}{dx}$$

If x is any real number and a is any positive real number, then

$$a^x = e^{x \ln a}$$

From this definition we obtain the following:

a) $\frac{d}{dx}a^x = a^x \ln a$ and $\frac{d}{dx}a^u = a^u \ln a \frac{du}{dx}$

b) $\frac{d}{dx}(\log_a x) = \frac{1}{x \ln a}$ and $\frac{d}{dx}\log_a |u| = \frac{1}{u \ln a}\frac{du}{dx}$

Sometimes it is useful to take the logs of a function and then differentiate since the computation becomes easier (as in the case of a product).

Steps in Logarithmic Differentiation

1.	$y = f(x)$	given
2.	$\ln y = \ln f(x)$	take logs and simplify
3.	$D_x(\ln y) = D_x(\ln f(x))$	differentiate implicitly
4.	$^1/_y D_x y = D_x(\ln f(x))$	
5.	$D_x y = f(x)D_x(\ln f(x))$	multiply by $y = f(x)$

To complete the solution it is necessary to differentiate ln $f(x)$. If $f(x) < 0$ for some x then step 2 is invalid and we should replace step 1 by $|y| = |f(x)|$, and then proceed.

Example:

$$y = (x+5)(x^4+1)$$

$$\ln y = \ln[(x+5)(x^4+1)] = \ln(x+5) + \ln(x^4+1)$$

$$\frac{d}{dx}\ln y = \frac{d}{dx}\ln(x+5) + \frac{d}{dx}\ln(x^4+1)$$

$$\frac{1}{y}\frac{dy}{dx} = \frac{1}{x+5} + \frac{4x^3}{x^4+1}$$

$$\frac{dy}{dx} = (x+5)(x^4+1)\left[\frac{1}{x+5} + \frac{4x^3}{x^4+1}\right]$$

$$= (x^4+1) + 4x^3(x+5)$$

This is the same result as obtained by using the product rule.

■ THE MEAN VALUE THEOREM

If f is continuous on $[a, b]$ and has a derivative at every point in the interval (a, b), then there is at least one number c in (a, b) such that

$$f'(c) = \frac{f(b) - f(a)}{b - a}$$

Notice in Figure 17 that the secant has slope

$$\frac{f(b) - f(a)}{b - a}$$

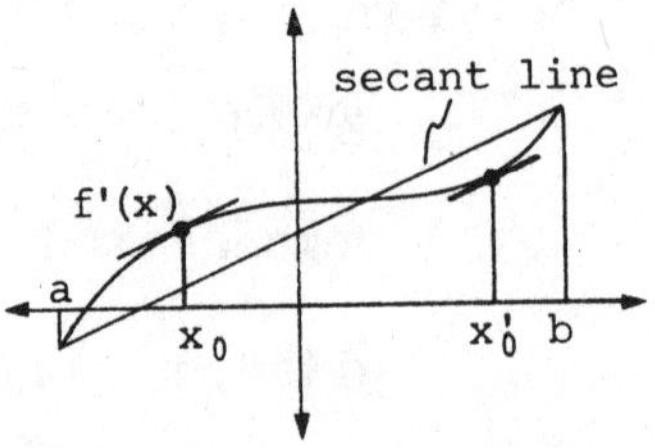

FIGURE 17

and $f'(x)$ has slope of the tangent to the point $(x, f(x))$. For some x_0 in (a, b) these slopes are equal.

Example:

If $f(x) = 3x^2 - x + 1$, find the point x_0 at which $f'(x)$ assumes its mean value in the interval [2, 4].

Recall the mean value theorem. Given a function $f(x)$ which is continuous in $[a, b]$ and differentiable in (a, b), there exists a point x_0 where $a < x_0 < b$ such that:

$$\frac{f(b) - f(a)}{b - a} = f'(x_0),$$

where x_0 is the mean point in the interval.

In our problem, $3x^2 - x + 1$ is continuous, and the derivative exists in the interval (2, 4). We have:

$$\frac{f(4) - f(2)}{4 - 2} = \frac{[3(4)^2 - 4 + 1] - [3(2)^2 - 2 + 1]}{4 - 2}$$

$$= f'(x_0),$$

or

$$\frac{45 - 11}{2} = 17 = f'(x_0) = 6x_0 - 1$$

$$6x_0 = 18$$

$$x_0 = 3.$$

$x_0 = 3$ is the point where $f'(x)$ assumes its mean value.

■ THEOREMS OF DIFFERENTIABLE FUNCTIONS

A) If $f(x)$ is differentiable at x_0, it is continuous there.

B) If $f(x)$ is continuous on the closed interval $[a, b]$, then there is a point $x' \in [a, b]$ for which

$$f(x') < f(x) \; (x : x \in [a, b])$$

C) If $f(x)$ is continuous on the closed interval $[a, b]$, then there is a point $x.$ in $[a, b]$ for which

$$f(x_0) \geq f(x) \; (x : x \in [a, b])$$

D) If $f(x)$ is an increasing function on an interval, then at each point x_0, where $f(x)$ is differentiable we have

$$f'(x_0) \geq 0$$

E) If $f(x)$ is strictly increasing on an interval, and suppose also that $f'(x_0) > 0$ for some x_0 in the interval, then the inverse function $f^{-1}(x)$ if it exists, is differentiable at the point $y_0 = f(x_0)$.

F) Chain Rule: If $f(x)$ is differentiable on the interval $[a, b]$, and $g(x)$ is a differentiable function in the range of f, then the composite function $h = g \circ f$ $(h(x) = g\,[f(x)]$ is also differentiable on $[a, b]$.

G) Suppose that $f(x)$, $g(x)$ are differentiable on the closed interval $[a, b]$ and that $f'(x) = g'(x)$ for all $x \in [a, b]$, then there is a constant c such that $f(x) = g(x) + C$.

H) Rolle's Theorem

If $f(x)$ is continuous on $[a, b]$, differentiable on (a, b), and $f(a) = f(b)$, then there is a point δ in (a, b) such that $f'(\delta) = 0$.

I) Mean Value Theorem

a) f is continuous on $[a, b]$

b) f is differentiable on (a, b) then there exists some point $\delta \in (a, b)$, such that

$$f'(\delta) = \frac{f(b) - f(a)}{b - a}.$$

■ L'HÔPITAL'S RULE

An application of the Mean Value Theorem is in the evaluation of

$$\lim_{x \to a} \frac{f(x)}{g(x)} \text{ where } f(a) = 0 \text{ and } g(a) = 0.$$

L'Hôpital's Rule states that if the

$$\lim_{x \to a} \frac{f(x)}{g(x)}$$

is an indeterminate form (i.e., $^0/_0$ or $^\infty/_\infty$), then we can differentiate the numerator and the denominator separately and arrive at an expression that has the same limit as the original problem.

Thus,

$$\lim_{x\to a}\frac{f(x)}{g(x)}=\lim_{x\to a}\frac{f'(x)}{g'(x)}$$

In general, if $f(x)$ and $g(x)$ have properties

1) $f(a)=g(a)=0$

2) $f^{(k)}(a)=g^{(k)}(a)=0$ for $k=1, 2, \ldots n;$ but

3) $f^{(n+1)}(a)$ or $g^{(n+1)}(a)$ is not equal to zero, then

$$\lim_{x\to a}\frac{f(x)}{g(x)}=\frac{f^{(n+1)}(x)}{g^{(n+1)}(x)}$$

B. APPLICATION OF THE DERIVATIVE

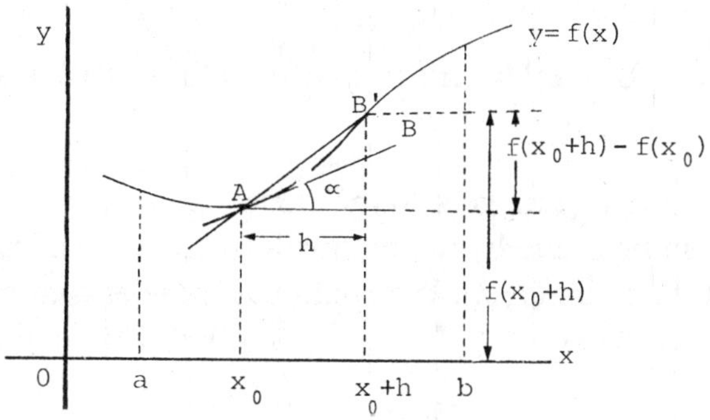

Graphical Interpretation of the derivative.

FIGURE 18

Graphically the derivative represents the slope of the tangent line *AB* to the function at the point $(x_0, f(x_0))$.

■ TANGENTS AND NORMALS

Tangents

A line which is tangent to a curve at a point "*a*", must have the same slope as the curve. That is, the slope of the tangent is simply

$$m=\lim_{h\to 0}\frac{f(a+h)-f(a)}{h}$$

Therefore, if we find the derivative of a curve and evaluate for a specific point, we obtain the slope of the curve and the tangent line to the curve at that point.

A curve is said to have a vertical tangent at a point (a, f(a)) if f is continuous at a and

$$\lim_{x \to a} |f'(x)| = \infty.$$

Normals

A line normal to a curve at a point must have a slope perpendicular to the slope of the tangent line. If $f'(x) \neq 0$ then the equation for the normal line at a point (x_0, y_0) is

$$y - y_0 = \frac{-1}{f'(x_0)}(x - x_0).$$

Example:

Find the slope of the tangent line to the ellipse $4x2 + 9y^2 = 40$ at the point (1, 2).

The slope of the line tangent to the curve $4x^2 + 9y^2 = 40$ is the slope of the curve and can be found by taking the derivative, $\frac{dy}{dx}$ of the function and evaluating it at the point (1, 2). We could solve the equation for y and then find y'. It is easier, however, to find y' by implicit differentiation. If

$$4x^2 + 9y^2 = 40,$$

then

$$8x + 18y(y') = 0.$$

$$18y(y') = -8x$$

$$y' = \frac{-8x}{18y} = \frac{-4x}{9y}.$$

At the point (1,2), x =1 and y = 2. Therefore, substituting these points into $y' = \frac{-4x}{9y}$, we obtain:

$$y' = \frac{-4(1)}{9(2)} = -\frac{2}{9}$$

The slope is $-^2/_9$.

■ MINIMUM AND MAXIMUM VALUES

If a function f is defined on an interval I, then

A) f is increasing on I if $f(x_1) < f(x_2)$ whenever x_1, x_2 are in I and $x_1 < x_2$.

B) f is decreasing on I if $f(x_1) > f(x_2)$ whenever $x_1 < x_2$ in I.

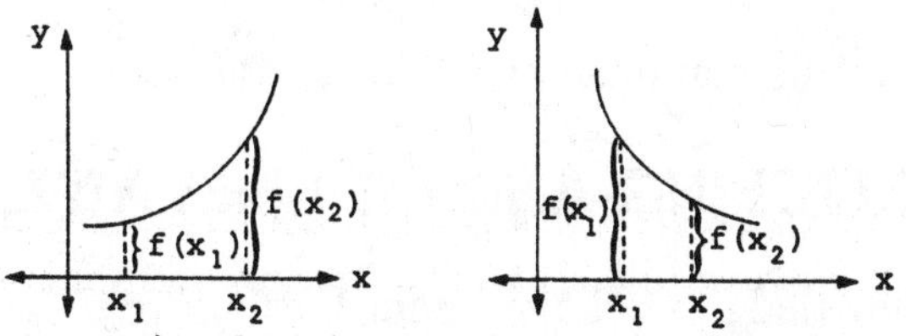

Increasing function   Decreasing function

FIGURE 19

C) f is constant if $f(x_1) = f(x_2)$ for every x_1, x_2 in I.

Suppose f is defined on an open interval I and c is a number in I then,

a) $f(c)$ is a local maximum value if $f(x) \leq f(c)$ for all x in I.

b) $f(c)$ is a local minimum value of $f(x) \geq f(c)$ for all x in I.

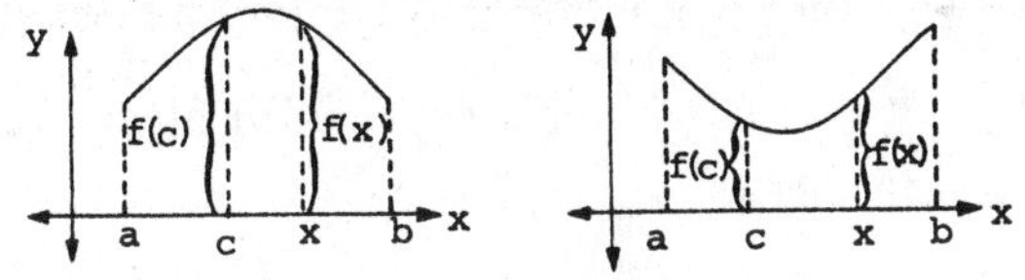

Maximum value f(c)   Minimum value f(c)

Fig. 6.5

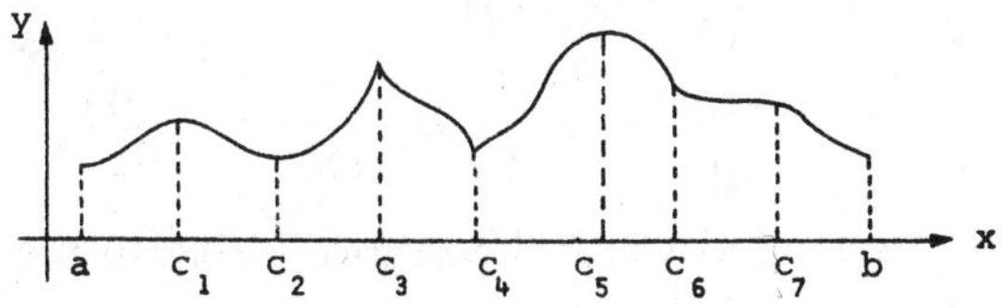

Fig. 6.6

FIGURE 20

Solving Maxima and Minima Problems

Step 1. Determine which variable is to be maximized or minimized (i.e., the dependent variable y).

Step 2. Find the independent variable x.

Step 3. Write an equation involving x and y. All other variables can be eliminated by substitution.

Step 4. Differentiate with respect to the independent variable.

Step 5. Set the derivative equal to zero to obtain critical values.

Step 6. Determine maxima and minima.

■ CURVE SKETCHING AND THE DERIVATIVE TESTS

Using the knowledge we have about local extrema and the following properties of the first and second derivatives of a function, we can gain a better understanding of the graphs (and thereby the nature) of a given function.

A function is said to be smooth on an interval (a, b) if both f' and f'' exist for all $x \in (a, b)$.

The First Derivative Test

Suppose that c is a critical value of a function, f, in an interval (a, b), then if f is continuous and differentiable we can say that,

A) if $f'(x) > 0$ for all $a < x < c$ and $f'(x) < 0$ for all $c < x < b$, then $f(c)$ is a local maximum.

B) if $f'(x) < 0$ for all $a < x < c$ and $f'(x) > 0$ for all $c < x < b$, then $f(c)$ is a local minimum.

C) if $f'(x) > 0$ or if $f'(x) < 0$ for all $x \in (a, b)$ then $f(c)$ is not a local extrema.

Concavity

If a function is differentiable on an open interval containing c, then the graph at this point is

A) concave upward (or convex) if $f''(c) > 0$;

B) concave downward if $f''(c) < 0$.

If a function is concave upward than f' is increasing as x increases. If the function is concave downward, f' is decreasing as x increases.

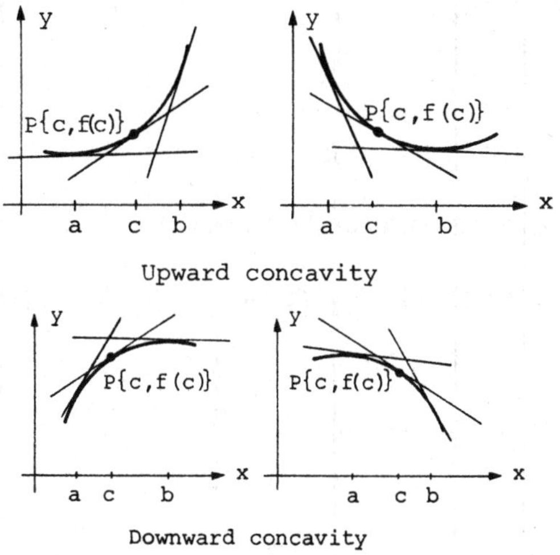

FIGURE 21

Points of Inflection

Points which satisfy $f''(x) = 0$ may be positions where concavity changes. These points are called the points of inflection. It is the point at which the curve crosses its tangent line.

Graphing a Function Using the Derivative Tests

The following steps will help us gain a rapid understanding of a function's behavior.

A) Look for some basic properties such as oddness, evenness, periodicity, boundedness, etc.

B) Locate all the zeroes by setting $f(x) = 0$.

C) Determine any singularities, $f(x) = \infty$.

D) Set $f'(x)$ equal to zero to find the critical values.

E) Find the points of inflection by setting $f''(x) = 0$.

F) Determine where the curve is concave, $f''(x) < 0$, and where it is convex $f''(x) > 0$.

G) Determine the limiting properties and approximations for large and small $|x|$.

H) Prepare a table of values x, $f(x)$, $f'(x)$ which includes the critical values and the points of inflection.

I) Plot the points found in Step H and draw short tangent lines at each point.

J) Draw the curve making use of the knowledge of concavity and continuity.

Example:

Determine the maxima and minima of $f(x) = x^3 - x$ in the interval from $x = -1$ to $x = 2$.

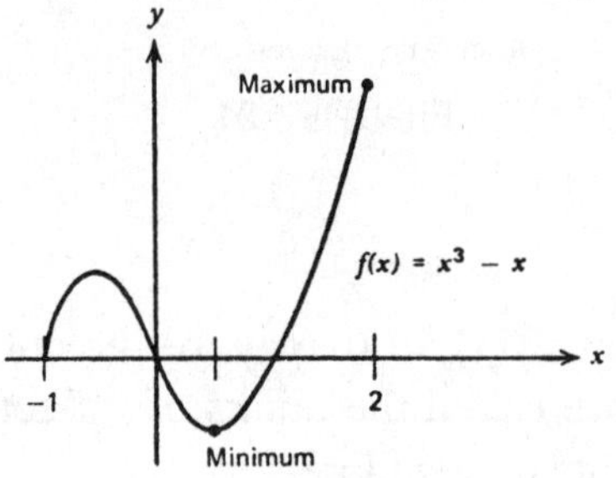

FIGURE 22

To determine the extreme points, we find $f'(x)$, equate it to 0, and solve for x to obtain the critical points. We have:

$$f'(x) = 3x^2 - 1 = 0. \quad x^2 = \frac{1}{3}.$$

Therefore, the critical values are $x = \pm\frac{1}{\sqrt{3}}$ Now

$$f\left(\frac{1}{\sqrt{3}}\right) = -\frac{2}{3\sqrt{3}} \text{ and } f\left(-\frac{1}{\sqrt{3}}\right) = \frac{2}{3\sqrt{3}}.$$

Evaluating f at the end points of the interval we have $f(-1) = 0$ and $f(2) = 6$. Therefore, $x = 2$, an end point, is the maximum point for f, and $x = \frac{1}{\sqrt{3}}$ is the minimum point as can be seen in Figure 22. The extreme values of f in $[-1, 2]$ are 6 and $-\frac{2}{3\sqrt{3}}$. The point $\left(-\frac{1}{\sqrt{3}}, \frac{2}{3\sqrt{3}}\right)$ is not an absolute maximum, but it is a relative maximum.

■ RECTILINEAR MOTION

When an object moves along a straight line we call the motion rectilinear motion. Distance s, velocity v, and acceleration a, are the chief concerns of the study of motion.

Velocity is the proportion of distance over time.

$$v = \frac{s}{t}$$

$$\text{Average velocity} = \frac{f(t_2) - f(t_1)}{t_2 - t_1}$$

where t_1, t_2 are time instances and $f(t_2) - f(t_1)$ is the displacement of an object.

Instantaneous velocity at time t is defined as

$$v - D\ s(t) = \lim_{h \to 0} \frac{f(t+h) - f(t)}{h}$$

We usually write

$$v(t) = \frac{ds}{dt}.$$

Acceleration, the rate of change of velocity with respect to time is

$$a(t) = \frac{dv}{dt}.$$

It follows clearly that

$$a(\text{t}) = v'(t) = s''(t).$$

When motion is due to gravitational effects, $g = 32.2$ ft/sec^2 or $g = 9.81$ m/sec^2 is usually substituted for acceleration.

Speed at time t is defined as $|v(t)|$. The speed indicates how fast an object is moving without specifying the direction of motion.

Example:

A particle moves in a straight line according to the law of motion:

$$s = t^3 - 4t^2 - 3t.$$

When the velocity of the particle is zero, what is its acceleration?

The velocity, v, can be found by differentiating this equation of motion with respect to t. Further differentiation gives the acceleration. Hence, the velocity, v, and acceleration, a, are:

$$v = \frac{ds}{dt} = 3t^2 - 8t - 3,$$

$$a = \frac{dv}{dt} = 6t - 8.$$

The velocity is zero when

$$3t^2 - 8t - 3 = (3t + 1)(t - 3) = 0,$$

from which

$$t = -\tfrac{1}{3} \text{ or } t = 3.$$

The corresponding values of the acceleration are

$$a = -10 \text{ for } t = -\tfrac{1}{3}, \text{ and}$$

$$a = +10 \text{ for } t = 3.$$

Example:

A particle moves in a plane according to the parametric equations of motion:

$$x = -t^2, y = t^3.$$

Find the magnitude and direction of the acceleration when $t = \tfrac{2}{3}$.

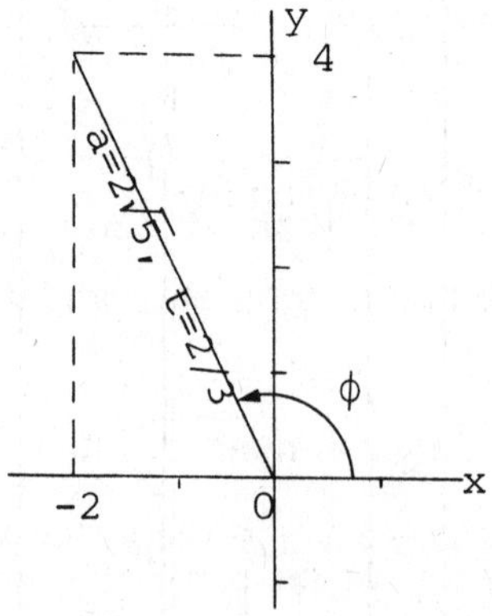

FIGURE 23

$$v_x = \frac{dx}{dt} = -2t,\ v_y = \frac{dy}{dt} = 3t^2.$$

Then,

$$a_x = \frac{dv_x}{dt} = -2,\ a_y = \frac{dv_y}{dt} = 6t.$$

At $t = {}^2/_3$, we obtain: $a_x = -2, a_y = 4$. Then,

$$a^2 = a_x^2 + a_y^2 = (-2)^2 + (4)^2 = 20.$$

$$a = 2\sqrt{5}$$

$$\tan\phi = \frac{4}{-2} = -2,\ \phi = 116°34',$$

since $\cos\phi = -\dfrac{2}{2\sqrt{5}}$ is negative, and

$\sin\phi = \dfrac{4}{2\sqrt{5}}$ is positive.

■ RATE OF CHANGE AND RELATED RATES

Rate of Change

In the last section we saw how functions of time can be expressed as velocity and acceleration. In general, we can speak about the rate of change of any function with respect to an arbitrary parameter (such as time in the previous section).

For linear functions $f(x) = mx + b$, the rate of change is simply the slope m.

For non-linear functions we define the

1) average rate of change between points c and d to be (see Figure 24)

$$\frac{f(d) - f(c)}{d - c}$$

2) instantaneous rate of change of f at the point x to be

$$f'(x) = \lim_{h \to 0} \frac{f(x + h) - f(x)}{h}$$

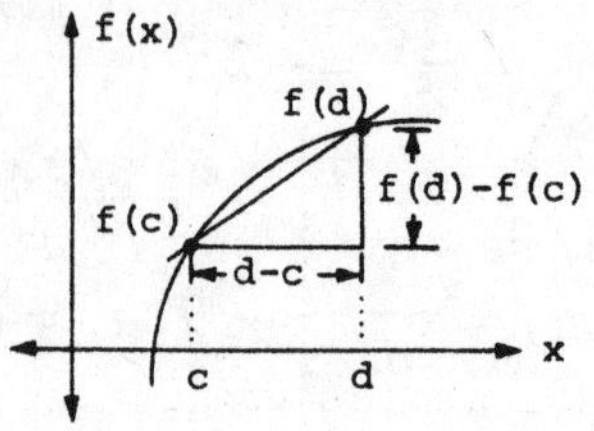

FIGURE 24

If the limit does not exist, then the rate of change of f at x is not defined.

The form, common to all related rate problems, is as follows:

A) Two variables, x and y are given. They are functions of time, but the explicit functions are not given.

B) The variables, x and y are related to each other by some equation such as $x^2 + y^3 - 2x - 7y^2 + 2 = 0$.

C) An equation which involves the rate of change $\frac{dx}{dt}$ and $\frac{dy}{dt}$ is obtained by differentiating with respect to t and using the chain rule.

As an illustration, the previous equation leads to

$$2x \frac{dx}{dt} + 3y^2 \frac{dy}{dt} - 2 \frac{dx}{dt} - 14y \frac{dy}{dt} = 0$$

The derivatives $\frac{dx}{dt}$ and $\frac{dy}{dt}$ in this equation are called the related rates.

EXAMPLE

A point moves on the parabola $6y = x^2$ in such a way that when $x = 6$ the abscissa is increasing at the rate of 2 ft. per second. At what rate is the ordinate increasing at that instant? See Figure 25.

Since

$$6y = x^2,$$

$$6 \frac{dy}{dt} = 2x \frac{dx}{dt}, \text{ or}$$

$$\frac{dy}{dt} = \frac{x}{3} \cdot \frac{dx}{dt}. \qquad (1)$$

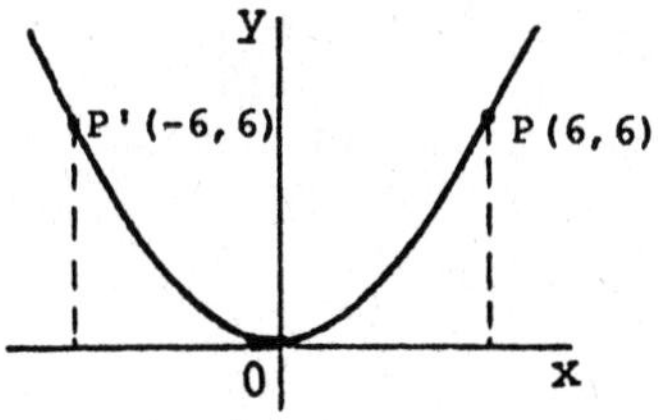

FIGURE 25

This means that, at any point on the parabola, the rate of change of ordinate = $(x/3)$ times the rate of change of abscissa. When $x = 6, \frac{dx}{dt} = 2$ ft. per second. Thus, substitution gives:

$$\frac{dy}{dt} = \frac{6}{3} \cdot 2 = 4 \ ft/\text{sec}.$$

CHAPTER 3

INTEGRAL CALCULUS

A. ANTIDERIVATIVES

Definition:

If $F(x)$ is a function whose derivative $F'(x) = f(x)$, then $F(x)$ is called the antiderivative of $f(x)$.

Theorem:

If $F(x)$ and $G(x)$ are two antiderivatives of $f(x)$, then $F(x) = G(x) + c$, where c is a constant.

Power Rule for Antidifferentiation

Let "a" be any real number, "r", any rational number not equal to –1 and "c" an arbitrary constant.

$$\text{If } f(x) = ax^r, \text{ then } F(x) = \frac{1}{r+1}\, x^{r+1} + c.$$

Theorem:

An antiderivative of a sum is the sum of the antiderivatives.

$$\frac{d}{dx}(F_1 + F_2) = \frac{d}{dx}(F_1) + \frac{d}{dx}(F_2) = f_1 + f_2$$

B. APPLICATIONS OF ANTIDERIVATIVES $y = y_0 e^{Kt}$: THE LAW OF EXPONENTIAL CHANGE.

Example:

In the course of any given year, the number y of cases of a disease is reduced by 10%. If there are 10,000 cases, today, about how many years will it take to reduce the number of cases to less than 1,000?

$$y = y_0 e^{Kt}$$

$y_0 = 10{,}000$ so, $y = 10{,}000\, e^{Kt}$. When $t = 1$, there are 10% fewer cases or 9,000 cases remaining so

$$9{,}000 = 10{,}000\, e^{K}$$

$$e^{K} = 0.9 \text{ therefore } K = \ln 0.9$$

Then

$$1{,}000 = 10{,}000\, e^{(\ln 0.9)t} \Rightarrow$$

$$.1 = e^{(\ln 0.9)t} \Rightarrow \ln .1 = \ln .9t$$

So

$$t = \frac{\ln 0.1}{\ln 0.9} \approx 21.9 \text{ years}$$

Another application of the antiderivative involves its use with velocity. The following problem illustrates this.

Example:

A body falls under the influence of gravity (gx 32 ft./sec^2) so that its speed is $v = 32t$. Determine the distance it falls in 3 sec. Let x = distance.

$$v = f(t) = 32t$$

The velocity is dependent on time because of the following general relationship:

$$v = gt + v_i$$

where v increases indefinitely as time goes on — neglecting air resistance and some other factors. The initial velocity v_i is zero in this case because the body starts from rest.

Assuming the distance covered is dx in time t, we can represent the velocity in a differential form:

$$\frac{dx}{dt} = v = 32t.$$

Integrating to find the relationship between x and t yields:

$$\int dx = \int 32t\, dt.$$

$$x = \frac{32t^2}{2} + C.$$

$x = 0$ when $t = 0$. Therefore, $0 = 16(0)^2 + C$, $C = 0$.

$$x = 16t^2.$$

The distance the body falls from the reference point,

$$x = 16t^2 = 16(3)^2 = 144 \text{ ft}.$$

C. TECHNIQUES OF INTEGRATION

■ TABLE OF INTEGRALS

$$\int \alpha\, dx = \alpha x + C.$$

$$\int x^n\, dx = \frac{1}{n+1} x^{n+1} + C,\ n \neq 1.$$

$$\int \frac{dx}{x} = \ln |x| + C.$$

$$\int e^x dx = e^x + C.$$

$$\int p^x dx = \frac{p^x}{\ln p} + C.$$

$$\int \ln x\, dx = x \ln x - x + C.$$

$$\int \cos x\, dx = \sin x + C.$$

$$\int \sin x\, dx = -\cos x + C.$$

$$\int \sec^2 x\, dx = \tan x + C.$$

$$\int \sec x \tan x\, dx = \sec x + C.$$

$\int \tan x \, dx = \ln |\sec x| + C.$

$\int \cot x \, dx = \ln |\sin x| + C.$

$\int \sec x \, dx = \ln |\sec x + \tan x| + C.$

$\int \operatorname{cosec} x \, dx = \ln |\operatorname{cosec} x - \cot x| + C.$

When integrating trigonometric functions, the power rule is often involved. Before applying the fundamental integration formulas, it also may be necessary to simplify the function. For that purpose, the common trigonometric identities are most often applicable as, for example, the half-angle formulas and the double-angle formulas. Again, no general rule can be given for finding the solutions. It takes a combination of experience and trial-and-error to learn what to substitute to arrive at the best solution method.

Example:

Integrate:

$$\int \cos x \, e^{2 \sin x} dx.$$

This problem is best solved by the method of substitution. We let $u = 2 \sin x$. Then $du = 2 \cos x$ dx. Substituting, we obtain:

$$\int \cos x \, e^{2 \sin x} dx = \frac{1}{2} \int e^{2 \sin x} (2 \cos x \, dx)$$

$$= \frac{1}{2} \int e^{u} \, du = \frac{1}{2} e^{u} + C$$

$$= \frac{1}{2} e^{2 \sin x} + C.$$

■ INTEGRATION BY PARTS

Differential of a product is represented by the formula

$$d(uv) = udv + vdu$$

Integration of both sides of this equation gives

$$uv = \int u \, dv + \int v \, du \qquad (1)$$

or

$$\int u \, dv = uv - \int v \, du \qquad (2)$$

Equation (2) is the formula for integration by parts.

Example:

Evaluate $\int x \ln x \, dx$

Let
$$u = \ln x \qquad dv = xdx$$
$$du = 1/x \, dx \qquad v = {}^1\!/_2 \, x^2$$

Thus,

$$\begin{aligned} \int x \ln x \, dx &= ({}^1\!/_2)\, x^2 \ln x - \int ({}^1\!/_2)x^2 \cdot ({}^1\!/_x)\, dx \\ &= ({}^1\!/_2)\, x^2 \ln x - {}^1\!/_2 \int \text{x dx} \\ &= ({}^1\!/_2)\, x^2 \ln x \; - ({}^1\!/_4)x^2 + c \end{aligned}$$

Integration by parts may be used to evaluate definite integrals. The formula is:

$$\int_a^b u \; dv = [uv]_a^b - \int_a^b v \; du$$

Example:

Integrate: $\int x \cdot \cos x \cdot dx.$

In this case we use integration by parts, the rule for which states:

$$\int u \, dv = uv - \int v \, du.$$

Let $u = x$ and $dv = \cos x \, dx$. Then $du = dx$ and

$$v = \int \cos x \cdot dx = \sin x.$$

$$\int u \cdot dv = uv - \int v \cdot du$$

becomes $$\int x \cdot \cos x \cdot dx = x \cdot \sin x - \int \sin x \cdot dx.$$

To integrate $\int \sin x \, dx$ we use the formula, $\int \sin u \, du = -\cos u + C$. This gives:

$$\int x \cdot \cos x \cdot dx = x \sin x - (-\cos \text{x}) + C$$

$$= x \sin \text{x} + \cos x + C.$$

■ PARTIAL FRACTIONS

To evaluate rational functions of the form

$$\int \frac{P(x)}{Q(x)}\,dx,$$

where P and Q are polynomials, we apply the following techniques:

1. Factor the denominator, $Q(x)$, into a product of linear and quadratic factors.

Example:

$$\begin{aligned} Q(x) &= x^3 + 2x^2 + x + 2 \\ &= x^3 + x + 2x^2 + 2 = x(x^2+1) + 2(x^2+1) \\ &= (x^2+1)\,(x+2) \end{aligned}$$

quadratic factor (x^2+1)   linear factor ($x+2$)

2. Rewrite $\frac{P}{Q}$ as a sum of simpler rational functions, each of which can be integrated.

If the degree of the numerator ($P(x)$) is larger than the degree of the denominator ($Q(x)$), we divide $P(x)$ by $Q(x)$ to obtain a quotient (polynomial of the form $\frac{P}{Q}$) plus a rational function (remainder divided by the divisor) in which the degree of the numerator is less than the degree of the denominator.

The decomposition of a rational function into the sum of simpler expressions is known as the method of partial fractions. Four ways in which the denominator can be factored are as follows:

1. The denominator $Q(x)$ can be decomposed to give distinct linear factors of the form

$$\frac{A_1}{x-a_1} + \frac{A_2}{x-a_2} + \ldots + \frac{A_n}{x-a_n}.$$

2. The denominator $Q(x)$ can be decomposed into linear factors of the form

$$\frac{A_1}{x-a} + \frac{A_2}{(x-a)^2} + \ldots + \frac{A_k}{(x-a)^k},$$

where some of the linear factors are repeated.

Example:

Decomposition of $Q(x) = (x-2)^3$ gives

$$\frac{A_1}{x-2} + \frac{A_2}{(x-2)^2} + \frac{A_3}{(x-2)^3}.$$

3. $Q(x)$ can be factored to give linear and irreducible quadratic factors. Each unrepeated quadratic factor has the form

$$\frac{Ax + B}{x^2 + bx + c}.$$

4. $Q(x)$ can be factored to give linear and quadratic factors where some of the quadratic factors can be repeated.

   In this case the fraction can be expressed as follows:

$$\frac{A_{1x} + B_1}{(x^2 + bx + c)} + \frac{A_{2x} + B_2}{(x^2 + bx + c)^2} + \ldots + \frac{A_{nx} + B_n}{(x^2 + bx + c)^n}$$

■ TRIGONOMETRIC SUBSTITUTION

If the integral contains expressions of the form

$$\sqrt{a^2 - x^2}\ ,\ \sqrt{a^2 + x^2}\ \text{ or }\ \sqrt{x^2 - a^2}\ ,$$

where $a > 0$, it is possible to transform the integral into another form by means of trigonometric substitution.

General Rules for Trigonometric Substitutions

1. Make appropriate substitutions.

2. Sketch a right triangle.

3. Label the sides of the triangle by using the substituted information.

4. The length of the third side is obtained by use of the Pythagorean Theorem.

5. Utilize sketch, in order to make further substitutions.

   A. If the integral contains the expression of the form $\sqrt{a^2 - x^2}$, make the substitution $x = a \sin \theta$.

$$\sqrt{a^2 - x^2} = \sqrt{a^2 - a^2 \sin^2\theta} = \sqrt{a^2(1 - \sin^2\theta)}$$

$$= \sqrt{a^2 \cos^2\theta} = a \cos\theta.$$

In trigonometric substitution the range of θ is restricted. For example, in the sine substitution the range of $\theta = -\pi/2 \leq \theta \leq \pi/2$. The sketch of this substitution is shown in Figure 26.

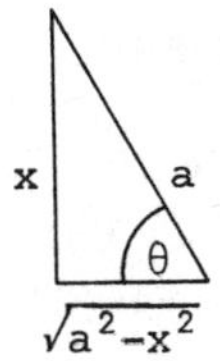

$x = a \sin\theta$, thus $\sin\theta = \frac{x}{a}$

FIGURE 26

B. If the integral contains the expression of the form $\sqrt{x^2 - a^2}$, make the substitution $x = a \sec\theta$. The sketch is shown in Figure 27.

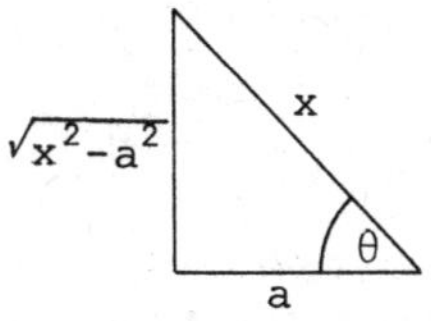

$x = a \sec\theta$

FIGURE 27

C. If the integral contains the expression of the form $\sqrt{a^2 + x^2}$, make the substitution $x = a \tan\theta$. The sketch is shown in Figure 28.

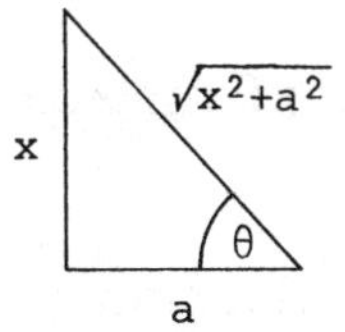

$x = a \tan\theta$

FIGURE 28

Example:

Evaluate $\int \frac{dx}{\sqrt{4+x}^{2}}$

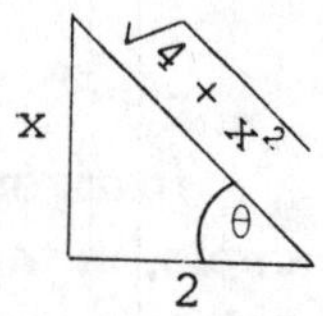

FIGURE 29

Let $x = 2\tan\theta$; $dx = 2\sec^2\theta\, d\theta$

Thus, $$\int \frac{dx}{\sqrt{4+x}^{2}} = \int \frac{2\sec^2\theta\, d\theta}{\sqrt{4+(2\tan\theta)^2}}$$

$$= \int \frac{2\sec^2\theta\, d\theta}{\sqrt{4(1+\tan^2\theta)}}$$

$$= \int \frac{2\sec^2\theta\, d\theta}{2\sqrt{\sec^2\theta}} = \int \sec\theta\, d\theta$$

$$= \ln|\sec\theta + \tan\theta| + c$$

To convert from θ back to x we use Figure 29 to find:

$$\sec\theta = \frac{\sqrt{4+x^2}}{2} \quad \text{and} \quad \tan\theta = \frac{x}{2}$$

Therefore,

$$\int \frac{dx}{\sqrt{4+x^2}} = \ln\left| \frac{\sqrt{4+x^2}}{2} + \frac{x}{2} \right| + c.$$

Summary of Trigonometric Substitutions

Given expression	Trigonometric substitution
$\sqrt{x^2-a^2}$	$x = a\sec\theta$
$\sqrt{x^2+a^2}$	$x = a\tan\theta$
$\sqrt{a^2-x^2}$	$x = a\sin\theta$

D. THE DEFINITE INTEGRAL

■ AREA

To find the area under the graph of a function f from a to b, we divide the interval $[a, b]$ into n subintervals, all having the same length $(b - a)/n$. This is illustrated in the following figure.

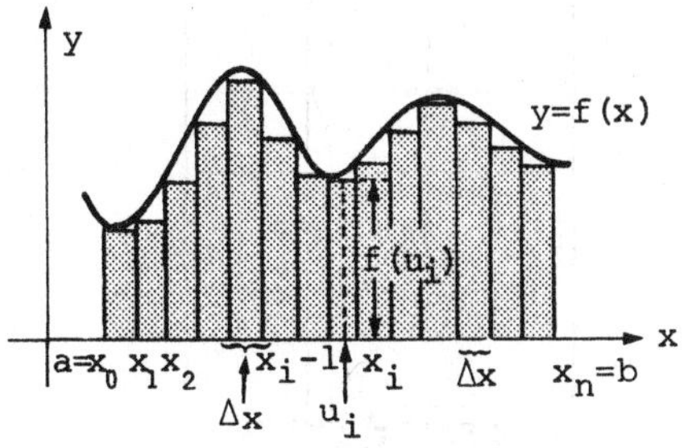

FIGURE 30

Since f is continuous on each subinterval, f takes on a minimum value at some number u_i in each subinterval.

We can construct a rectangle with one side of length $[x_{i-1}, x_i]$, and the other side of length equal to the minimum distance $f(u_i)$ from the x–axis to the graph of f.

The area of this rectangle is $f(u_i)\ \Delta x$. The boundary of the region formed by the sum of these rectangles is called the inscribed rectangular polygon.

The area (A) under the graph of f from a to b is

$$A = \lim_{\Delta x \to 0} \sum_{i=1} f(u_i)\Delta x.$$

The area A under the graph may also be obtained by means of circumscribed rectangular polygons.

In the case of the circumscribed rectangular polygons the maximum value of f on the interval $[x_{i-1}, x_i]$, v_i, is used.

Note that the area obtained using circumscribed rectangular polygons should always be larger than that obtained using inscribed rectangular polygons.

■ DEFINITION OF DEFINITE INTEGRAL

Definition:

Let f be a function that is defined on a closed interval $[a, b]$ and let P be a partition of $[a, b]$. A Riemann Sum of f for P is any expression R_p of the form,

$$R_p = \sum_{i=1}^{n} f(w_i)\Delta x_i ,$$

where w_i is some number in $[x_{i-1}, x_i]$, for $i = 1, 2, \ldots, n$.

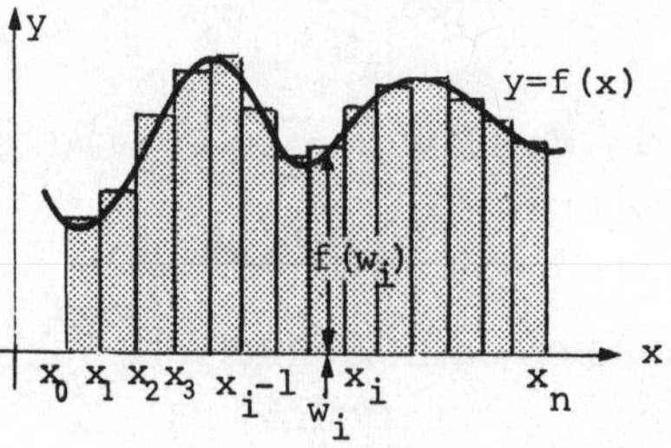

FIGURE 31

Definition:

Let f be a function that is defined on a closed interval $[a, b]$. The definite integral of f from a to b, denoted by

$$\int_a^b f(x)\,dx$$

is given by

$$\int_a^b f(x)\,dx = \lim_{\|P\| \to 0} \sum_i f(w_i)\,\Delta x_i ,$$

provided the limit exists.

Theorem:

If f is continuous on $[a, b]$, then f is integrable on $[a, b]$.

Theorem:

If $f(a)$ exists, then

$$\int_a^a f(x)\,dx = 0.$$

■ PROPERTIES OF THE DEFINITE INTEGRAL

A) If f is integrable on $[a, b]$, and k is any real number, then kf is integrable on $[a, b]$ and

$$\int_a^b kf(x)\,dx = k\int_a^b f(x)\,dx.$$

B) If f and g are integrable on $[a,b]$, then $f+g$ is integrable on $[a, b\}$ and

$$\int_a^b [f(x)+g(x)]\,dx = \int_a^b f(x)\,dx + \int_a^b g(x)\,dx.$$

C) If $a < c < b$ and f is integrable on both $[a, c]$ and $[c, b]$, then f is integrable on $[a, b]$ and

$$\int_a^b f(x)\,dx = \int_a^c f(x)\,dx + \int_c^b f(x)\,dx.$$

D) If f is integrable on a closed interval and if a, b, and c are any three numbers in the interval, then

$$\int_a^b f(x)\,dx = \int_a^c f(x)\,dx + \int_c^b f(x)\,dx.$$

E) If f is integrable on $[a, b]$ and if $f(x) \geq 0$ for all x in $[a, b]$, then

$$\int_a^b f(x)\,dx \geq 0.$$

■ THE FUNDAMENTAL THEOREM OF CALCULUS

The fundamental theorem of calculus establishes the relationship between the indefinite integrals and differentiation by use of the mean value theorem.

Mean Value Theorem for Integrals

If f is continuous on a closed interval $[a, b]$, then there is some number P in the open interval (a, b) such that

$$\int_a^b f(x)\,dx = f(P)\,(b-a)$$

To find $f(P)$ we divide both sides of the equation by $(b-a)$ obtaining

$$f(P) = \frac{1}{b-a}\int_a^b f(x)\,dx.$$

Definition of the Fundamental Theorem

Suppose f is continuous on a closed interval $[a, b]$, then

a) If the function G is defined by:

$$G(x) = \int_a^x f(t)\,dt\ ,$$

for all x in $[a, b]$, then G is an antiderivative of f on $[a, b]$.

b) If F is any antiderivative of f, then

$$\int_a^b f(x)\,dx = F(b) - F(a)$$

E. APPLICATIONS OF THE INTEGRAL

■ AREA

If f and g are two continuous functions on the closed interval $[a, b]$, then the area of the region bounded by the graphs of these two functions and the ordinates $x = a$ and $x = b$ is

$$A = \int_a^b [f(x) - g(x)]\,dx.$$

where $\qquad f(x) \geq 0 \quad$ and $\quad f(x) \geq g(x)$

$$a \leq x \leq b$$

This formula applies whether the curves are above or below the x–axis.

The area below $f(x)$ and above the x–axis is represented by

$$\int_a^b f(x)$$

The area between g (x) and the x–axis is represented by $\int g(x)$.

Example:

Find the area of the region bounded by the curves $y = x^2$ and $y = \sqrt{x}$.

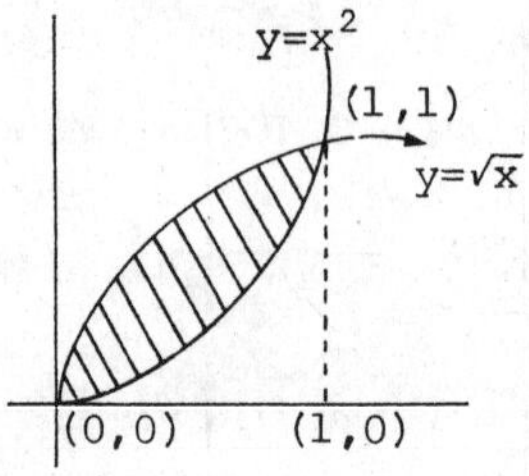

FIGURE 32

$$\text{Area} = A = \int_0^1 (\sqrt{x} - x^2)\, dx$$

$$= \int_0^1 \sqrt{x}\, dx = \int_0^1 x^2\, dx$$

$$= \left[\frac{2}{3} x^{\frac{3}{2}} - \frac{1}{3} x^3 \right]_0^1$$

$$A = \left[\frac{2}{3} - \frac{1}{3} \right] = \frac{1}{3}$$

■ AREAS IN POLAR COORDINATES

The area (A) of a region bounded by the curve $r = f(\theta)$, and by the lines $\theta = a$ and $\theta = b$ is given by the formula:

$$A = \frac{1}{2} \int_a^b r^2 d\theta = \frac{1}{2} \int_a^b [f(\theta)]^2\, d\theta.$$

When finding the area,

1. Sketch graph of the polar equations given.
2. Shade region for which area is sought.
3. Determine limits.
4. Solve using the equation for area.

Example:

Find the area outside the circle $r = 2a \cos \theta$ and inside the cardioid $r = a(1 + \cos \theta)$.

The required area is split evenly into two equal parts, above and below the x–axis. Therefore, to obtain the total area we can multiply the value for the area above the x–axis by 2. The area above the x–axis may be split into two parts and expressed as the sum of the area in the first quadrant (area of the cardioid minus the area of the circle, where θ goes from 0 to $\pi/2$)

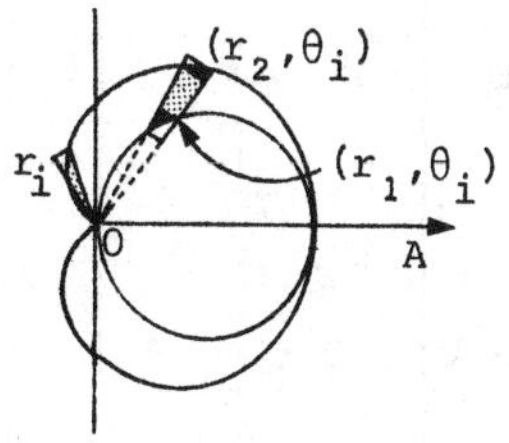

FIGURE 33

and the area of the second quadrant (the area of the cardioid alone, where θ goes from $\pi/2$ to π).

Thus, $\text{Area} = A = \frac{1}{2}\int_a^b r^2 d\theta = \frac{1}{2}\int_a^b [f(\theta)]^2\, d\theta$

$$A_{\text{Total}} = 2\int_0^{\frac{\pi}{2}} \frac{1}{2}[a(1+\cos\theta)]^2\, d\theta - 2\int_0^{\frac{\pi}{2}} \frac{1}{2}(2a\cos\theta)^2\, d\theta$$

$$+ 2\int_{\frac{\pi}{2}}^{\pi} \frac{1}{2}[a(1+\cos\theta)]^2 d\theta$$

$$A_{\text{Total}} = a^2\int_0^{\frac{\pi}{2}} (1 + 2\cos\theta + \cos^2\theta)\, d\theta - a^2\int_0^{\frac{\pi}{2}} 4\cos^2\theta\, d\theta$$

$$+ a^2\int_{\frac{\pi}{2}}^{\pi} (1 + 2\cos\theta + \cos^2\theta) d\theta$$

$$A_{\text{Total}} = a^2\int_0^{\frac{\pi}{2}} (1 + 2\cos\theta - 3\cos^2\theta)\, d\theta$$

$$+ a^2\int_{\frac{\pi}{2}}^{\pi} (1 + 2\cos\theta + \cos^2\theta) d\theta$$

Substitute $\cos^2\theta = \frac{1+\cos^2 2\theta}{2}$ and integrate to obtain

$$A_{\text{Total}} = a^2\left[2\sin\theta - \frac{\theta}{2} - \frac{3\sin 2\theta}{4}\right]_0^{\frac{\pi}{2}}$$

$$+ a^2\left[2\sin\theta + \frac{3\theta}{2} + \frac{\sin 2\theta}{4}\right]_{\frac{\pi}{2}}^{\pi}$$

$$A_{\text{Total}} = a^2\left(2 - \frac{\pi}{4}\right) + a^2\left(\frac{3\pi}{4} - 2\right) = \frac{\pi a^2}{2}.$$

■ VOLUME OF A SOLID OF REVOLUTION

If a region is revolved about a line, a solid called a solid of revolution is generated. The axis of revolution is the line about which the revolution takes place.

There are several methods by which we may obtain the volume of a solid of revolution. We shall now discuss three such methods.

1. Disk Method

The volume of a solid generated by the revolution of a region about the x–axis is given by the formula

$$V = \pi \int_a^b [f(x)]^2 \, dx,$$

provided that f is a continuous, nonnegative function on the interval $[a, b]$.

2. Shell Method

This method applies to cylindrical shells exemplified by

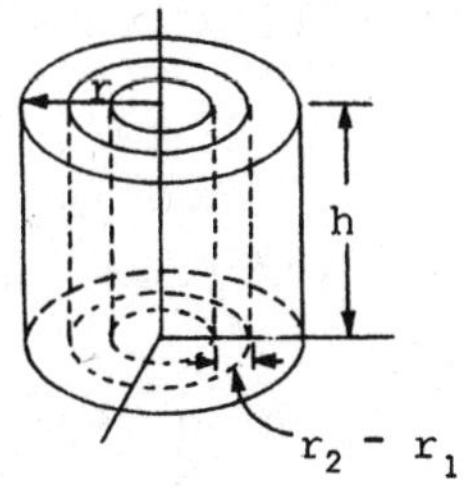

FIGURE 34

The volume of a cylindrical shell is

$$\begin{aligned} V &= \pi r_2^2 \, h - \pi r_1^2 \, h \\ &= \pi(r_2 + r_1)\,(r_2 - r_1)\, h \\ &= 2\pi\left(\frac{r_2 + r_1}{2}\right)(r_2 - r_1)\, h \end{aligned}$$

where r_1 = inner radius

r_2 = outer radius

h = height.

Let $r = \frac{r_1 + r_2}{2}$ and $\Delta r = r_2 - r_1$, then the volume of the shell becomes

$$V = 2\pi \, rh\Delta \, r$$

The thickness of the shell is represented by Δr and the average radius of the shell by r.

Thus,

$$V = 2\pi \int_a^b x f(x)\, dx$$

is the volume of a solid generated by revolving a region about the y-axis. This is illustrated by Figure 35.

3. Parallel Cross Sections

A cross section of a solid is a region formed by the intersection of a solid by a plane. This is illustrated by Figure 36.

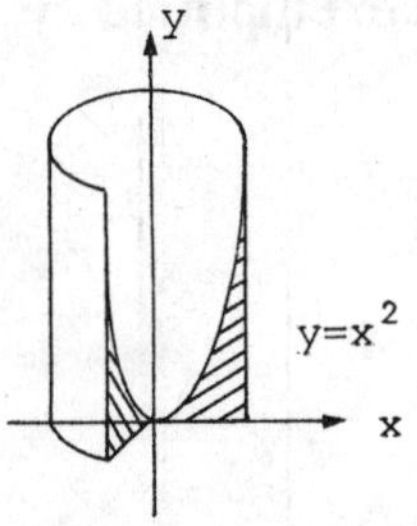

FIGURE 35

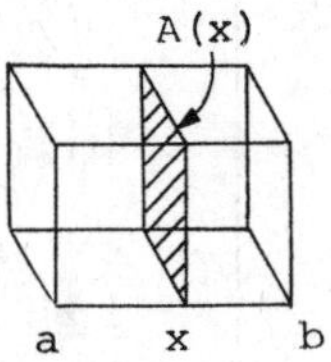

FIGURE 36

If x is a continuous function on the interval $[a, b]$, then the volume of the cross sectional area $A(x)$ is

$$V = \int_a^b A(x)\, dx.$$

■ AREA OF SURFACE OF REVOLUTION

A surface of revolution is generated when a plane is revolved about a line.

If f' and g' are two continuous functions on the interval $[a, b]$ where $g(t) = 0$, $x = f(t)$ and $y = g(t)$ then, the surface area of a plane revolved about the x–axis is given by the formula

$$S = \int_a^b 2\pi\, g(t) \sqrt{[f'(t)]^2 + [g'(t)]^2}\, dt$$

Since $x = f(t)$ and $y = g(t)$,

$$S = \int_a^b 2\pi\, y \sqrt{\left(\frac{dx}{dt}\right)^2 + \left(\frac{dy}{dt}\right)^2}\, dt$$

If the plane is revolved about the y–axis, then the surface area is

$$S = \int_a^b 2\pi\, x \sqrt{\left(\frac{dx}{dt}\right)^2 + \left(\frac{dy}{dt}\right)^2}\; dt$$

These formulas can be simplified to give the following:

$$S = 2\pi y \int_a^b ds$$

for revolution about the x–axis, and

$$S = 2\pi x \int_a^b ds$$

for revolution about the y–axis.

In the above equations, ds is given as $ds = \sqrt{1 + f'(x)^2}\; dx$.

■ IMPROPER INTEGRALS

$$\int_a^\infty f(x)\, dx = \lim_{t \to \infty} \int_a^t f(x)\, dx,$$

if the limit exists.

$$\int_{-\infty}^a f(x)\, dx = \lim_{t \to -\infty} \int_t^a f(x)\, dx,$$

if the limit exists.

The above two expressions are improper integrals since one of their limits is not a real number.

Improper integrals either converge or diverge.

They converge when the limit on the right-hand side of the equation exists as t goes to infinity.

They diverge when the limit on the right-hand side of the equation does not exist as t goes to infinity.

$$\int_{-\infty}^{+\infty} f(x)\, dx = \int_{-\infty}^a f(x)\, dx + \int_a^\infty f(x)\, dx$$

The above integral converges if and only if both integrals on the right-hand side of the equation are convergent.

Another form of an improper integral is one in which the integrand does not exist for some value on the closed interval of integration.

Example:

If f is continuous on the half-open interval $[a, b)$ and becomes infinite or undefined at b, then, by definition,

$$\int_a^b f(x)\,dx = \lim_{t \to b^-} \int_a^t f(x)\,dx,$$

provided the limit exists.

Likewise, if f is continuous on the half-open interval $(a, b]$ and becomes infinite or undefined at a, then by definition,

$$\int_a^b f(x)\,dx = \lim_{t \to a^+} \int_t^b f(x)\,dx,$$

provided the limit exists.

As previously stated, the above integral converges if the limit on the right-hand side of the expression exists, and diverges otherwise.

CHAPTER 4

SEQUENCES AND SERIES

A. SEQUENCES OF REAL NUMBERS AND FUNCTIONS; CONVERGENCE

■ SEQUENCES

1) Definition of a sequence

A sequence, S_n, is a particular kind of function, $f : Z^+ \rightarrow Y$, whose independent variable n ranges over the set of positive integers. Thus a sequence, $\{S_n\}$, is a set of real numbers $s_1, s_2, s_3, \ldots$ in a one-to-one correspondence with the natural numbers.

2) Limits of a sequence

The limit L of a sequence S_n is defined as

$$\lim_{n \to \infty} S_n = L,$$

if and only if, for all $\varepsilon > 0$, there exists an N, such that $| S_n - L | < \varepsilon$ for all $n > N$.

If the limit of the sequence exists, the sequence is called convergent; otherwise it is called divergent.

$\lim_{n \to \infty} S_n = \infty$ if for all $M > 0$, there exists an $N > 0$, such that $S_n > M$, for all $n > N$.

$\lim_{n \to \infty} S_n = -\infty$ if for all $M > 0$, there exists an $N > 0$ such that $S_n < -M$, for all $n > N$.

3) Bounded Sequences

A sequence, S_n, is called bounded above if $S_n \leq M$, for $n = 1, 2, 3, \ldots$. The constant M (independent of n) is called an upper bound. If $S_n \geq m$ for all $n = 1, 2, 3, \ldots$ the sequence is bounded below, and m is called the lower bound. If $m \leq S_n \leq M$ the sequence is called bounded.

4) Monotonic Sequences

A sequence, $\{S_n\}$, is called:

a) monotonically increasing, if $S_{n+1} \geq S_n$ for all $n \in N$.

b) strictly monotonically increasing, if $S_{N+1} > S_N$ for all $n \in N$.

c) monotonically decreasing if $S_{N+1} \leq S_N$ for all $n \in N$.

d) strictly monotonically decreasing if $S_{n+1} \leq S_n$ for all $n \in N$.

Theorem:

Every bounded monotonic sequence of real numbers has a limit.

B. SERIES OF REAL NUMBERS

■ DEFINITION OF INFINITE SERIES

If $a_0, a_1, a_2, \ldots$ is an infinite sequence then an infinite series is the sum

$$\sum_{n=0}^{\infty} a_n = a_0 + a_1 + a_2 + \ldots \tag{1}$$

The numbers $a_0, a_1, a_2, \ldots$ are the terms of the series, where a_n is defined as the general term.

For an infinite series, $\sum_{n=0}^{\infty} a_n$, to be of practical use, it must be convergent.

If the partial sum, $S_n = a_0 + a_1 + \ldots + a_n$ is given and $\lim_{n \to \infty} S_n = L$, then the series $\sum_{n=0}^{\infty} a_n$ converges to L. A series that is not convergent is called divergent.

Two kinds of series which are often used are:

A) Geometric series:

$$\sum_{n=1}^{\infty} ar^{n-1} = a + ar + ar^2 + \ldots$$

where a and r are constants. This series converges to $s = \frac{a}{1-r}$ if $|r| < 1$ and diverges if $|r| \geq 1$. The sum of the first n terms is given by

$$S_n = \frac{a(1-r^n)}{1-r}.$$

B) The k series

$$\sum_{n=0}^{\infty} \frac{1}{n^k} + \frac{1}{1^k} + \frac{1}{2^k} + \frac{1}{3^k} + \ldots,$$

where k is a constant. This series is convergent for $k > 1$ and divergent for $k \leq 1$. For $k = 1$, the series becomes $1 + {}^1/_2 + {}^1/_3 + {}^1/_4 + \ldots$, which diverges and is called the harmonic series.

■ TESTS FOR CONVERGENCE

Comparison Test

a) Convergence

Suppose that Σa_n is a convergent series with $a_n > 0$ for all n, then a series Σb_n also converges if $a_n \geq b_n \geq 0$ for all $n > N$, for some N.

b) Divergence

If Σa_n diverges and $a_n \leq b_n$ for all $n > N$, then Σb_n also diverges.

Ratio Test

If the series Σa_n has positive terms, and if

$$\lim_{n \to \infty} \left| \frac{a_{n+1}}{a_n} \right| = L,$$

then the series Σa_n converges absolutely if $L < 1$, and Σa_n diverges if $L > 1$. $L = 1$ the test is inconclusive.

Integral Test

Let $f(x)$ be a function which is positive, continuous and non-increasing as x increases for all values of $x \geq N$, where N is some fixed positive integer. Then the series $\Sigma a_n = \Sigma f(n)$ converges or diverges according to the integral

$$\lim_{R \to \infty} \int_N^R f(x)\, dx \qquad (*)$$

If (*) converges or diverges, then the series Σa_n converges or diverges correspondingly.

■ POWER SERIES, CONVERGENCE

One of the most important series is the power series. A power series in powers of $(x - c)$ is a series of the form

$$\sum_{n=0}^{\infty} a_n(x-c)^n = a_0 + a_1(x-c) + a_2(x-c)^2 + \ldots \qquad (2)$$

Letting $c = 0$, the power series takes the form

$$\sum_{n=0}^{\infty} a_n x^n = a_0 + a_1 x + a_2 x^2 + \ldots \qquad (3)$$

Of importance in the study of power series is the notion of radius of convergence, R, which can be often found by the ratio test. In general, a power series converges for $|x| < R$, diverges for $|x| > R$, and may or may not converge for $|x| = R$. For $R = 0$, the series converges only for $x = 0$. If $R = \infty$ the series converges for all values of x.

The series

$$\sum_{n=0}^{\infty} a_n x^n$$

is absolutely and uniformly convergent if $|x| < R$.

For the two convergent power series

$$\sum_{n=0}^{\infty} a_n x^n \text{ and } \sum_{n=0}^{\infty} b_n x^n,$$

the following theorems are valid:

A) The series can be added or subtracted term by term.

B) These series can be multiplied to obtain the series

$$\sum_{n=0}^{\infty} c_n x^n, \text{ where } c_n = \sum_{n=0}^{\infty} a_k b_{n-k} = a_0 b_n + a_1 b_{n-1} + \ldots + a_n b_0$$

C) The series

$$\sum_{n=0}^{\infty} a_n x^n$$

can be divided by the series

$$\sum_{n=0}^{\infty} b_n x^n \; (b_0 \neq 0)$$

to obtain the series

$$\sum_{n=0}^{\infty} c_n x^n,$$

whose coefficients may be found by the process of division or by solving the system

$$b_0 c_0 = a_0$$

$$b_0 c_1 + b_1 c_0 = a_1$$

$$\vdots$$

for $$c_0, c_1, \ldots, c_n.$$

D) If

$$\sum_{n=0}^{\infty} a_n x^n \text{ and } \sum_{n=0}^{\infty} b_n x^n,$$

then $a_n = b_n$ for all n.

■ ALTERNATING SERIES

An alternating series is a series in which the terms are alternately positive and negative. Thus, if $u_1 - u_2 + u_3 - u_4 + \ldots$ is an alternating series, and if

$$\lim_{n \to \infty} u_n = 0,$$

the series is convergent.

Example

Test the alternating series:

$$\frac{1+\sqrt{2}}{2} - \frac{1+\sqrt{3}}{4} + \frac{1+\sqrt{4}}{6} - \frac{1+\sqrt{5}}{8} + \ldots$$

for convergence.

An alternating series is convergent if (a) the terms, after a certain nth term, decrease numerically, i.e., $u_{n+1} < u_n$, and (b) the general term approaches 0 as n becomes infinite. Therefore, we determine the nth term of the given alternating series. By discovering the law of information, we find that the general term is

$$\pm\frac{1+\sqrt{n+1}}{2n}.$$

Therefore, the preceding term is

$$\pm\frac{1+\sqrt{n}}{2(n-1)}.$$

To satisfy condition (a) stated above, we must show that:

$$\frac{1+\sqrt{n+1}}{2n}<\frac{1+\sqrt{n}}{2(n-1)}.$$

Obtaining a common denominator for both these terms,

$$\frac{1}{2}\cdot\frac{(1+\sqrt{n+1})\,(n-1)}{n(n-1)}<\frac{(1+\sqrt{n})\,(n)}{n(n-1)}\cdot\frac{1}{2}.$$

Since the denominators are the same, to prove condition (a) we must show:

$$1+\sqrt{n+1}\;(n-1)<(1+\sqrt{n})\;(n),$$

which is obvious, since subtracting 1 from n has a greater effect than adding 1 to $\sqrt{n}$. Since $u_{n+1} < u_n$, we have the first condition for convergence.

Now we must show that

$$\lim_{n\to\infty}\frac{1+\sqrt{n}}{2n-2}=0.$$

We find that

$$\lim_{n\to\infty}\frac{1+\sqrt{n}}{2n-2}=\frac{\infty}{\infty},$$

which is an indeterminate form. We therefore apply L'Hôpital's Rule, obtaining:

$$\lim_{n\to\infty}\frac{\frac{1}{2}n^{-\frac{1}{2}}}{2}=\lim_{n\to\infty}\frac{1}{4\sqrt{n}}=0.$$

Since both conditions hold, the given alternating series is convergent.

C. SERIES OF FUNCTIONS, POWER SERIES

■ THEOREM ON POWER SERIES

A) Abel's Theorem

If the series

$$\sum_{n=0}^{\infty} a_n x^n$$

converges at R, then it converges uniformly on the closed interval $0 \le x \le R$. The conclusion holds for $-R \le x \le 0$ if the series converges at $x = -R$.

B) Abel's Limit Theorem

If the series

$$\sum_{n=0}^{\infty} a_n x^n$$

converges at $x = x_0$, where x_0 may be an interior point or an endpoint of the interval of convergence, then

$$\lim_{x \to x_0} \left\{ \sum_{n=0}^{\infty} a_n x^n \right\} = \sum_{n=0}^{\infty} \lim_{x \to x_0} a_n x^n = \sum_{n=0}^{\infty} a_n x_0^n$$

If x_0 is a left-hand endpoint it is proper to write $x \to x_0^+$ and for a right-hand endpoint $x \to x_0^-$.

C) If the series

$$\sum_{n=0}^{\infty} a_n x^n$$

has a radius of convergence $R > 0$, then the series converges uniformly on the closed interval $[-r, r]$, where $0 \le r < R$.

D) If a function is defined as

$$f(x) = \sum_{n=0}^{\infty} a_n x^n,$$

then the integral of this function

$$\left(\int_a^b f(x)\, dx \right)$$

is equal to the series obtained by integrating the original power series term by term, or

$$\int_a^b \left(\sum_{n=0}^{\infty} a_n x^n \right) dx = \sum_{n=0}^{\infty} \frac{a_n}{n+1} (b^{n+1} - a^{n+1})$$

If the function

$$f(x) = \sum_{n=0}^{\infty} a_n x^n$$

has a radius of convergence $R > 0$, then it is differentiable term by term or,

$$f'(x) = \sum_{n=0}^{\infty} a_n \frac{d}{dx}(x^n) = \sum_{n=1}^{\infty} n a_n x^{n-1}$$

for $|x| < R$,

■ TAYLOR AND MacLAURIN SERIES

If the function $f(x)$ is continuous in a closed interval $[ab]$ and its derivatives $f'(x), f''(x), \ldots, f^n(x)$ and $f^{n+1}(x)$ exist, then the function $f(x)$ can be represented by a series expansion of $f(x)$ about the point $x = a$, or

$$f(x) = \sum_{n=0}^{\infty} \frac{f^n(a)}{n!} (x-a)^n \tag{4}$$

The function may also be represented by

$$\sum_{k=0}^{\infty} \frac{f^k(a)}{K!} + R_{n+1}$$

where R_{n+1} is the remainder.

Lagrange's form of the remainder is

$$R_{n+1} = \frac{f^{n+1}(\delta)}{(n+1)!} (x-a)^{n+1} \tag{5}$$

Cauchy's form is

$$R_{n+1} = \frac{f^{n+1}(\delta)}{n!} (x-\delta)^n (x-a)$$

$$x < \delta < a \tag{6}$$

If

$$\lim_{n \to \infty} R_{n+1} = 0,$$

then the series (4) is called the Taylor series.

If $a = 0$, equation (4) often is called the MacLaurin series expansion of f(x).

■ POWER SERIES

A power series is a series of the form

$$c_0 + c_1(x-a) + c_2(x-a)^2 + \ldots + c_n(x-a)^n$$

in which a and c_i, $i = 1, 2, 3$, etc. are constants.

The notations

$$\sum_{n=0}^{\infty} c_n(x-a)^n \quad \text{and} \quad \sum_{n=0}^{\infty} c_n x^n$$

are used to describe power series.

A power series $\Sigma c_n x^n$ is said to converge:

1) at x_1 if and only if $\Sigma c_n x^n$ converges

2) on the set S if and only if $\Sigma c_n x^n$ converges for each $x \in S$.

If $\Sigma c_n x^n$ converges at $x_1 \neq 0$, then it converges absolutely whenever $|x| < |x_1|$. If $\Sigma c_n x^n$ diverges at x_1, then it diverges for $|x| > |x_1|$.

Calculus of Power Series

If the series $\Sigma c_n x^n$ converges on the interval $(-a, a)$, then

$$\Sigma \frac{d}{dx}(c_n x^n) = \Sigma\, n c_n x^{n-1}$$

also converges on $(-a, a)$.

The Differentiation of Power Series

If

$$f(x) = \sum_{n=0}^{\infty} c_n x^n$$

for all x in $(-a, a)$, then f is differentiable on $(-a, a)$, and

$$f'(x) = \sum_{n=1}^{\infty} n c_n x^{n-1}$$

for all x in $(-a, a)$.

A power series defines an infinite differentiable function in the interior of its interval of convergence.

The derivatives of this function may be obtained by differentiating term by term.

Integrating Term by Term

If

$$f(x) = \Sigma c_n x^n$$

converges on the interval $(-a, a)$, then

$$g(x) = \Sigma \frac{c_n}{n+1} x^{n+1}$$

converges on $(-a, a)$, and

$$\int f(x)\, dx = g(x) + c.$$

The equations for term-by-term integration are expressed as either

$$\int (\Sigma c_n x^n)\, dx = \left(\Sigma \frac{c_n}{n+1} x^{n+1}\right) + c$$

for indefinite integrals or

$$\int_a^b (\Sigma c_n x^n)\, dx = \Sigma \left(\int_a^b c_n x^n\, dx\right)$$

$$= \Sigma \frac{c_n}{n+1} \left(b^{n+1} - a^{n+1}\right)$$

for definite integrals (provided $[a, b]$ is contained in the interval of convergence).

CHAPTER 5

ELEMENTARY DIFFERENTIAL EQUATIONS

A. FIRST-ORDER, VARIABLE SEPARABLE

A differential equation is of the order of the highest derivative involved. For example, a second-order equation involves only the first and second derivatives. Differential equations can have constant coefficients, or it can have coefficients that are functions of the variables. A differential equation can also be homogeneous, or it can be non-homogeneous.

The solution of a differential equation can present a difficult task, and for this reason numerous methods have been developed in the attempt to systematize their solutions. The simplest differential equations can be handled by the separation of variables, in which each variable is on only one side of the equation. This leads to direct integration. For the linear equation, a sum of solutions known as the complementary function and the particular function may be used. For homogeneous equations, substitution is often useful. Sometimes, integrating factors can be employed.

Example:

Solve the differential equation: $\dfrac{d_2y}{dx^2} = \cos\ 2x.$

$$\frac{dy}{dx} = \frac{1}{2}\sin\ 2x + a\,.$$

Hence $y = -\,{}^1/_4\cos\ 2x + ax = b$ is the general solution. This solution is obtained by setting $p = \frac{dy}{dx}$, and hence

$$\frac{dp}{dx} = \frac{d^2y}{dx}.$$

If the given equation had been expressed as (y'', y', y), we would (by the chain rule) have used

$$\frac{d^2y}{dx^2} = \frac{dp}{dy}\frac{dy}{dx} = p\frac{dp}{dy}.$$

Substituting

$$\frac{d^2y}{dx^2} = \frac{dp}{dx}$$

in the given differential equation, and integrating yields an expression from which we solve for p. Substituting $\frac{dy}{dx}$ back for p, we obtain the first-order differential equation. Further integration gives the desired general solution. Once we are used to this technique, we can automatically write down the first-order and the general equations.

Example:

Obtain the general solution for:

$$\frac{dy}{dx} = e^x + y.$$

The given differential equation is of the general form:

$$\frac{dy}{dx} + py = Q,$$

where p and Q are constants and functions of x only. In this case, $p = -1$ and $Q = e^x$. This differential equation is of degree one and is called a linear differential equation. To find the general solution, we first let Q be identically zero. Hence,

$$\frac{dy}{dx} + py = 0,$$

from which, upon separating the variables and integrating, we obtain:

$$\ln y + \int p\, dx = \ln c,$$

or

$$\ln\left(\frac{c}{y}\right) = e^{\int p\, dx}.$$

$$c = y\, e^{\int p\, dx}.$$

Now, we can write:

$$\left(\frac{dy}{dx} + py\right)e^{\int p\,dx} = \frac{d}{dx}\left(y\,e^{\int p\,dx}\right) = Q\,e^{\int p\,dx}.$$

Using the substitution method to integrate the left-hand side of the above differential equation, we let

$$v = x^2 + 1 \qquad w = y^2 - 1$$

$$dv = 2x\,dx \qquad dw = 2y\,dy.$$

Therefore, the given equation becomes:

$$\frac{1}{2}\frac{dv}{v} + \frac{1}{2}\frac{dw}{w} = 0.$$

Integrating, we have:

$$\frac{1}{2}\ln v + \frac{1}{2}\ln w = k$$

or

$$\frac{1}{2}\ln(x^2 + 1) + \frac{1}{2}\ln(y^2 - 1) = k,$$

putting $k = {}^1/_2 \ln C$, we may write this:

$$\ln[(x^2 + 1)(y^2 - 1)] = \ln C,$$

from which we have

$$(x^2 + 1)(y^2 - 1) = C.$$

This expression is the required general solution of the given differential equation.

■ APPLICATIONS WITH INITIAL CONDITIONS

Solve the equation:

$$\frac{d^2y}{dx^2} + 16y = 0,$$

subject to the initial conditions: $y = 0$ and $\frac{dy}{dx} = 5$ when $x = 0$.

This is a second-order, homogeneous differential equation of the form,

$$\frac{d^2y}{dx^2} + a\frac{dy}{1dx} + a_2y = 0,$$

with $a_1 = 0$ and $a_2 = 16$.

Assuming $y = ke^{mx}$ is the general solution, and, since

$$\frac{d^2 y}{dx^2} = km^2 e^{mx},$$

we obtain

$$\frac{d^2 y}{dx^2} + 16y = ke^{mx}(m^2 + 16) = 0.$$

Taking $k = 0$ leads to trivial solution. A non-trivial solution is found by the auxiliary equation:

$$m^2 + 16 = 0$$

with roots $m = \pm 4i$.

The solution $y_1 = k_1 e^{iax}$ or $y_2 = k_2 e^{-4x}$ is adequate, but as we are looking for the general solution, the sum of all possible solutions is of importance. Therefore

$$y = y_1 + y_2$$

or

$$y = k_1 e^{i4x} + k_2 e^{-i4x}$$

is the desired general solution.

THE ADVANCED PLACEMENT EXAMINATION IN

CALCULUS BC

TEST I

$$3x^2 + 2\left[2xy^2 + x^2 2y dy\right] + y + x dy = 0$$

$$3x^2 + 4xy^2 + 4x^2 y dy + y + x dy = 0$$

$$\frac{-3x^2 - 4xy^2 - y}{4x^2 y + x} = 4x^2 y dy + x dy$$

$$= dy(4x^2 y + x)$$

$$\frac{-3 + -4 + -1}{4 + 1} = \frac{-8}{5}$$

ADVANCED PLACEMENT CALCULUS BC EXAM I

SECTION I

PART A

Time: 45 minutes
25 questions

End 2:35

DIRECTIONS: Each of the following problems is followed by five choices. Solve each problem, select the best choice, and blacken the correct space on your answer sheet.

NOTE:

Unless otherwise specified, the domain of function *f* is assumed to be the set of all real numbers *x* for which *f*(*x*) is a real number.

1. If $x^3 + 2x^2y^2 + xy = 7$, then at the point (1, 1), y' is

(A) -1

(B) $\frac{4}{5}$

(C) $-\frac{4}{5}$

(D) $-\frac{8}{5}$

(E) 0

2. Which of the following series are convergent?

I. $1 + \frac{1}{2^2} + \frac{1}{3^2} + \dots + \frac{1}{n^2} + \dots$

II. $1 + \frac{1}{\sqrt{2}} + \frac{1}{\sqrt{3}} + \dots + \frac{1}{\sqrt{n}} + \dots$

III. $\frac{1}{5} + \frac{1}{6} + \frac{1}{7} + \dots + \frac{1}{n+4} + \dots$

(A) I only

(B) II only

(C) I, II, and III

(D) II and III only

(E) none

3. $\int \sqrt{4 - x^2}\, dx =$

(A) $2 \cos^{-1} \frac{x}{2} + C$

(B) $\frac{x}{2}\sqrt{4 - x^2} + C$

(C) $2 \sin^{-1} \frac{x}{2} + \frac{x}{2}\sqrt{4 - x^2} + C$

(D) $2 \ln \left| x + \sqrt{4 - x^2} \right| + C$

(E) $2 \cos^{-1} \frac{x}{2} + \frac{x}{2}\sqrt{4 - x^2} + C$

4. $\lim_{x \to 0} \frac{1 - \cos x}{x^2}$ is

(A) 0

(B) $\frac{1}{2}$

(C) 1

(D) 2

(E) nonexistent

5. $\frac{1}{2}\int_2^4 \frac{2x + 4}{\sqrt{x^2 + 4x}}\, dx$ is approximately:

(A) −4.010

(B) −2.193

(C) 2.193

(D) 4.010

(E) 4.000

6. Let $f(x) = x^3$. Find the value of x_1 that satisfies the Mean Value Theorem on the closed interval [1, 3].

(A) 1.414

(B) 1.732

(C) 2.351

(D) 2.000

(E) 2.082

7. A particle moves in the xy - plane so that at any time, t, its coordinates are $x = t^3 - t^2$ and $y = t^4 - 5t^2$. At $t = 1$ its acceleration vector is:

(A) (0, 4)

(B) (0, 2)

(C) (2, 4)

(D) (− 4, − 2)

(E) (4, 2)

$dx = 3t^2 - 2t \Rightarrow 6t - 2$

$dy = 4t^3 - 10t \Rightarrow 12t^2 - 10$

$6 - 2 = 4$

$12 - 10 = 2$

8. At what value of x does $f(x) = \frac{x^3}{3} - x^2 - 3x + 5$ have a relative minimum?

(A) − 1 only

(B) 0 only

(C) + 1 only

(D) 3 only

(E) − 1 and 3

$x^2 - 2x - 3 = 0$

$2x - 2$

$(x - 3)(x + 1)$

$x = 3$ or -1

9.

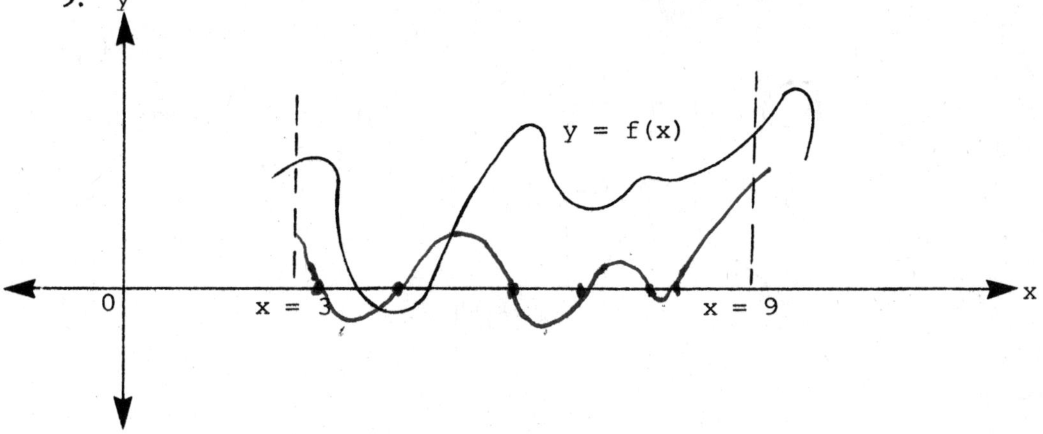

The graph of $y = f(x)$ on the closed interval [3, 9] is shown above. How many points of inflection does the graph have on this interval?

(A) two

(B) three

(C) four

(D) five

(E) six

10. If $\int f(x)e^x\,dx = f(x)e^x - \int 2x\,e^x\,dx$, then $f(x)$ could be:

(A) $2x$

(B) x^2

(C) $-x^2$

(D) e^x

(E) 2

11. $\int \frac{1}{(x-2)(x+3)}\,dx =$

(A) $\frac{1}{5} \ln \frac{|x+3|}{|x-2|} + C$

(B) $\frac{1}{5} \ln \frac{|x-2|}{|x+3|} + C$

(C) $\frac{1}{5} \ln |(x-2)(x+3)| + C$

(D) $(\ln |x-2|)(\ln |x+3|) + C$

(E) $(\ln |x+2|)(\ln |x-3|) + C$

12. If f and g are twice differentiable functions such that $g(x) = \ln (f(x))$ and $g''(x) = h(x) / (f(x))^2$, then $h(x) =$

(A) $f(x)f''(x) - 2f'(x)$

(B) $f(x)f''(x) - f'(x)$

(C) $f(x)[f''(x)]^2 - f'(x)$

(D) $f(x)f''(x) - [f'(x)]^2$

(E) $[f(x)f''(x) - f'(x)]^2$

13. Suppose that $f(x)$ is continuous for $a \le x \le b$, and let $\{a = x_0 < x_1 < x_2 < \ldots < x_n = b\}$ be a subdivision of $[a, b]$ into n equal intervals of length $h = (b - a)/n$. Then $\int_a^b f(x)\,dx$ approximately equals:

(A) $h[f(x_0) + 2f(x_1) + 2f(x_2) + \ldots + 2f(x_{n-1}) + f(x_n)]$

(B) $2h[f(x_0) + 2f(x_1) + 2f(x_2) + \ldots + 2f(x_{n-1}) + f(x_n)]$

(C) $\frac{h}{2}[f(x_0) + 2f(x_1) + 2f(x_2) + \ldots + 2f(x_{n-1}) + f(x_n)]$

(D) $h^2[f(x_0) + f(x_1) + f(x_2) + \ldots f(x_n)]$

(E) None of the above

14. An antiderivative of $\dfrac{x}{\sqrt{16 + x^2}}$ is

(A) $x\sqrt{16 + x^2}$

(B) $x(16 + x^2)$

(C) $\ln|16 + x^2|$

(D) $\sqrt{16 + x^2}$

(E) $\left(\frac{1}{2}\ln|16 + x^2|\right)(\ln x)$

15. The area of a region enclosed by the polar curve $r = \cos(2\theta)$ for $0 \leq \theta \leq \frac{\pi}{2}$ is

(A) 1.571

(B) 3.142

(C) 0.393

(D) 0.785

(E) 1.000

16. The length of the arc of $y = \frac{x^{5/2}}{5}$ from $x = 0$ to $x = 2$ is given by

(A) $\frac{1}{2}\int_0^2 (4 + x^3)^{\frac{1}{2}}\, dx$

(B) $\frac{1}{2}\int_0^2 (4 + x^3)\, dx$

(C) $\int_0^2 (1 + x^3)\, dx$

(D) $\int_0^2 (4 + x^3)^{\frac{1}{2}}\, dx$

(E) $\frac{1}{2}\int_0^2 (1 + x^3)^{\frac{1}{2}}\, dx$

17. An equation of the line normal to the graph of $y = 7x^4 + 2x^3 + x^2 + 2x + 5$ at the point where $x = 0$ is

(A) $x + 2y = 10$

(B) $2x + y = 10$

(C) $5x + 5y = 2$

(D) $2x - y = -5$

(E) $2x + y = -10$

18. If $\frac{dy}{dt} = t^2 - t - 1$ and if $y = 0$ when $t = 1$, what is the value of y when $t = 0$?

(A) $\frac{7}{6}$

(B) $\frac{8}{7}$

(C) $-\frac{4}{5}$

(D) $\frac{1}{2}$

(E) $\frac{4}{7}$

19. The area of the region between the graph of $y = 3x^2 + 3$ and the x- axis, from $x = 1$ to $x = 3$ is

(A) 36

(B) 32

(C) 27

(D) 24

(E) 21

20. Properties of the definite integral are:

I. $\int_a^b cf(x)\,dx = c\int_a^b f(x)\,dx$

II. $\int_a^b f(x)\,dx = -\int_b^a f(x)\,dx$

III. $\int_b^a [f(x)\cdot g(x)]\,dx = \int_a^b f(x)\,dx \cdot \int_a^b g(x)\,dx$

(A) I only

(B) II only

(C) III only

(D) I, II, and III

(E) I and II only

21. The region in the first quadrant between the x-axis and the graph $y = x^2$ from $x = 0$ to $x = 4$, is rotated about the line $x = 4$. The volume of the resulting solid of revolution is given by

(A) $\int_0^4 2\pi x^2(4-x)\,dx$

(B) $\int_0^4 \pi x^2(4-x)\,dx$

(C) $\int_0^4 2\pi x\,(4-x)\,dx$

(D) $\int_0^4 2\pi x\,(x-4)^2\,dx$

(E) $\int_0^8 \pi\left(4+\sqrt{16+y}\right)^2 dy$

22. $\lim_{x \to 0} x \ln x$ is

(A) 0

(B) e^3

(C) ln 3

(D) 1

(E) nonexistent

23. The general solution for the equation $\frac{dy}{dx} + y = x$ is :

(A) $y = x + 1 + Ce^{-x}$

(B) $y = x + 2 - Ce^{-x}$

(C) $y = x - e^{-x} + Ce^{-x}$

(D) $y = xe^{-x} + 1 + Ce^{-x}$

(E) $y = x - 1 + Ce^{-x}$

24. $\int_{-1}^{2} \frac{8dx}{x^3}$ is

(A) 3

(B) -3

(C) 8

(D) 0

(E) nonexistent

25. If C is a positive integer, then

$$\lim_{C\to\infty} \frac{1}{c}\left[\frac{1}{c} + \frac{2}{c} + \ldots + \frac{5c}{c}\right]$$ can be expressed as:

(A) $\int_0^1 x^2 dx$

(B) $\int_0^5 \frac{dx}{x}$

(C) $\int_{-5}^5 x dx$

(D) $\int_0^\infty x dx$

(E) $\int_0^5 x dx$

SECTION I

PART B

Time: 45 minutes
15 questions

DIRECTIONS: Calculators may be used for this section of the test. Each of the following problems is followed by five choices. Solve each problem, select the best choice, and blacken the correct space on your answer sheet.

NOTES:

1. Unless otherwise specified, answers can be given in unsimplified form.
2. The domain of function *f* is assumed to be the set of all real numbers *x* for which *f*(*x*) is a real number.

26. At each point (x, y) on a curve, the slope of the curve is $3x^2 (y - 6)$. If the curve contains the point $(0, 7)$, then its equation is:

(A) $y = 6e^{x^3}$

(B) $y = x^3 + 7$

(C) $y = 6e^{x^3} + 7$

(D) $y^2 = x^3 + 6$

(E) $y = e^{x^3} + 6$

27. Use the calculator to find $\int_{0.1}^{0.2} \sqrt{2}X^{-6}\, dx$.

(A) 14

(B) 53

(C) 3.5

(E) 25

(D) 0.8

28. The coefficient of x^3 in the Taylor series for $f(x) = \ln x$ about $x = 1$ is:

(A) $\frac{1}{6}$

(D) $\frac{1}{3}$

(B) $\frac{2}{3}$

(E) $\frac{1}{4}$

(C) $\frac{1}{2}$

29. The position of a particle moving along a straight line at any time t is given by $s(t) = 2t^3 - 4t^2 + 2t - 1$. The lowest rate of movement within the time interval [0,2] is:

(A) 4.25

(D) –1.5

(B) 0.5

(E) 3

(C) –0.67

$6t^2 - 8t + 2$

$0 = 12t - 8$

$8 = 12t$

$\overline{12} \quad \overline{12}$

30. For $-1 < x \le 1$, if $f(x) = \sum_{m=1}^{\infty} \frac{(-1)^{m+1} x^{3m-2}}{3m-2}$,

then $f'(x) =$

(A) $\sum_{m=1}^{\infty} (-1)^{m+1} x^{3m}$

(B) $\sum_{m=1}^{\infty} (-1)^{m+1} x^{3m-3}$

(C) $\sum_{m=1}^{\infty} (-1)^{3m} x^{3m}$

(D) $\sum_{m=1}^{\infty} (-1)^{m} x^{3m-3}$

(E) $\sum_{m=1}^{\infty} (-1)^{m} x^{3m}$

31. The acceleration of a particle moving on a line is $a(t) = t^{-\frac{1}{2}} + 3t^{\frac{1}{2}}$. The distance travelled by the particle from $t = 0$ to $t = 9.61$ is approximately

(A) 632.15

(B) 65.78

(C) 20.21

(D) 300.1

(E) 78.25

32. Which of the following is equal to $\int \frac{1}{x^2 + 9} dx$?

(A) $\arctan \frac{x}{3} + C$

(B) $\arcsin \frac{x}{3} + C$

(C) $\frac{1}{3} \arctan \frac{x}{3} + C$

(D) $\sqrt{x^2 + 9} + C$

(E) $\frac{1}{6} \ln \frac{|3 + x|}{|3 - x|} + C$

33. Let $f(x) = 3x^2 - 12x + 7$. If $f(x) = 0$, then x equals

(A) 1 and 2

(B) –2.28 and 1

(C) 3 and 2.5

(D) 0.71 and 3.28

(E) 1 and –6

$0 = 3x^2 - 12x + 7$

34. If f is a function such that $\lim_{x \to 5} \frac{f(x) - f(5)}{x - 5} = 0$ which of the following must be true?

(A) The limit of $f(x)$ as x approaches 5 does not exist.

(B) $f(5) = 0$

(C) f is continuous at $x = 0$.

(D) f' at $x = 5$ is 0.

(E) f is not defined at $x = 5$.

35. Let $f(x) = x^3 - x$. If $f'(-x) = -f'(x)$, find x.

(A) -1 and 1

(B) 0 only

(C) All x

(D) ± 0.58

(E) None

36. If $f(x) = x^2\left(\ln\left(x^3\right)\right)$, then $f'(3) =$

(A) 12.296

(B) 0.333

(C) 0.111

(D) 20.108

(E) 28.775

37. Find the derivative of $\cos^3 2x$.

(A) $3\cos^2 2x$

(B) $-6\cos^2 2x \sin 2x$

(C) $3\sin^2 2x$

(D) $-3\cos^2 2x \sin 2x$

(E) $3\cos 2x \sin 2x$

38. $\int \cos(3x+1)\,dx =$

(A) $3\sin(3x+1) + C$

(B) $\sin(3x+1) + C$

(C) $\frac{1}{3}\sin(3x+1) + C$

(D) $-\frac{1}{3}\sin(3x+1) + C$

(E) $-\sin(3x+1) + C$

39. What are all the values of x for which the series

$$x - \frac{x^2}{2^2} + \frac{x^3}{3^2} - \frac{x^4}{4^2} + \ldots \text{ converges?}$$

(A) All values of x

(B) $0 \le x \le 2$

(C) $0 < x < 2$

(D) $0 < x < 1$

(E) $-1 \le x \le 1$

40. If $f(x) = \dfrac{x}{\cot x}$, then $f'\left(\dfrac{\pi}{4}\right) =$

(A) $1 - \frac{\pi}{2}$

(B) $1 + \frac{\pi}{2}$

(C) $\frac{\pi}{2} - 1$

(D) 2

(E) $\frac{3}{4}$

ADVANCED PLACEMENT CALCULUS BC EXAM I

SECTION II

Time: 1 hour and 30 minutes
6 questions†

DIRECTIONS: Show all your work. Grading is based on the methods used to solve the problems as well as the accuracy of your final answers. Please make sure all procedures are clearly shown.

NOTES:

1. ln *x* denotes the natural logarithm of *x* (that is, logarithm to the base *e*).

2. Unless otherwise specified, the domain of function *f* is assumed to be the set of all real numbers *x* for which *f*(*x*) is a real number.

† The practice tests in this book incorporate Section II free-response solutions that approximate the content breakdown you will encounter on the AP exam. The overall timing and formatting of the practice tests mirror the actual test; examinees should note, however, that this section is split into two parts on the AP exam. Furthermore, prospective examinees should pay attention to restrictions on calculator use. For details, consult current official College Board materials in print or on the Web.

1. $\lim_{x \to a} f(x) = l$ if for each $\varepsilon > 0$ there exists $\delta > 0$ such that if $0 < |x - a| < \delta$, then $|f(x) - l| < \varepsilon$

(a) Find δ for $\lim_{x \to 2} (2x - 1) = 3$

(b) Sketch the graph of $f(x) = 2x - 1$ indicating δ and ε on the axes below.

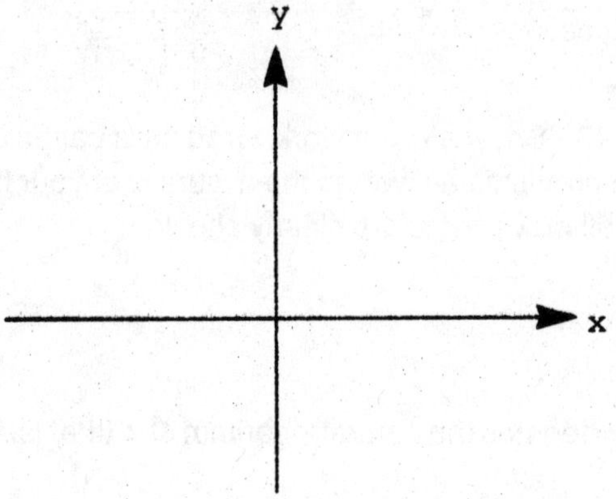

2. Given the circle $x^2 + y^2 = 25$, find the average value of y in the first quadrant when y is expressed as:

(a) a function of x

(b) a function of the angle $\theta = \angle P0Q$

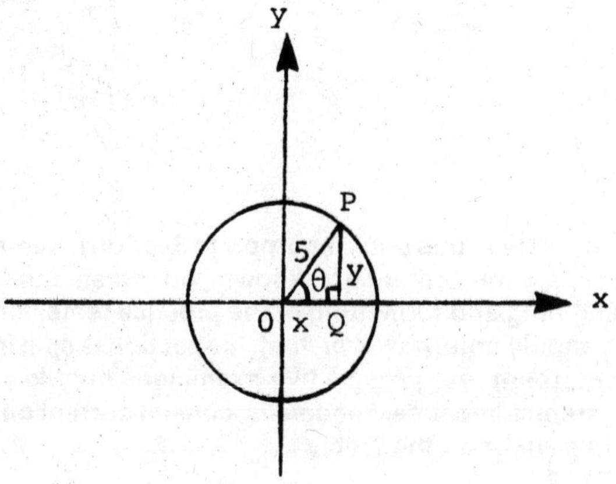

3. Function $f(x) = 2x^2 + x^3$.

(a) Find the local maximum of $f(x)$.

(b) Find the local minimum of $f(x)$.

(c) Evaluate $\int_{-2}^{1} f(x)$.

4. Given $y = x^3 - 6x^2 + 9x - 2$.

(a) Find the critical values of x.

(b) Find the x-coordinate of the relative maximum point of the graph.

(c) Find the x-coordinate of the relative minimum point of the graph.

(d) Sketch the graph on the axes below.

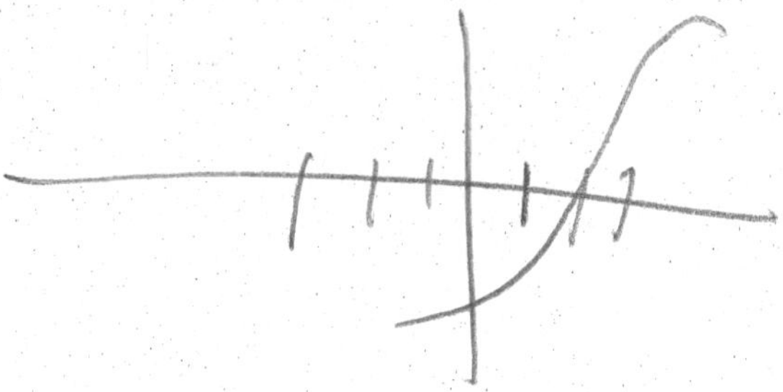

5. Given the ellipse $x = 8\cos\theta$

$$y = \sqrt{2}\sin\theta$$

(a) Find the equation of the line tangent to the ellipse at $\theta = 45°$.

(b) Find the equation of the line normal to the ellipse at $\theta = 45°$.

6. Consider the differential equation $\dfrac{dy}{dt} = -0.4Y$.

(a) Find the general solution of the differential equation.

(b) Find the solution when $y = y_0$ at $t = 0$.

(c) Find the value of t when $y = \dfrac{y_0}{2}$.

ADVANCED PLACEMENT CALCULUS BC EXAM I

ANSWER KEY

SECTION I

1.	D	21.	A
2.	A	22.	A
3.	C	23.	E
4.	B	24.	E
5.	C	25.	E
6.	E	26.	E
7.	E	27.	B
8.	D	28.	D
9.	D	29.	C
10.	B	30.	B
11.	B	31.	A
12.	D	32.	C
13.	C	33.	D
14.	D	34.	D
15.	C	35.	D
16.	A	36.	E
17.	A	37.	B
18.	A	38.	C
19.	B	39.	E
20.	E	40.	B

SECTION II

See Detailed Explanations of Answers.

ADVANCED PLACEMENT CALCULUS BC EXAM I

SECTION I

DETAILED EXPLANATIONS OF ANSWERS

1. (D)

Differentiate implicitly

$$3x^2 + 2\left(x^2 \cdot 2y\frac{dy}{dx} + y^2 2x\right) + \frac{xdy}{dx} + y = 0$$

$$\frac{dy}{dx}(4x^2y + x) = -(3x^2 + 4xy^2 + y)$$

$$\frac{dy}{dx} = -\frac{(3x^2 + 4xy^2 + y)}{4x^2y + x}$$

Substitute $(x, y) = (1, 1)$

$$\frac{dy}{dx} = \frac{-(3 + 4 + 1)}{(4 + 1)} = \frac{-8}{5}$$

2. (A)

A series with positive and negative terms is convergent if the series converges absolutely. Compare each given series with $1 + \frac{1}{2} + \frac{1}{2^2} + \frac{1}{2^3}, + \ldots$

which is known to be convergent.

The terms of the series above are <u>never less than</u> the corresponding terms of <u>I only</u>. Hence, <u>only</u> I is convergent.

3. (C)

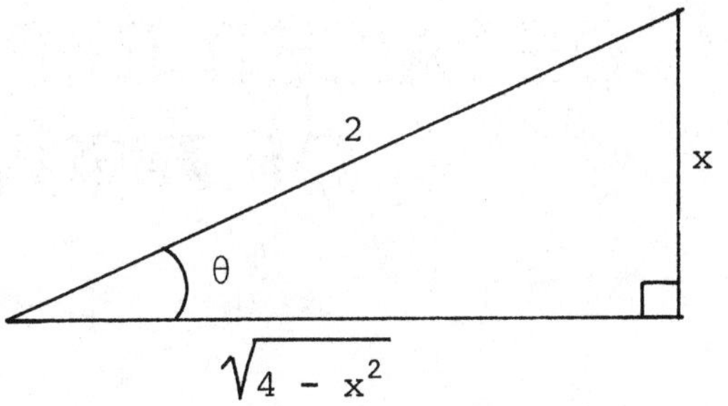

Using trigonometric substitution:

$$\sin\theta = \frac{x}{2}, x = 2\sin, dx = 2\cos\theta d\theta$$

$$\sqrt{4-x^2} = \sqrt{4-4\sin^2\theta} = 2\sqrt{1-\sin^2\theta} = 2\cos\theta$$

$$\int\sqrt{4-x^2}\,dx = 4\int\cos^2\theta d\theta.$$

Since $\cos^2\theta = (1+\cos 2\theta)/2$,

$$= 2\int(1+\cos 2\theta)d\theta = 2\theta + \sin 2\theta + C$$

$$= 2\theta + 2\sin\theta\cos\theta + C,$$

Since $\sin 2\theta = 2\sin\theta\cos\theta$

$$= 2\sin^{-1}\frac{x}{2} + \frac{x}{2}\sqrt{4-x^2} + C$$

4. (B)

By L'Hôpital's rule:

$$\lim_{x \to 0} \frac{1 - \cos x}{x^2} = \lim_{x \to 0} \frac{\sin x}{2x}.$$ Since this limit is also an indeterminate form, we can use L' Hôpital's rule again:

$$= \lim_{x \to 0} \frac{\cos x}{2} = \frac{1}{2}$$

5. (C)

Let $u = x^2 + 4x$ If $x = 4$ then $u = 32$

$du = (2x + 4)\,dx$ If $x = 2$ then $u = 12$

Substitute: $$\frac{1}{2}\int_{12}^{32} \frac{du}{u^{1/2}} = \frac{1}{2}\int_{12}^{32} u^{1/2}\,du = \frac{1}{2}\left[\frac{u^{1/2}}{\frac{1}{2}}\right]_{12}^{32}$$

$$= u^{\frac{1}{2}}\Big|_{12}^{32} = \sqrt{32} - \sqrt{12} = 4\sqrt{2} - 2\sqrt{3} =$$

$$= 2.193$$

6. (E)

$f(x) = x^3$ $f(b) = f(3) = 27$

$f'(x_1) = 3x_1^2$ $f(a) = f(1) = 1$

$$f(b) - f(a) = (b - a)f'(x_1)$$

$$27 - 1 = (3 - 1)\left(3x_1^2\right)$$

$$x = \sqrt{\frac{13}{3}} = 2.082$$

7. (E)

We know that $s(t) = (x(t), y(t))$ is the position function of a moving point P, with the velocity of P at the time t defined to be

$$v(t) = \lim_{h \to 0} \frac{s(t+h) - s(t)}{h}$$

Thus, for accleration, velocity, and position we have:

$$a(t) = v'(t) = s''(t) = (x''(t), y''(t))$$

$x(t) = t^3 - t^2$ $\quad$ $y(t) = t^4 - 5t^2$

$x''(t) = 6t - 2$ $\quad$ $y''(t) = 12t^2 - 10$

For $t = 1$, $x = 4$ and $y = 2$, so $a(1) = (4, 2)$

8. (D)

$$f'(x) = x^2 - 2x - 3 = (x+1)(x-3)$$

$(x+1)(x-3) = 0 \Rightarrow x = -1$ and 3 are critical values. The numbers -1 and 3 divide the x-axis into 3 intervals, from $-\infty$ to -1, -1 to 3, and 3 to $-\infty$.
$f(x)$ has a relative minimum value at $x = x_1$, if and only if $f'(x_1) = 0$ and the sign of $f'(x)$ changes from $-$ to $+$ as x increases through x_1.

If $-1 < x < 3$ then $f'(x) = -$
If $x = 3$ then $f'(x) = 0$
If $x > 3$ then $f'(x) = +$

$\therefore f(3)$ is a relative minimum.

9. (D)

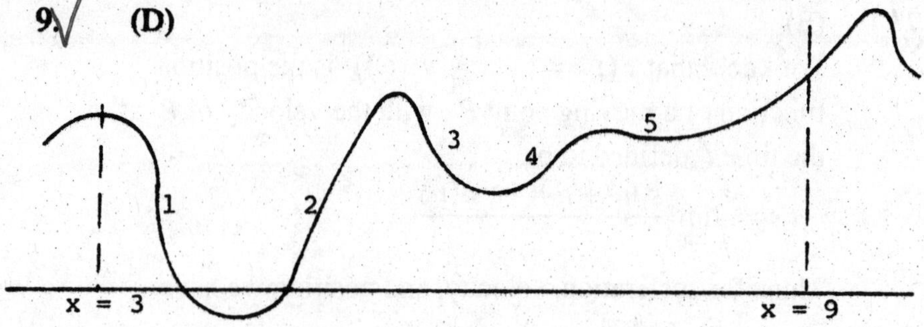

The point where a curve changes from concave upward to concave downward, or vice versa, is called a point of inflection.

10. (B)

Recognize the form as integration by parts:

$$\int u\,dv = uv - \int v\,du$$

$$u = f(x) \Rightarrow du = f'(x)dx$$

$$dv = e^x dx \Rightarrow v = e^x$$

$$\therefore f'(x) = 2x \text{, and } f(x) = x^2$$

11. (B)

Use partial fractions:

Let $\frac{1}{(x-2)(x+3)} = \frac{A}{(x-2)} + \frac{B}{(x+3)}$

then $1 = A(x+3) + B(x-2)$

$1 = (A+B)x + (3A-2B)$

$0 = A+B \Rightarrow A = -B$

$1 = 3A - 2B \Rightarrow 1 = 3A + 2A = 5A$

$A = \frac{1}{5}$ and $B = -\frac{1}{5}$

$$\int \frac{\frac{1}{5}}{x-2}\,dx + \int \frac{\left(-\frac{1}{5}\right)}{x+3}\,dx$$

$$= \frac{1}{5}(\ln|x-2| - \ln|x+3|) + C$$

$$= \frac{1}{5}\ln\left|\frac{x-2}{x+3}\right| + C$$

DNA

12. (D)

$g(x) = \ln(f(x))$ $\qquad$ $g''(x) = h(x)/(f(x))^2$

$g'(x) = \frac{f'(x)}{f(x)}$ $\qquad$ $h(x) = g''(x)(f(x))^2$

$$g''(x) = \frac{f(x)f''(x) - (f'(x))^2}{(f(x))^2} \Rightarrow h(x)$$

$$= \left(\frac{f(x)f''(x) - (f'(x))^2}{(f(x))^2}\right)(f(x))^2$$

So $h(x) = f(x)f''(x) - (f'(x))^2$

13. (C)

According to the Trapezoidal Rule:

$$\int_a^b f(x)\,dx \approx \frac{h}{2}[f(x_0) + 2f(x_1) + 2f(x_2) + \dots$$

$$+ 2f(x_{n-1}) + f(x_n)]$$

14. (D)

Let $u = 16 + x^2$

$du = 2x\,dx$

then

$$\int \frac{x}{\sqrt{16+x^2}}dx = \int \frac{x}{2x\sqrt{u}}du = \frac{1}{2}\int \frac{du}{\sqrt{u}} = \frac{1}{2}\int u^{\frac{-1}{2}}du$$

$$= \frac{1}{2}\frac{u^{1/2}}{1/2} + C = u^{1/2} + C$$

$= \sqrt{16+x^2} + C$. Letting $C = 0$, we see that

$\sqrt{16+x^2}$ is an antiderivative.

15. (C)

$$\frac{1}{2}\int_0^{\frac{\pi}{2}} r^2\,d\theta = \frac{1}{2}\int_0^{\frac{\pi}{2}} (\cos 2\theta)^2\,d\theta = \frac{1}{4}\int_0^{\pi} \cos^2\phi\,d\phi$$

Where we use the substitution $2\theta = \phi$.

if $\theta = \frac{\pi}{2}$, then $\phi = \pi$.

if $\theta = 0$, then $\phi = 0$

Then use the identity $\cos^2\phi = \frac{1}{2} + \frac{1}{2}\cos 2\phi$,

$$\frac{1}{4}\int_0^{\pi} \cos^2\phi \, d\phi = \frac{1}{4}\int_0^{\pi}\left(\frac{1}{2} + \frac{1}{2}\cos 2\phi\right)d\phi$$

$$= \frac{1}{4}\left[\frac{\phi}{2} + \frac{1}{4}\sin 2\phi\right]\Big|_0^{\pi}$$

$$= \frac{1}{4}\left(\frac{\pi}{2} + 0 - 0 - 0\right)$$

$$= \frac{\pi}{8} = 0.393$$

16. (A)

$$f(x) = \frac{x^{5/2}}{5} \quad f'(x) = \frac{x^{3/2}}{2}, \ [f'(x)]^2 = \frac{x^3}{4}$$

$$s = \int_a^b [1 + f'(x)^2]^{1/2} dx = \int_0^2 \left[1 + \frac{x^3}{4}\right]^{1/2} dx$$

$$= \frac{1}{2}\int_0^2 [4 + x^3]^{\frac{1}{2}} dx$$

17. (A)

$f(x) = 7x^4 + 2x^3 + x^2 + 2x + 5$. If we substitute $x = 0$, then $y = 5$.

$$f'(x) = 28x^3 + 6x^2 + 2x + 2$$

$f'(0) = 2$, so slope of normal line is $-\frac{1}{2}$ (negative/reciprocal)
and equation of normal line is $y - 5 = -\frac{1}{2}(x - 0)$, by point-slope formula

$2y - 10 = -x$

$x + 2y = 10$

18\. (A)

$\int dy = \int (t^2 - t - 1)dt$

$y = \frac{t^3}{3} - \frac{t^2}{2} - t + C$

Substitute : $y = 0$ and $t = 1$

$0 = \frac{1}{3} - \frac{1}{2} - 1 + C$

$C = \frac{7}{6}$

So $y = \frac{t^3}{3} - \frac{t^2}{2} - t + \frac{7}{6}$

and when $t = 0$,

$y = \frac{7}{6}$

19\. (B)

$\int_1^3 (3x^2 + 3) = [x^3 + 3x]_1^3 = 27 + 9 - 1 - 3$

$= 32$

20. (E)

III is not a property of the definite integral. For example let $f(x) = x$, $g(x) = \frac{1}{x}$. Then

$$\int_a^b f(x) \cdot g(x)dx = \int_a^b x \cdot \frac{1}{x}dx = \int_a^b dx = b - a,$$

but $\int_a^b f(x)dx \cdot \int_a^b g(x)dx = \int_a^b xdx \cdot \int_a^b \frac{1}{x}dx$

$$= \frac{x^2}{2}\Big|_a^b - \ln|x|\Big|_a^b = \frac{b^2}{2} - \frac{a^2}{2} + \ln\left|\frac{b}{a}\right| \neq b - a$$

21. (A)

By the shell method : $v = \int_a^b 2\pi x f(x)dx$

The product $2\pi x f(x)$ gives the lateral area of a cylindrical surface of radius x and height $f(x)$.
The thin strip shown in the figure will sweep out a thin shell of radius 4-x when revolved about the line $x = 4$.
The height of the shell is $h = y = x^2$

$$v = \int_0^4 2\pi x^2(4 - x)dx$$

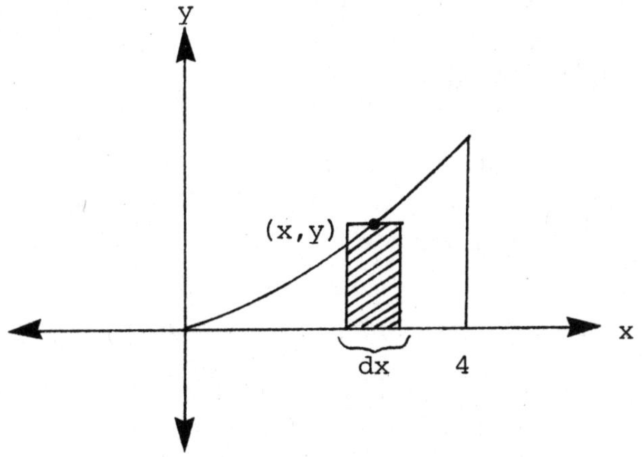

22. (A)

$$F(x) = x \ln x = \frac{\ln x}{\frac{1}{x}}$$

$$f(x) = \ln x \qquad g(x) = \frac{1}{x}$$

$$f'(x) = \frac{1}{x} \qquad g'(x) = -\frac{1}{x^2}$$

Use L' Hôpital's Rule :

$$\lim_{x \to 0} F(x) = \lim_{x \to 0} \frac{f(x)}{g(x)} = \lim_{x \to 0} \frac{f'(x)}{g'(x)} = \lim_{x \to 0} \frac{\frac{1}{x}}{-\frac{1}{x^2}}$$

$$= \lim_{x \to 0} (-x) = 0$$

DNA

23. (E)

Multiply given equation by

$$e^x \frac{dy}{dx} + e^x y = e^x x$$

$$\Rightarrow (ye^x)' = e^x x$$

Integrate both sides.

$$e^x y = (x - 1)e^x + C$$

$$y = x - 1 + Ce^{-x}$$

24. (E)

The function is not continuous at $x = 0$, which lies in the interval $[-1, 2]$. Therefore, the integral is nonexistent by the Fundamental Theorem of Calculus.

25. (E)

$$\lim_{c \to \infty} \frac{1}{c}\left[\frac{1}{c} + \frac{2}{c} + \ldots \frac{5c}{c}\right] =$$

$$\lim_{c \to \infty} \frac{1}{c^2}(1 + 2 + \ldots + 5c)$$

The sum of the integers from 1 to n equals $n(n+1)/2$

Let $n = 5c$; then $\lim_{c \to \infty} \frac{1}{c^2}[5c(5c+1)/2]$

$= \lim_{c \to \infty} \frac{5}{2}\left(5 + \frac{1}{c}\right) = \frac{25}{2}$. Also, $\int_0^5 x dx = \left[\frac{x^2}{2}\right]_0^5 = \frac{25}{2}$.

26. (E)

Solve the differential equation $\frac{dy}{dx} = 3x^2(y - 6)$

Separate variables : $3x^2 dx = \frac{dy}{(y-6)}$, and integrate

$$3\int x^2 dx = \int \frac{dy}{(y-6)}$$

$$x^3 = \ln(y - 6) + C$$

$$\ln(y - 6) = x^3 - C$$

$$y - 6 = e^{x^3} - C$$

$$y = e^{x^3 - C} + 6$$

Let $A = e^{-c}$, then $y = Ae^{x^3} + 6$

Substitute in (0, 7) : $7 = A + 6$

$A = 1 = e^{-c} \Rightarrow c = 0$

Therefore, $y = e^{x^3} + 6$

27. (B)

You can solve this equation directly by using

fnInt($\sqrt{2}$X^(−6), *x*, 0.1, 0.2)

Pressing ENTER, 53 will be given.

28. (D)

The coefficients for the power series of $f(x)$ about $x = b$

are given by : $a_n = \dfrac{f^{(n)}}{n!}$

$$f(x) = \ln x \qquad f(1) = 0$$

$$f'(x) = \frac{1}{x} \qquad f'(1) = 1$$

$$f''(x) = -\frac{1}{x^2} \qquad f''(1) = -1$$

$$f'''(x) = \frac{2}{x^3} \qquad f'''(1) = 2$$

$$a_3 = \frac{f'''(1)}{3!} = \frac{2}{3!} = \frac{1}{3}$$

29. (C)

The rate of movement of the particle is the velocity $s'(t)$. Use your graphic calculator to draw both $s(t)$ and $s'(t)$.

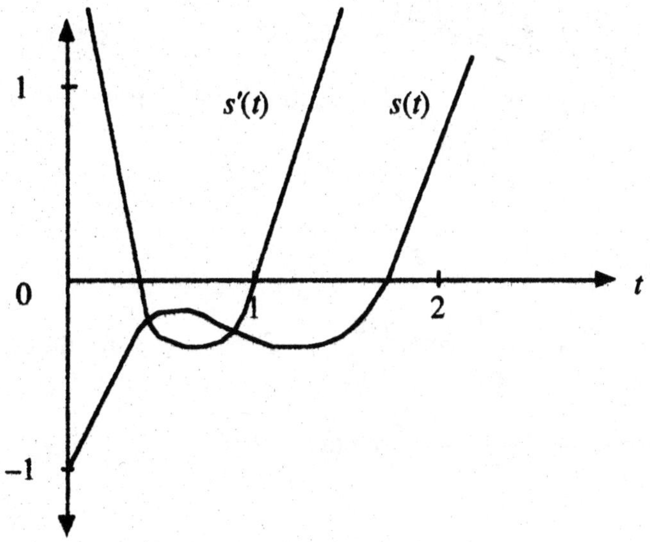

Readjusting the viewing window to $[0,1] \cdot [-1,0]$ and tracing $s'(t)$ to the minimum, you can get the lowest rate of movement –0.67.

30. (B)

We can differentiate the power series term by term:

$$\frac{d}{dx}\left(\frac{x^{3m-2}}{3m-2}\right) = x^{3m-3}$$

The constant term $(-1)^{m+1}$ is unchanged.

31. (A)

In order to find the distance travelled, you have to know the average velocity of the particle. But velocity is the integral of acceleration, i.e.,

$$\int_0^{9.61} t^{-\frac{1}{2}} + 3t^{\frac{1}{2}}, \text{ or } fnInt\ (X\text{^}\ (-0.5) + 3\ X\text{^}0.5, X, 0, 9.61)$$

which gives 65.78. Hence, the distance travelled is 65.78 · 9.61 ≈ 632.15 .

32. (C)

$\int \frac{du}{u^2 + a^2} = \frac{1}{a}\arctan\left(\frac{u}{a}\right) + C$ is a standard integration formula. $\int \frac{dx}{x^2 + 9} = \frac{1}{3}\arctan\frac{x}{3} + C$

33. (D)

Draw the graph of $f(x)$ in the window [–10,10] · [–10,10].

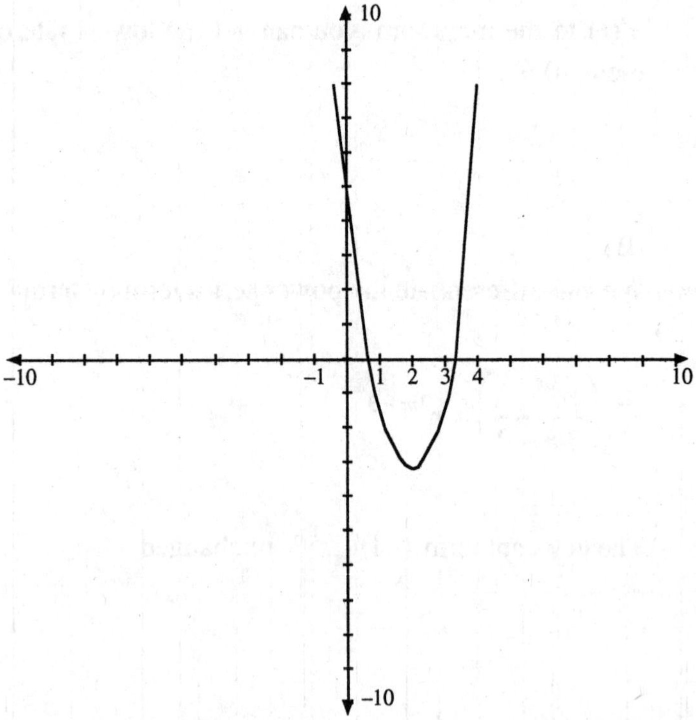

Obviously, when $f(x) = 0$, x can be either between 0 and 1 or between 3 and 4. Change the viewing window to $[0,4]\cdot[-1,1]$ and trace the coordinates on the graph. You can find $x = 0.71$, $x = 3.28$.

34. (D)

$$f'(5) = \lim_{x \to a} \frac{f(x) - f(a)}{x - a}. \text{ Let } a = 5;$$

$$f'(5) = \lim_{x \to 5} \frac{f(x) - f(5)}{x - 5} = 0 \text{ so } f'(5) = 0$$

35. (D)

Draw the graph of $f(x)$ and $f'(x)$.

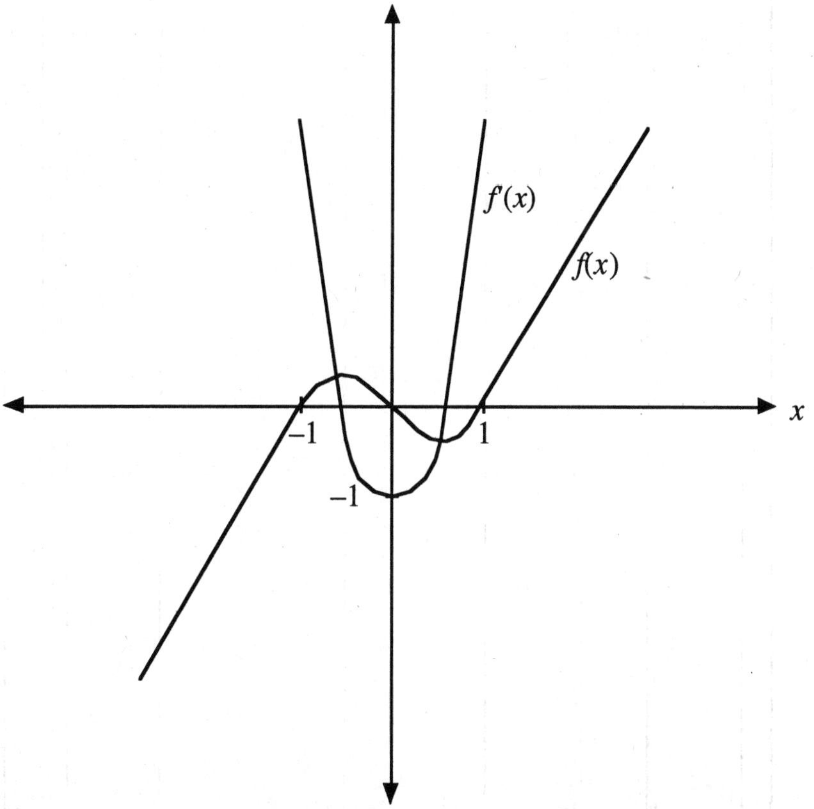

From the graph $f'(x)$, $f'(-x) = -f'(x)$ only holds when $f'(-x) = f'(x) = 0$. Set the viewing window to [–1,1] · [–0.5, 0.5] and trace the value of x to where $f'(x) = 0$. x should be –0.58 and 0.58 .

36. (E)

$$f'(x) = x^2\left(\frac{1}{x^3}\right)(3x^2) + 2x\ln(x^3)$$

$$= 3x + 2x \ln (x^3)$$

$$f'(3) = 3(3) + 2(3) \ln (3^3)$$

$$= 9 + 6 \ln 27$$

Calculator: [27] [ln] × [6] + [9] = 28.775

37. (B)

$$\frac{d}{dx}\cos^3 2x = 3(\cos 2x)^2 \frac{d}{dx}(\cos 2x)$$

$$= 3\cos^2 2x(-2\sin 2x)$$

$$= -6\cos^2 2x \sin 2x$$

38. (C)

$u = 3x + 1$ $\quad \frac{1}{3}\int \cos u\, du = \frac{1}{3}\sin(3x+1) + C$

$du = 3dx$

$\frac{1}{3}du = dx$

39. (E)

The nth term of the series is $(-1)^{n+1}x^n/n^2$.

$$\rho = \lim_{n\to\infty}\left|\frac{a_{n+1}}{a_n}\right| = \lim_{n\to\infty}\left|\frac{(-1)^{n+2}x^{n+1}/(n+1)^2}{(-1)^{n+1}x^n/n^2}\right|$$

$$= \lim_{n\to\infty}\left|\frac{-n^2}{(n+1)^2}x\right| = |x|$$

So, $\rho = |x|$ is the radius of convergence.

If $x = \rho < 1$, then we have convergence, and the interval of convergence is (–1,1).

We now check the endpoints of the interval.

When $x = 1$, series is $1 - \frac{1}{2^2} + \frac{1}{3^2} + \frac{1}{4^2} \ldots$, it converges.

When $x = 1$, series is $-1 - \frac{1}{2^2} - \frac{1}{3^2} - \frac{1}{4^2} \ldots$ it converges.

(Can compare both series to $\sum_{n=0}^{\infty}\frac{1}{2^n}$ in absolute values.)

$\therefore$ the series converges on [–1,1].

40. (B)

$$\frac{d}{dx}f(x) = \frac{\cot x - x\left(-\csc^2 x\right)}{\cot^2 x} = \frac{\cot x + x\csc^2 x}{\cot^2 x}$$

Substitute $\frac{\pi}{4}$ for x: $\frac{1+\pi/4\left(\sqrt{2}\right)^2}{1^2} = 1 + \frac{\pi}{2}$

ADVANCED PLACEMENT CALCULUS BC EXAM I

SECTION II

DETAILED EXPLANATIONS OF ANSWERS

1. (a)

Let $\epsilon > 0$ be given. We want to find $\delta > 0$ such that if $0 < |x - 2| < \delta$, then $|(2x - 1) - 3| < \epsilon$.

We need to establish a connection between $|(2x - 1) - 3|$ and $|x - 2|$.

The connection is : $|(2x - 1) - 3| = |2x - 4|$

so that $|(2x - 1) - 3| = 2|x - 2|$

To make $|(2x - 1) - 3|$ less than ϵ, make $|x - 2|$ twice as small. This suggests that we choose $\delta = \frac{1}{2}\epsilon$.

(b)

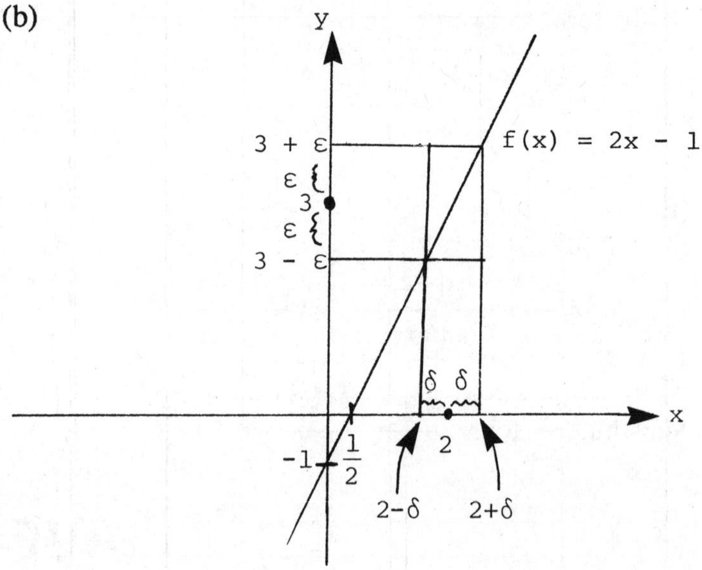

2. (a)

$x^2 + y^2 = 25$

$y = \sqrt{25 - x^2},\ a = 0, b = 5$

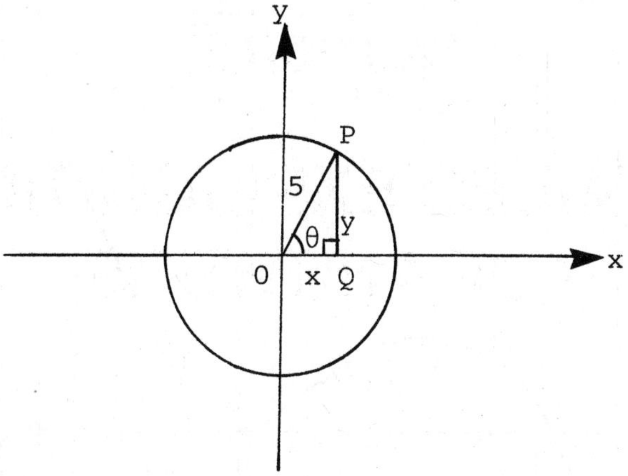

$$\bar{y} = \frac{\int_a^b y\,dx}{b-a} = \frac{\int_0^5 \sqrt{25 - x^2 dx}}{5-0} =$$

$$= \frac{\frac{1}{2}\left[x\sqrt{25 - x^2} + 25\sin^{-1}\left(\frac{x}{5}\right)\right]_0^5}{5}$$

$$= \frac{1}{5}\cdot\frac{1}{2}\left(25\cdot\frac{\pi}{2}\right) = \frac{5}{4}\pi$$

(b)

$y = 5\sin\theta, a = 0, b = \frac{\pi}{2}$

$$\bar{y} = \frac{\int_0^{\frac{\pi}{2}} 5\sin\theta\,d\theta}{\frac{\pi}{2} - 0} = \frac{5[-\cos\theta]_0^{\frac{\pi}{2}}}{\frac{\pi}{2}} = \frac{10(1)}{\pi} = \frac{10}{\pi}$$

3. (a)
Draw the graph of $f(x)$.

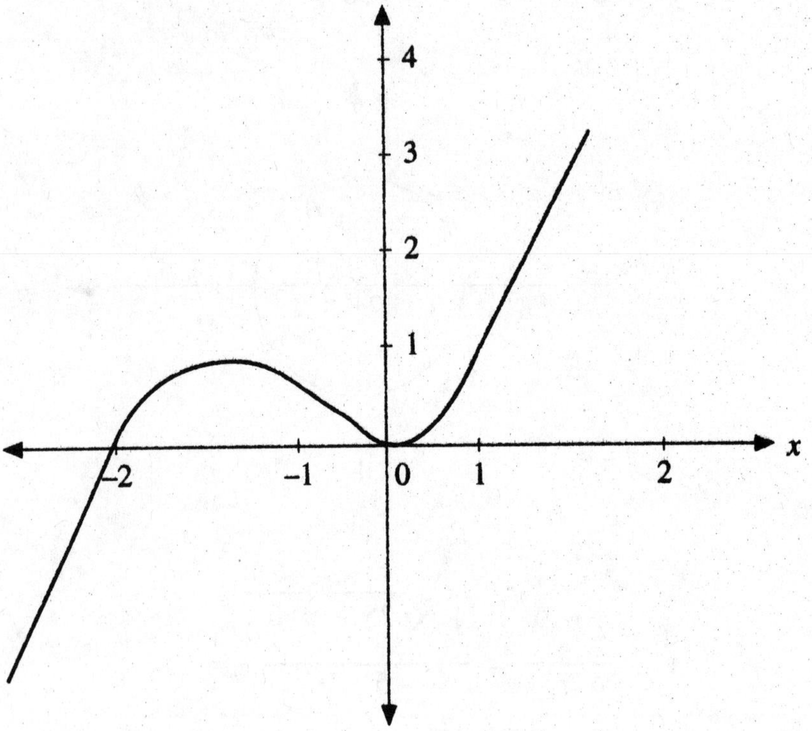

$f(x)$ has a local maximum in $-2 < t < -1$. By using viewing window $[-2, 0] \cdot [0,2]$, the value of this maximum can be found to be 1.19 at $x = -1.35$.

(b)
In the graph, it can be easily seen that $f(x)$ has a local minimum at $x = 0$, its values equal 0.

(c)

By using your calculator, $\int_{-2}^{1} f(x)$ can easily be solved by *fnInt* (2X^2 + X^3, X, –2, 1) which gives 2.25 .

Hence, $\int_{-2}^{1} 2x^2 + x^3\, dx = 2.25$.

4. (a)

$y = x^3 - 6x^2 + 9x - 2$

$f'(x) = 3x^2 - 12x + 9 = 3(x^2 - 4x + 3)$

$= 3(x-1)(x-3).$

Therefore, the critical values are $x = 1$ and 3.

(b)

$f''(x) = 6x - 12$

$f''(1) = 6 - 12 = -6$

Since $f''(1) < 0$, the x-coordinate of the relative maximum is 1.

(c)

$f''(3) = 18 - 12 = 6$

Since $f''(3) > 0$, the x-coordinate of the relative minimum is 3.

(d)

If $x = 1$, then $f(1) = 1 - 6 + 9 - 2$

$= 2$.

if $x = 3$, then $f(3) = 27 - 54 + 27 - 2$

$$= -2$$

if $x = 2$, then $f(2) = 8 - 24 + 18 - 2$

$$= 0$$

$\therefore$

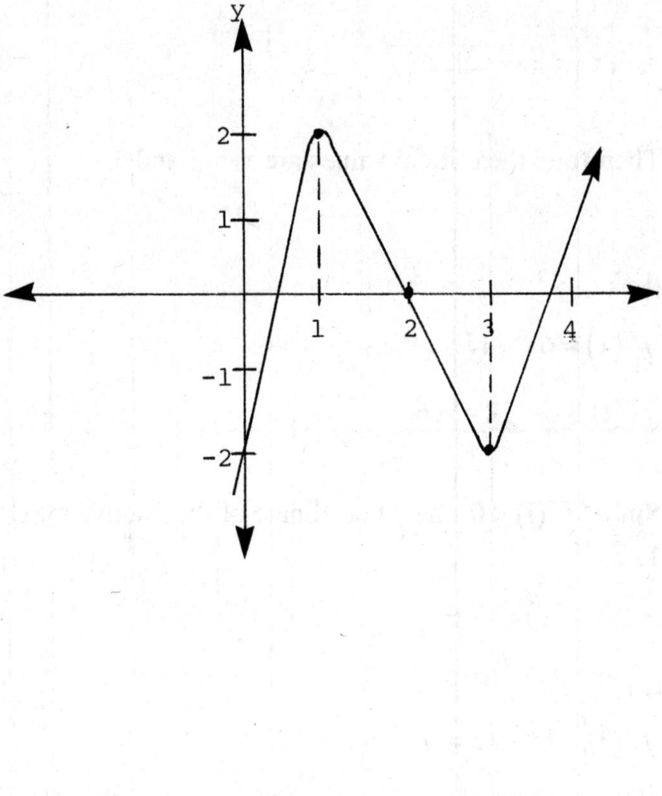

5. (a)

$$\frac{dx}{d\theta} = -8\sin\theta, \quad \frac{dy}{d\theta} = \sqrt{2}\cos\theta$$

$$\frac{dy}{dx} = \frac{dy/d\theta}{dx/d\theta} = -\frac{\sqrt{2}\cos\theta}{8\sin\theta} = \frac{-\sqrt{2}}{8}\cot\theta$$

$$m = \frac{-\sqrt{2}}{8}\cot 45° = -\frac{\sqrt{2}}{8}$$

$$x_1 = 8\cos 45° = 8\sqrt{2}/2 = 4\sqrt{2}$$

$$y_1 = \sqrt{2}\sin 45° = \sqrt{2}\cdot\sqrt{2}/2 = 1$$

$$y - y_1 = m(x - x_1)$$

$$y - 1 = -\frac{\sqrt{2}}{8}(x - 4\sqrt{2})$$

$$\sqrt{2}x + 8y = 16$$

(b)

$$y - y_1 = -\frac{1}{m}(x - x_1)$$

$$y - 1 = \frac{8}{\sqrt{2}}(x - 4\sqrt{2})$$

$$4\sqrt{2}x - y = 31$$

6. (a)

$$\frac{dy}{dt} = -0.4y$$

$$\frac{dy}{y} = -0.4\,dt$$

$\ln y = -0.4t + C$ or $y = e^{-0.4t + C}$

Let $e^c = A, \quad Y = Ae^{-0.4t}$

(b)

When $t = 0,\ y = y_0$
From (a), when $t = 0,\ y = A \ \therefore A = y_0,$ thus the solution is
$y = y_0 e^{-0.4t}$

(c)

From (b), $\dfrac{y_0}{2} = y_0 e^{-0.4t}$

$$\frac{1}{2} = e^{-0.4t}$$

$$-\ln 2 = -0.4t$$

$$\therefore t = \frac{\ln 2}{0.4} = \frac{5}{2}\ln 2$$

THE ADVANCED PLACEMENT EXAMINATION IN

CALCULUS BC

TEST II

ADVANCED PLACEMENT CALCULUS BC EXAM II

SECTION I

PART A

Time: 45 minutes
25 questions

DIRECTIONS: Each of the following problems is followed by five choices. Solve each problem, select the best choice, and blacken the correct space on your answer sheet.

NOTE:

Unless otherwise specified, the domain of function *f* is assumed to be the set of all real numbers *x* for which $f(x)$ is a real number.

1. If $y = f(x) = x^3 + \ln x$, what is y' ?

(A) $3x^2 \ln x + x^2$

(B) $\frac{1}{4}x^4 + \frac{1}{x}$

(C) $3x^2 + \frac{1}{x}$

(D) $3x^2 + x \ln x$

(E) None of the above

2. Given that $x'(t) = t^2 + 3t$ and $x(1) = 5$, what is $x(t)$?

(A) $2t + 3$

(B) $\frac{1}{3}t^3 + \frac{3}{2}t^2$

(C) $\frac{1}{2}t^3 + 3t^2 + \frac{3}{2}$

(D) $\frac{1}{3}t^3 + \frac{3}{2}t^2 + \frac{19}{6}$

(E) Cannot be determined

3. If $2x^3 + 3xy + e^y = 6$, what is y' when $x = 0$?

(A) -0.896

(B) 0.896

(C) 1.792

(D) -1.792

(E) 0

4. $\int_0^2 |x^2 - x|\,dx =$

(A) $\frac{2}{3}$

(B) $-\frac{2}{3}$

(C) $\frac{1}{2}$

(D) 0

(E) 1

5. Which of the values of x below are minima of $f(x) = x^3 - 3x$ on the interval $[-2, 2]$?

(A) -2

(B) 1

(C) -1

(D) -2 and -1

(E) -2 and 1

6. The BEST method to evaluate $\int_2^3 \frac{dx}{x^2 - x}$ is

(A) Integration by parts

(B) Partial fractions

(C) Completing the square

(D) Substitution

(E) None of the above

7. If a particle moves on the x - axis according to $x(t) = 2t - t^2$, how far to the right will it get ?

(A) 1

(B) 0

(C) -1

(D) 2

(E) -2

8. Given that $\cos x = \sum_{n=0}^{\infty} \frac{(-1)^n x^{2n}}{(2n)!}$ what is $\cos(3x^2)$?

(A) $\sum_{n=0}^{\infty} \frac{x^{4n}}{(2n)!}$

(B) $\sum_{n=0}^{\infty} \frac{(-9x)^{2n}}{(2n)!}$

(C) $\sum_{n=0}^{\infty} \frac{(-1)^n x^{2n}}{(2n)!}$

(D) $\sum_{n=0}^{\infty} \frac{-9x^{4n}}{(2n)!}$

(E) $\sum_{n=0}^{\infty} \frac{(-9)^n x^{4n}}{(2n)!}$

9. The area of one leaf of the rose $r = \sin 3\theta$ is

(A) $\frac{\pi}{12}$

(B) $\frac{\pi}{6}$

(C) $\frac{\pi}{4}$

(D) $\frac{\pi}{3}$

(E) $\frac{\pi}{2}$

10. As x approaches 2 from the left, $\left(1 - \frac{x}{2}\right)^{2-x}$ approaches

(A) 0

(B) $\frac{1}{e}$

(C) 1

(D) e

(E) No limit

11. $\int_0^1 \frac{dx}{x^2 - 4} =$

(A) ln 3 - ln 4

(B) $\frac{8}{9}$

(C) $\frac{\pi}{2}$

(D) $-\frac{1}{4}\ln 3$

(E) $-4\ln(-3)$

12. A funnel is in the shape of a circular cone with the height equal to the diameter (both 6 inches). Liquid is being poured through it at the rate of 2 cubic inches per minute when it becomes clogged. How fast is the level of liquid rising when it is 2 inches deep ? (The volume of a cone is $\frac{1}{3}\pi r^2 h$)

(A) $\frac{1}{\pi}$ in/min

(B) $\frac{2}{\pi}$ in/min

(C) 1 in/min

(D) $\frac{\pi}{2}$ in/min

(E) π in/min

13. $\int \frac{dx}{x^2 + a^2} =$

(A) $a \tan^{-1} ax + C$

(B) $\frac{1}{a} \tan^{-1} \frac{x}{a} + C$

(C) $\tan^{-1} x + C$

(D) $\tan^{-1} \frac{x}{a} + C$

(E) $\tan^{-1} ax + C$

14. The function of $f(x) = |x^2 - 2x|$ has a relative minimum at which values of x ?

(A) 1

(B) 0

(C) 2

(D) 0 and 2

(E) 0,1, and 2

15. If $y = x^2 + 3x + 5$ and $x = \sin t$, what is $\frac{dy}{dt}$ when $t = \pi$?

(A) 0

(B) 3

(C) 2

(D) -3

(E) 1

16. If $f(x) = \sum_{n=0}^{\infty} a_n (x-1)^n$ for some constants a_n, which of the following could be the interval of convergence for f?

(A) $[0, 1]$

(B) $\left[\frac{1}{2}, 2\right)$

(C) $(0,2]$

(D) $\left(0, \frac{3}{2}\right)$

(E) $(0,4]$

17. $\int_0^1 x^2 e^{x^3} dx$ is approximately:

(A) 0.906

(B) 0.573

(C) 1.718

(D) 8.155

(E) 5.155

18. If $y = x^{x^2}$, then $y'(2)$ is approximately:

(A) 76.361

(B) 64.000

(C) 54.181

(D) 4.773

(E) None of the above

19. The area between the line $y = x$ and the curve $y = \frac{1}{2}x^2$ is

(A) 1

(B) $\frac{1}{2}$

(C) $\frac{2}{3}$

(D) $\frac{3}{2}$

(E) 2

20. $\frac{d}{dx}\left(x^4 \ln\left(4x^4\right)\right)$ at $x = 1$ is:

(A) 5.545

(B) 22.181

(C) 38.181

(D) 9.545

(E) 4.000

21. If $e^x = \sum_{n=0}^{\infty} \frac{x^n}{n!}$, then $\sum_{n=1}^{\infty} \frac{(-1)^n x^{2n}}{n!}$ must be

(A) e^{-x^2}

(B) $\cos x$

(C) $1 - e^{-x^2}$

(D) $e^{-x^2} - 1$

(E) None of the above

22. $\int_{-1}^{1} \ln(x + 2)\,dx$ is approximately:

(A) 1.554

(B) 4.661

(C) 1.296

(D) 0.296

(E) diverges

23. If $x, y > 0$ and $y' = xy$, then $y =$

(A) Ke^{x}

(B) Ke^{x^2}

(C) Kx^2

(D) $Ke^{\frac{x^2}{2}}$

(E) Ke^{2x^2}

24. If the movement of a particle in the plane is $x(t) = \sin t$, $y(t) = \cos^2 t$, if t is in the interval $[0,\pi]$, when is it stationary ?

(A) 0

(B) $\frac{\pi}{2}$

(C) $\frac{\pi}{4}$

(D) $\frac{3\pi}{4}$

(E) π

$x'(t) = \cos t$

$y'(t) = 2\cos t(-\sin t)$

25. An ellipse with semiaxes a and b has area πab. If the area is 9π (held constant), how fast is b increasing when $a = 1$ and a is decreasing at $\frac{1}{2}$ units/minute?

(A) $4\frac{1}{2}$ units/minute

(B) $\frac{2}{9}$ units/minute

(C) 3π units/minute

(D) 3 units/minute

(E) Cannot tell

$9\pi = \pi ab$

$ab = 9$

$1b = 9$

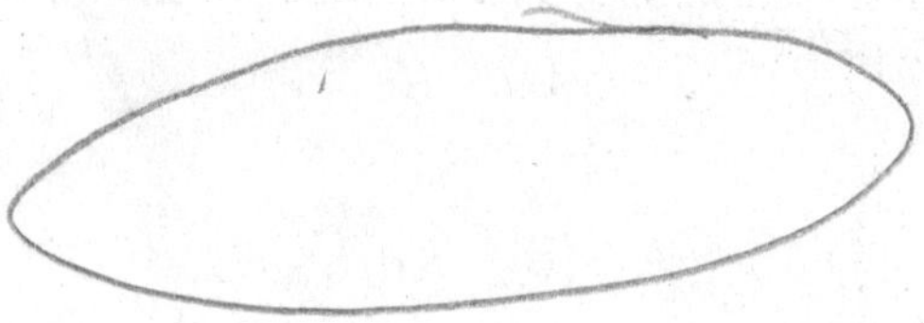

$dA = \pi(da\,b + a\,db)$

$0 = \pi(-\tfrac{1}{2}(9) + (1)db)$

$= \pi(-\frac{9}{2} + db)$

SECTION I

PART B

Time: 45 minutes
15 questions

DIRECTIONS: Calculators may be used for this section of the test. Each of the following problems is followed by five choices. Solve each problem, select the best choice, and blacken the correct space on your answer sheet.

NOTES:

1. Unless otherwise specified, answers can be given in unsimplified form.
2. The domain of function *f* is assumed to be the set of all real numbers *x* for which *f*(*x*) is a real number.

26. $\lim_{h \to 0} \frac{e^{1+h} - e}{h} =$

(A) 0

(B) $\frac{1}{e}$

(C) 1

(D) e

(E) Does not exist

27. Let $f(x) = 2\sqrt{x}$. If $f(c) = f'(c)$, then c equals

(A) 0

(B) 0.82

(C) 1.2

(D) 0.49

(E) 2.1

28. $\int_{-\frac{\pi}{2}}^{\frac{\pi}{2}} \frac{\cos^2\theta}{2} d\theta$ represents

(A) The area of a semicircle

(B) The area of a circle

(C) The area of a cardioid

(D) The area of one leaf of a rose

(E) None of these

29. The area under the first arch $f(x) = \sin x \ln x$ for $x \geq 0$ is

(A) –0.24

(B) 0.26

(C) 1.5

(D) –1.75

(E) 5.7

30. The curve $y = x^2$ between $x = 1$ and $x = 2$ is rotated around the y-axis. What volume is generated between it and the y-axis ?

(A) $\frac{15\pi}{2}$

(B) $\frac{5\pi}{2}$

(C) 9π

(D) $\frac{9\pi}{2}$

(E) 3π

31. Let $f(x) = x^3 - 2x$. The relationship between its local minimum and local maximum is

(A) $f_{min} = 2f_{max}$

(D) $f_{min} = 1.5f_{max}$

(B) $f_{min} = f_{max}$

(E) $f_{min} = \sqrt{f_{max}}$

(C) $f_{min} = -f_{max}$

$f'(x) = 3x^2 - 2$

$x = -.81606$

$.816$

32. $\int_0^{\pi} x \sin 2x \, dx =$

(A) 0

(D) $-\frac{\pi}{2}$

(B) $\frac{\pi}{2}$

(E) $1 + \frac{\pi}{2}$

(C) π

33. Estimate the "highest" rate of change for the function $y = \sqrt{1-x}$ inside $0 \le x \le 0.8$.

(A) -1.14

(B) 5

y'

$\frac{32}{5} - \frac{1}{5} = \frac{31}{5}$

(C) 0

(D) –3

(E) –2

34. The function $f(x) = x - (x)$ ([x] means greatest integer $\leq x$) satisfies which of these?

(A) Continuous at all non-integer values of x

(B) Periodic of period 1

(C) $f(0) = 0$

(D) $f(x) = x$ if $0 < x < 1$

(E) All of these

35. If $f(x) = x^{\frac{1}{3}} \ln x$, then $f'(2)$ equals

(A) –0.75

(D) 0

(B) 0.95

(E) 0.75

(C) 0.25

36. $\lim_{x \to 0} \frac{\sin 2x - 2x}{x^3} =$

(A) Does not exist

(B) 1

(C) $-\frac{4}{3}$

(D) ∞

(E) $-\infty$

37. Let $x(t) = \frac{1}{2}\left(e^t + e^{-t}\right), y(t) = \frac{1}{2}\left(e^t - e^{-t}\right)$ generate a curve from $t = -1$ to $t = 1$. What is the length of this arc?

(A) $\sqrt{2}\int_0^1 \sqrt{e^{2t} + e^{-2t}}\, dt$

(B) $\int_{-1}^1 \sqrt{e^{2t} - e^{-2t}}\, dt$

(C) $\sqrt{2}\int_0^1 \sqrt{e^{2t} - 1}\, dt$

(D) $\sqrt{2}\int_0^1 \sqrt{e^{2t} - e^{-2t}}\, dt$

(E) $\sqrt{2}\int_{-2}^2 \sqrt{e^t + e^{-t}}\, dt$

38. If n is a positive integer, then $\lim_{n \to \infty} \sum_{K=1}^{n} \frac{K}{n^2} =$

(A) π

(B) 1

(C) $\frac{1}{2}$ (D) $\frac{1}{\pi}$

(E) 0

39. If y is a function of x, $y' = y^2$ and $y(1) = 1$, then y is

(A) $\frac{1}{x}$

(B) $\frac{1}{2-x}$

(C) $\frac{1}{1-x}$

(D) $\frac{1}{x^2}$

(E) $\frac{2}{1+x}$

40. If a is a constant, then $\int_0^{\infty} xe^{ax}\,dx$

(A) always diverges

(B) always converges

(C) converges if $a > 0$

(D) converges if $a < 0$

(E) None of these

ADVANCED PLACEMENT CALCULUS BC EXAM II

SECTION II

Time: 1 hour and 30 minutes
6 questions†

DIRECTIONS: Show all your work. Grading is based on the methods used to solve the problems as well as the accuracy of your final answers. Please make sure all procedures are clearly shown.

NOTES:

1. ln *x* denotes the natural logarithm of *x* (that is, logarithm to the base *e*).

2. Unless otherwise specified, the domain of function *f* is assumed to be the set of all real numbers *x* for which *f*(*x*) is a real number.

1. Construct an isosceles triangle with two equal sides which are equal to the positive real number a. Call the other side $2x$.

   (a) What is the area, A, of such a triangle?

   (b) What is $\frac{dA}{dx}$?

† The practice tests in this book incorporate Section II free-response solutions that approximate the content breakdown you will encounter on the AP exam. The overall timing and formatting of the practice tests mirror the actual test; examinees should note, however, that this section is split into two parts on the AP exam. Furthermore, prospective examinees should pay attention to restrictions on calculator use. For details, consult current official College Board materials in print or on the Web.

(c) When is $\frac{dA}{dx} = 0$?

(d) Is this value minimum or maximum?

2. We want to know $\sqrt[3]{65}$.

(a) Write a series for $x^{\frac{1}{3}}$ near 64.

(b) Write the remainder after n terms.

(c) Decide how many terms to keep to achieve 4-digit accuracy.

3. Let $f(x) = \ln(x^2 - x - 6)$.

(a) The domain of $f(x)$ is $b < x < a$. Find a and b.

(b) Find $f(5)$.

(c) Find $f'(-3)$.

4. The curve $y = x^{\frac{1}{2}}$ is bounded by the x-axis, $x = 0$, and $x = 4$.

(a) Determine the area under the curve.

(b) Determine the volume of the solid generated when the curve is rotated about the x-axis.

5. Suppose $xy + \sin x + e^y = 0$

(a) How many values of x_0 are there such that $(x_0, 0)$ satisfies this equation?

(b) List one such value of x_0.

(c) Find y' at that point.

(d) Find y'' at that point.

6. A particle is traveling along the x - axis subject to an acceleration of $2 - \sin t$. When $t = 0$, its velocity and position are both zero.

(a) What is its velocity at time t ?

(b) What is its position at time t ?

(c) Is the motion bounded or unbounded ?

ADVANCED PLACEMENT CALCULUS BC EXAM II

ANSWER KEY

SECTION I

1.	C	21.	D
2.	D	22.	C
3.	B	23.	D
4.	E	24.	B
5.	E	25.	A
6.	B	26.	D
7.	A	27.	D
8.	E	28.	B
9.	A	29.	A
10.	C	30.	A
11.	D	31.	C
12.	B	32.	D
13.	B	33.	A
14.	D	34.	E
15.	D	35.	B
16.	C	36.	C
17.	B	37.	A
18.	A	38.	C
19.	C	39.	B
20.	D	40.	D

SECTION II

See Detailed Explanations of Answers.

ADVANCED PLACEMENT CALCULUS BC EXAM II

SECTION I

DETAILED EXPLANATIONS OF ANSWERS

1. (C)

$y' = 3x^2 + \frac{1}{x}$

2. (D)

$x(t) = \int (t^2 + 3t)\,dt$

$= \frac{1}{3}t^3 + \frac{3}{2}t^2 + c$

Since $x(1) = 5 = \frac{1}{3} + \frac{3}{2} + c$, $c = 5 - \frac{1}{3} - \frac{3}{2} = \frac{19}{6}$
$x = \frac{1}{3}t^3 + \frac{3}{2}t^2 + \frac{19}{6}$

ONA

3. (B)

Using implicit differentiation

$6x^2 + 3xy' + 3y + e^y y' = 0$ so

$$y' = -\frac{6x^2 + 3y}{3x + e^y}$$

$y(0) = \ln 6$, hence

$$y'(0) = \frac{-3\ln 6}{6} = -\frac{1}{2}\ln 6 = 0.896$$

4. (E)

$$\int_0^2 |x^2 - x|\, dx = \int_0^1 (x - x^2)\, dx + \int_1^2 (x^2 - x)\, dx$$

$$= \left(\frac{x^2}{2} - \frac{x^3}{3}\right)\Big|_0^1 + \left(\frac{x^3}{3} + \frac{x^2}{2}\right)\Big|_1^2$$

$$= \frac{1}{6} + \frac{1}{6} + \frac{8}{3} - 2 = 1$$

5. (E)

$f'(x) = 3x^2 - 3 = 0$ when $x = \pm 1$.

$f''(x) = 6x \quad f''(-1) < 0,\ -1$ so -1 is a maxima

$f''(1) > 0,\ 1$ so 1 is a minima

$f(1) = 1 - 3 \cdot 1 = -2$

Check endpoints :

$f(2) = 2^3 - 3 \cdot 2 = 2$

$f(-2) = (-2)^3 - 3(-2) = -2$

$\therefore x = 1, -2$

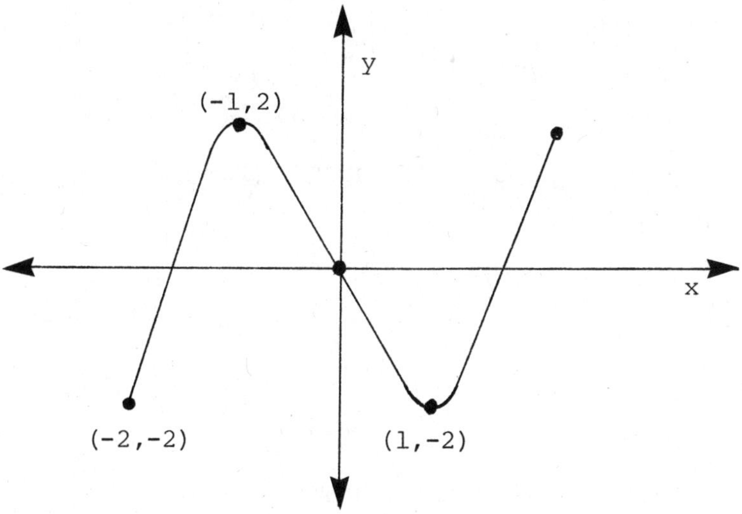

6. (B)

Partial fractions is the simplest method:

$$\frac{1}{x^2 - x} = \frac{1}{x(x-1)} = \frac{-1}{x} + \frac{1}{x-1}.$$

There exists no obvious choice for u and dv in parts.

Completing the square would be feasible, but it is a longer process:

$$\frac{dx}{x^2 - x} = \frac{dx}{x^2 - x + \frac{1}{4} - \frac{1}{4}}$$

$$= \frac{dx}{\left(x - \frac{1}{2}\right)^2 - \frac{1}{4}} = \frac{du}{u^2 - \frac{1}{4}},$$

No substitution looks promising.

7. (A)

$$\frac{dx}{dt} = 2 - 2t = 0 \text{ at } t = 1$$

$$\frac{d^2x}{dt^2} = -2 \text{ so } t = 1 \text{ is a max, } x(1) = 1$$

8. (E)

Substitute $3x^2$ for x in the series:

$$\cos(3x^2) = \sum_{n=0}^{\infty} \frac{(-1)^n (3x^2)^{2n}}{(2n)!} = \sum_{n=0}^{\infty} \frac{(-9)^n x^{4n}}{(2n)!}$$

9. (A)

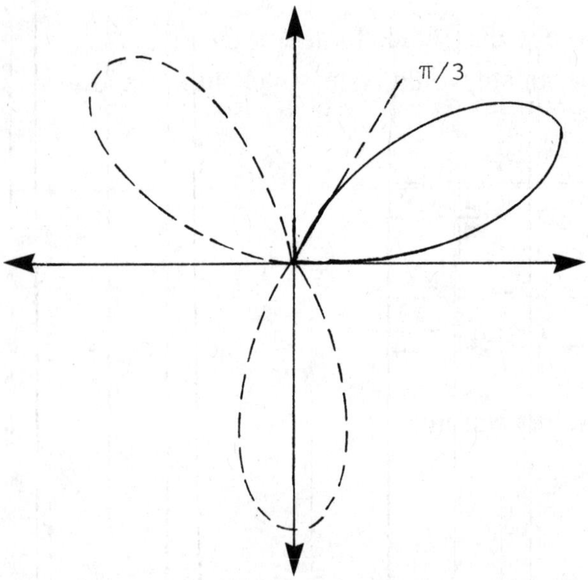

$$A = \int_{\theta_1}^{\theta_2} \frac{1}{2} r^2 d\theta$$

$$= \int_0^{\pi/3} \frac{\sin^2 3\theta}{2} d\theta$$

$$= \int_0^{\pi/3} \frac{1}{4}(1 - \cos 6\theta)d\,\theta = \left(\frac{\pi}{4}\theta - \frac{1}{24}\sin 6\theta\right)\Big|_0^{\pi/3} = \frac{\pi}{12}$$

where we use identity

$$\sin^2 3\theta = \frac{1 - \cos 6\theta}{2}$$

10. (C)

$$\lim_{x \to 2^-} \left(1 - \frac{x}{2}\right)^{2-x} = \lim_{x \to 2^-} e^{(2-x)\ln(1-x/2)}$$

$$= e^{\lim_{x \to 2^-} (2x)\ln\left(1 - \frac{x}{2}\right)}$$

We see $(2 - x)\ln\left(1 - \frac{x}{2}\right) = \dfrac{\ln((2-x)/2)}{\frac{1}{2-x}}$,

so we will find $\lim_{x \to 2^-} \dfrac{\ln\left(\frac{2-x}{2}\right)}{\frac{1}{2-x}}$

This is indeterminate, so by L' Hôpital's Rule:

$$\lim_{x \to 2^-} \frac{-1/(2-x)}{-1/(2-x)^2} = \lim_{x \to 2^-} (2 - x) = 0.$$

So $\lim_{x \to 2^-} \left[1 - \frac{x}{2}\right]^{2-x} = e^0 = 1.$

11. (D)
Using partial fractions

Let $\frac{1}{x^2 - 4} = \frac{A}{x - 2} + \frac{B}{x + 2}$

then $1 = A(x + 2) + B(x - 2)$
$\therefore 0 = A + B$, and $1 = 2A - 2B$
Solving these two equations, we have $A = \frac{1}{4}, B = -\frac{1}{4}$.

so $\int_0^1 \frac{dx}{x^2 - 4} = \int_0^1 \frac{\frac{1}{4}dx}{x - 2} - \int_0^1 \frac{\frac{1}{4}dx}{x + 2}$

$= \frac{1}{4}\ln|x - 2|\Big|_0^1 - \frac{1}{4}\ln|x + 2|\Big|_0^1$

$= \frac{1}{4}\ln 1 - \frac{1}{4}\ln 2 - \frac{1}{4}\ln 3 + \frac{1}{4}\ln 2 = -\frac{1}{4}\ln 3$

12. (B)

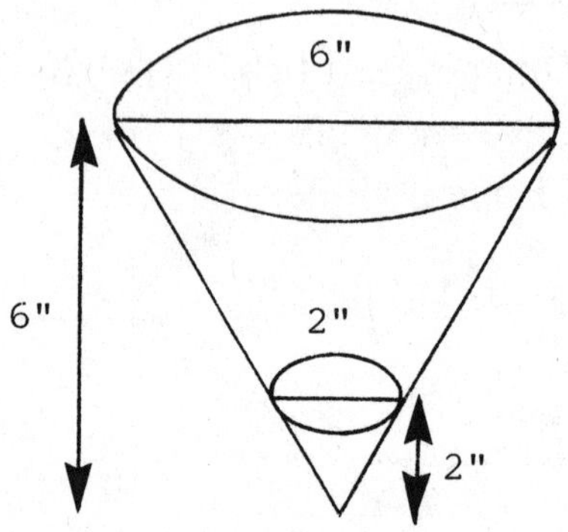

$V = \frac{1}{3}\pi r^2 h$. But the shape has

$h = 2r, V = \frac{2}{3}\pi r^3$,

$\frac{dV}{dt} = \frac{dv}{dr}\frac{dr}{dt} = 2$

$2\pi r^2 \frac{dr}{dt} = 2$

(given information)

so $\pi r^2 \frac{dr}{dt} = 1$ and $\frac{dr}{dt} = \frac{1}{\pi r^2}$.

Since $h = 2r$ and $h = 2$, we have $r = 1$ and $\frac{dr}{dt} = \frac{1}{\pi}$

So, $\frac{dh}{dt} = \frac{dh}{dr}\frac{dr}{dt} = 2\frac{dr}{dt} = \frac{2}{\pi}$ in/min.

13. (B)

If you have trouble remembering which integration formula is correct, substitute $x = a \tan \theta$.

$$\int \frac{dx}{x^2 + a^2} = \int \frac{a \sec^2 \theta \, d\theta}{a^2(\tan^2 \theta + 1)} = \int \frac{d\theta}{a}$$

$$= \frac{\theta}{a} + C = \frac{1}{a} \tan^{-1} \frac{x}{a} + C .$$

14. (D)

$f(x)$ has three critical points: $x = 0$, 1, and 2. $f'(1) = 0$ while $f'(0)$ and $f'(2)$ do not exist. $f(1) = 1$, $f(0) = f(2) = 0$, $\therefore f(x)$ has a relative minimum at $x = 0$ and $x = 2$.

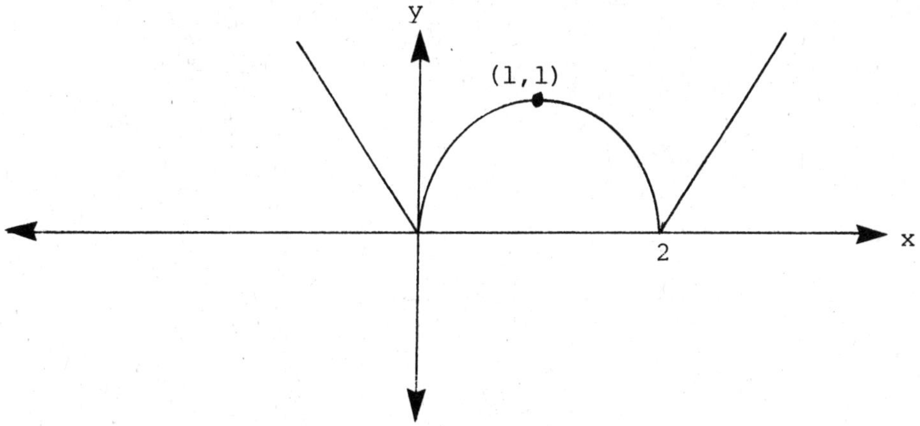

15. (D)

$$\frac{dy}{dx} = 2x + 3, \frac{dx}{dt} = \cos t \text{ , and}$$

$$\frac{dy}{dt} = \frac{dy}{dx} \cdot \frac{dx}{dt} = (2 \sin t + 3) \cos t \text{ .}$$

When $t = \pi$, $\sin t = 0$ and $\cos t = -1$, so

$$\frac{dy}{dt} = (0 + 3)(-1) = -3$$

16. (C)

The interval of convergence of a power series must be centered at the value "a" in $(x - a)^n$ (except possibly for the end points). Since $a = 1$, the only possibility is (C).

17. (B)

Integrate by substitution. Let $x^3 = u$, $dx \cdot 3x^2dx = du$, $x^2dx = \frac{1}{3}du$.

When $x = 0$, $u = 0$; when $x = 1$, $u = 1$.

$$\int_0^1 x^2e^{x^3}dx = \frac{1}{3}\int_0^1 e^u du$$

$$\text{so } \int_0^1 x^2e^{x^3}dx = \frac{1}{3}e^u \Big|_0^1 = \frac{1}{3}(e - 1) = 0.573$$

18. (A)

Take the natural log of both sides and use logarithmic differentiation. So, $\ln y = x^2 \ln x$

$$\frac{y'}{y} = x^2 \cdot \frac{1}{x} + 2x \ln x = x + 2x \ln x$$

$$y' = x^{x^2}(x + 2x \ln x)$$

$$y'(2) = 2^{2^2}(2 + 2(2)\ln(2))$$

$$= 2^4(2 + 4\ln 2) = 76.361$$

19. (C)

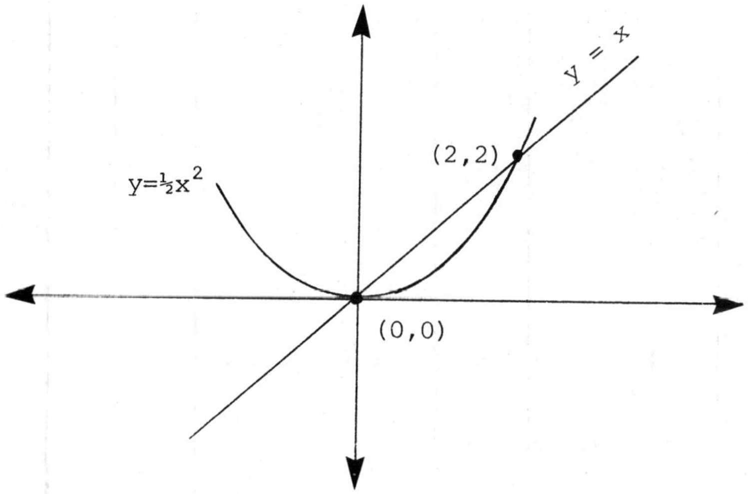

The curve is below the line, so

$$\text{Area} = \int_0^2 \left(x - \frac{1}{2}x^2\right) dx = \left(\frac{x^2}{2} - \frac{x^3}{6}\right)\Big|_0^2 = 2 - \frac{8}{6} = \frac{2}{3}.$$

20. (D)

Using the product rule,

$$\frac{d}{dx}\left[x^4 \ln\left(4x^4\right)\right] = x^4 \cdot \frac{16x^3}{4x^4} + 4x^3 \ln\left(4x^4\right)$$

$$= 4x^3 + 4x^3 \ln(4x^4)$$

$$= 4x^3(1 + \ln(4x^4))$$

$$\left.\frac{d}{dx}\right|_1 = 4(1)^3(1 + \ln(4 \times 1))$$

$$= 4(1 + \ln 4) = 9.545$$

21. (D)

Notice that $\sum_{n=1}^{\infty} \frac{(-1)^n x^{2n}}{n!} = \sum_{n=1}^{\infty} \frac{\left(-x^2\right)^n}{n!}$

$$= \sum_{n=0}^{\infty} \frac{\left(-x^2\right)^n}{n!} - 1$$

$$= e^{-x^2} - 1$$

22. (C)

$\int_{-1}^{1} \ln(x+2)dx = \int_{1}^{3} \ln(u)du$ if $u = x + 2$. Let $du = dg$

and $\ln u = f$, then

$$\int_{1}^{3} \ln(u)du = \int_{1}^{3} fdg = fg\Big|_1^3 - \int_{1}^{3} gdf$$

$$\int_{1}^{3} \ln(u)du = \int_{1}^{3} fdg = fg\Big|_1^3 - \int_{1}^{3} gdf$$

$$= (u \ln u - u)\Big|_1^3$$

$$= 3\ln 3 - 3 - (1 \times \ln 1 - 1) = 3\ln 3 - 2 = 1.296$$

23. (D)

$\frac{y'}{y} = x \Rightarrow \frac{dy}{y} = xdx \Rightarrow \int \frac{dy}{y} = \int xdx \Rightarrow$

$\ln|y| = \frac{x^2}{2} + c.$

Since $y > 0$, $y = e^{\frac{x^2}{2} + c} = Ke^{\frac{x^2}{2}}$, where $K = e^c$.

24. (B)

We want the velocity factor,

$\left(\frac{dx}{dt}, \frac{dy}{dt}\right) = (0,0)$, so $\frac{dx}{dt} = \cos t = 0 \Rightarrow t = \frac{\pi}{2}$,

and $\frac{dy}{dt} = 2\cos t\,(-\sin t) = -\sin 2t = 0 \Rightarrow 2t = 0, \pi$

so $t = 0, \frac{\pi}{2.}$

In order to make $\frac{dx}{dt} = 0$ and $\frac{dy}{dt}$ at the same time, t must be $\frac{\pi}{2.}$

25. (A)

The area of an ellipse $= \pi ab$, so $\pi ab = 9\pi, b = \frac{9}{a}$.

Thus $\frac{db}{dt} = \frac{-9}{a^2}\frac{da}{dt} = -9 \cdot \left(-\frac{1}{2}\right) = 4\frac{1}{2}$

26. (D)

Let $f(x) = e^x$, then $\lim_{h \to 0} \frac{e^{1+h} - e}{h}$

$= \lim_{h \to 0} \frac{f(1+h) - f(1)}{h} = f'(1) = e^x\big|_{x=1}$

$= e$

27. (D)

Draw both graphs of $f(x)$ and $f'(x)$.

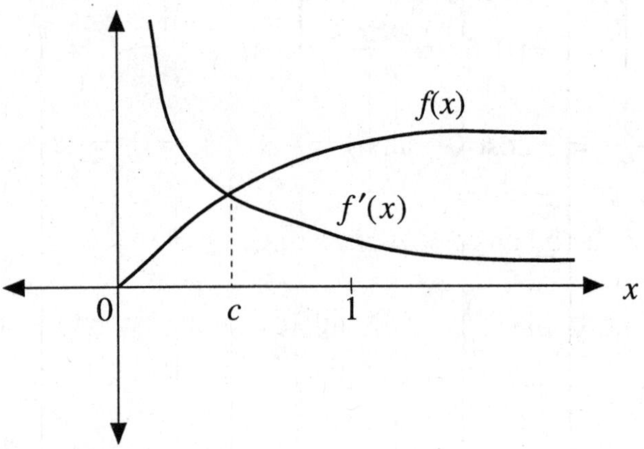

By tracing on the graph to the point where $x = c$, you can find that $c = 0.49$.

28. (B)

Note that area $= \int_{\theta_1}^{\theta_2} \frac{r^2}{2} d\theta$, so

$r = \cos\theta$

$r^2 = r\cos\theta$

$x^2 - x + y^2 = 0$

$\left(x - \frac{1}{2}\right)^2 + y^2 = \left(\frac{1}{2}\right)^2$

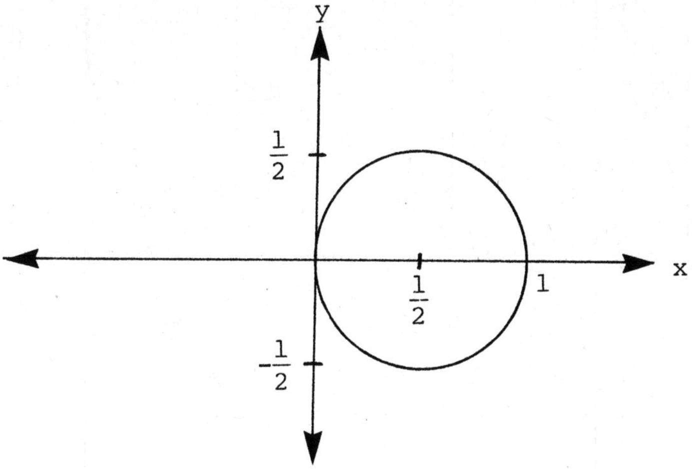

It is a circle of radius $\frac{1}{2}$ centered at $\left(\frac{1}{2},0\right)$.

29. (A)
Draw the graph of $f(x) = \sin x \ln x$.

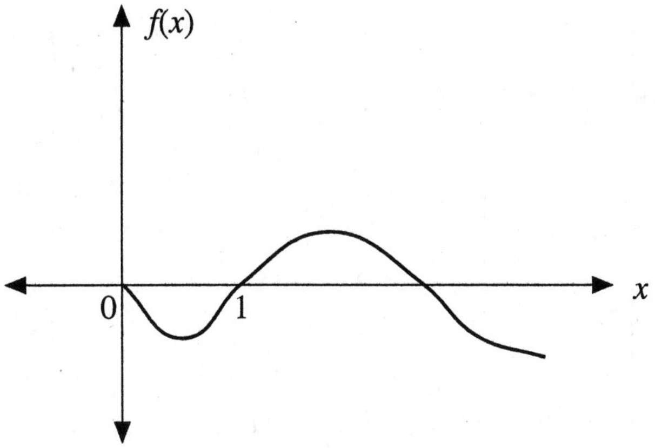

The area under the first arch is $\int_0^1 \ln x \sin x$. So, *fnInt* (sin x ln x, x, 0, 1) which gives –0.2398 .

30. (A)

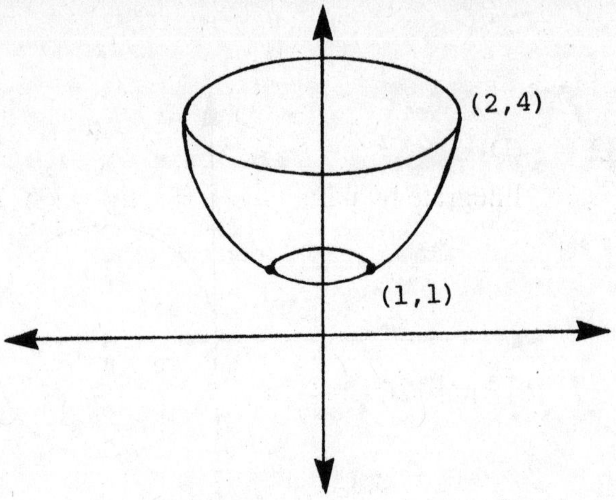

When $x = 1, y = 1$
When $x = 2, y = 4$.

$V = \int_1^4 \pi r^2 dy$. But $r = x$ so $r^2 = x^2 = y$,

$$V = \int_1^4 \pi y dy = \frac{\pi}{2} y^2 \Big|_1^4 = \frac{15\pi}{2}$$

31. (C)
Draw the graph of $f(x)$.

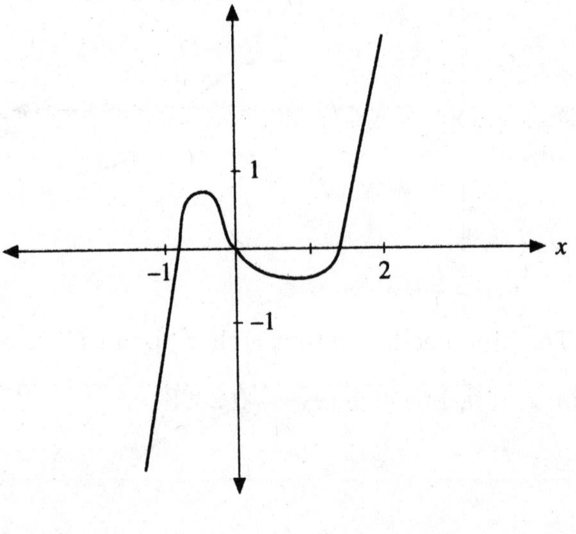

By tracing the x and y values on the graph, you can find $f_{\text{min}} = -1.087 = -f_{\text{max}}$.

32. (D)

Integrate by parts: let $f = x$, $dg = \sin 2x\ dx$. Then $df = dx$,

$g = -\frac{1}{2}\cos 2x.$

$$\int_0^{\pi} f dg = fg\Big|_0^{\pi} - \int_0^{\pi} g df$$

$$= -\frac{x}{2}\cos 2x\Big|_0^{\pi} - 0 + \int_0^{\pi}\frac{1}{2}\cos 2x\,dx$$

$$= -\frac{\pi}{2} + \frac{\sin 2x}{4}\Big|_0^{\pi} = -\frac{\pi}{2}.$$

It is negative because we are integrating the following:

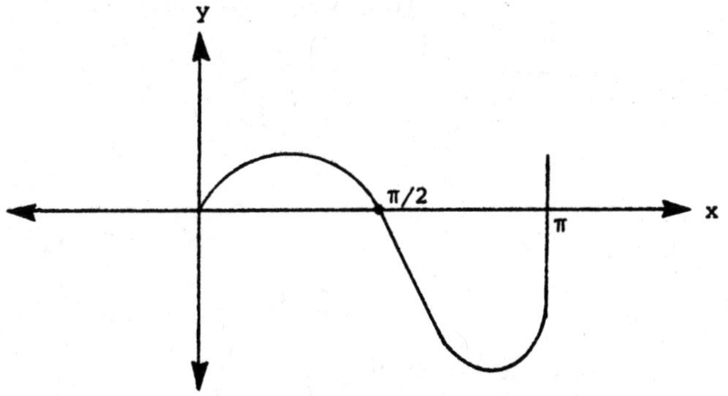

33. (A)

Draw graphs of both y and y'.

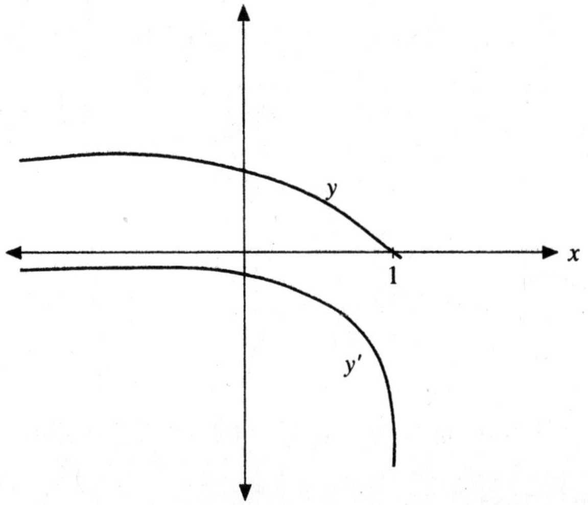

The rate of change, from the graph of y', increases negatively as x goes toward 1. So, inside $0 \le x \le 0.8$, the highest rate of change is $y'(0.8) = -1.14$.

34. (E)

The graph of $f(x)$ is:

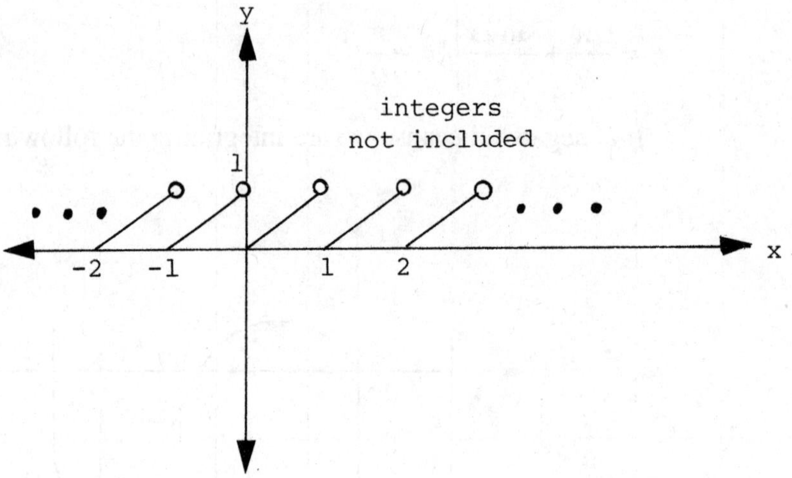

It satisfies (A), (B), (C), and (D).

35. (B)

Use the calculator directly to find $f'(2)$. For example, *der* 1 (X^0.5 ln X, X, 2) gives 0.95 .

36. (C)

Indeterminate form $\frac{0}{0}$, so by L' Hôpital's Rule:

$$\lim_{x\to 0}\frac{\sin 2x - 2x}{x^3} = \lim_{x\to 0}\frac{2\cos 2x - 2}{3x^2} = \frac{0}{0}$$

Apply L' Hôpital again:

$$\lim_{x\to 0}\frac{-4\sin 2x}{6x} = \lim_{x\to 0}\frac{-8\cos 2x}{6} = -\frac{4}{3}$$

37. (A)

$$s = \int_{-1}^{1}\sqrt{(x'(t))^2 + (y'(t))^2}\,dt$$

$$= \int_{-1}^{1}\left[\frac{1}{4}\left(e^t - e^{-t}\right)^2 + \frac{1}{4}\left(e^t + e^{-t}\right)^2\right]^{\frac{1}{2}} dt$$

$$= \frac{1}{2}\int_{-1}^{1}\left(e^{2t} - 2 + e^{-2t} + e^{2t} + 2 + e^{-2t}\right)^{\frac{1}{2}} dt$$

$$= \frac{\sqrt{2}}{2}\int_{-1}^{1}\left(e^{2t} + e^{-2t}\right)^{\frac{1}{2}} dt$$

$$= \sqrt{2}\int_{0}^{1}\sqrt{e^{2t} + e^{-2t}}\,dt$$

38. (C)

$\sum_{K=1}^{n}\frac{K}{n^2} = \frac{1}{n}\sum_{K=1}^{n}\frac{K}{n}$ is a Riemann sum for $\int_0^1 x\,dx$.

Thus $\lim_{n\to\infty} \sum_{K=1}^{n} \frac{K}{n^2} = \int_0^1 x dx$

$$= \frac{x^2}{2}\Big|_0^1$$

$$= \frac{1}{2}$$

39. (B)

$dy = y^2 dx, \frac{dy}{y^2} = dx, \int \frac{dy}{y^2} = \int dx.$

Thus $-\frac{1}{y} = x + c.$

Since $y(1) = 1,\ -1 = 1 + c,\ c = -2 =$

$-\frac{1}{y} = x - 2,\ y = \frac{1}{2-x}.$

40. (D)

Integrating by parts,

$$\int_0^\infty xe^{ax} dx = \lim_{b\to\infty} \left\{ \frac{xe^{ax}}{a}\Big|_0^b - \int_0^b \frac{1}{a} e^{ax} dx \right\}$$

$$= \lim_{b\to\infty} \left(\frac{be^{ab}}{a} - \frac{e^{ab}}{a^2} + \frac{1}{a^2} \right).$$

In order to have $e^{ab} \to 0$ as $b \to \infty$ we must have $a < 0$.

ADVANCED PLACEMENT CALCULUS BC EXAM II

SECTION II

DETAILED EXPLANATIONS OF ANSWERS

1.

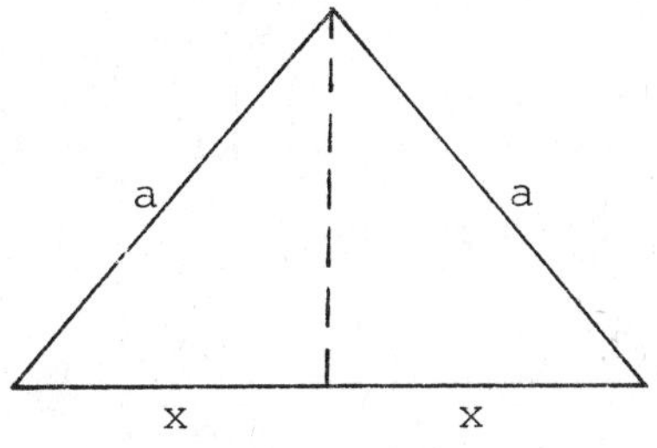

(a) $A = 2\left(\frac{1}{2}x\sqrt{a^2 - x^2}\right) = x\sqrt{a^2 - x^2}$

(b) $\frac{dA}{dx} = \sqrt{a^2 - x^2} - \frac{x^2}{\sqrt{a^2 - x^2}} = \frac{a^2 - 2x^2}{\sqrt{a^2 - x^2}}$

(c) Let $\frac{dA}{dx} = 0$, we have $x = \pm\frac{a}{\sqrt{2}}$.

$x = -\frac{a}{\sqrt{2}}$ is not applicable.

(d) As x ranges between $x = 0$ (no triangle) and $x = a$ (no triangle) the area increases and decreases. It must be a max.

2. (a) Let $f(x) = x^{\frac{1}{3}}$, $x_0 = 64$, then

$$x^{\frac{1}{3}} = 64^{\frac{1}{3}} + \frac{1}{3}(64)^{\frac{-2}{3}}(x-64) + \left(\frac{1}{3}\right)\left(\frac{-2}{3}\right)(64)^{\frac{-5}{3}} \cdot$$

$$\frac{(x-64)^2}{2!} + \ldots + \frac{f^{(n)}(64)}{n!}(x-64)^n + \ldots$$

(b) $$R_n = \frac{f^{n+1}(\xi)}{(n+1)!}(x-64)^{n+1} = \frac{(x-64)^{n+1}}{(n+1)!}$$

$$\left(\frac{1}{3}\right)\left(\frac{-2}{3}\right)\left(\frac{-5}{3}\right)\cdots\left(\frac{1-3n}{3}\right)\xi^{\frac{-2-3n}{3}}$$

(c) Since $x = 65$, $x - 64 = 1$, $64 \le \xi \le 65$, we may use 64 to estimate the remainder.

$$|R_1| \le \frac{2}{9} \cdot \frac{1}{2} \cdot \frac{1}{4^5} = \frac{1}{9.4^5} = \frac{1}{9(1024)}, \text{ too big.}$$

$$|R_2| \le |R_1| \cdot \frac{5}{3} \cdot \frac{1}{3} \cdot \frac{1}{4^3} = \frac{5}{9 \cdot 64 \cdot 9 \cdot 1024} < .00005$$

3. (a) Draw the graph of $y = x^2 - x - 6$.

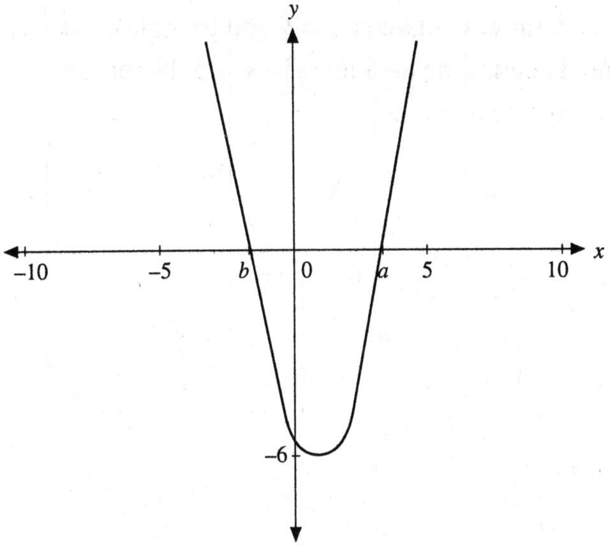

The function ln $(x^2 - x - 6)$ requires $x^2 - x - 6 > 0$. By tracing down the graph, you can easily see that $b = -2$, $a = 3$.

(b) Draw the graph $f(x) = \ln(x^2 - x - 6)$ for $x \geq 3$.

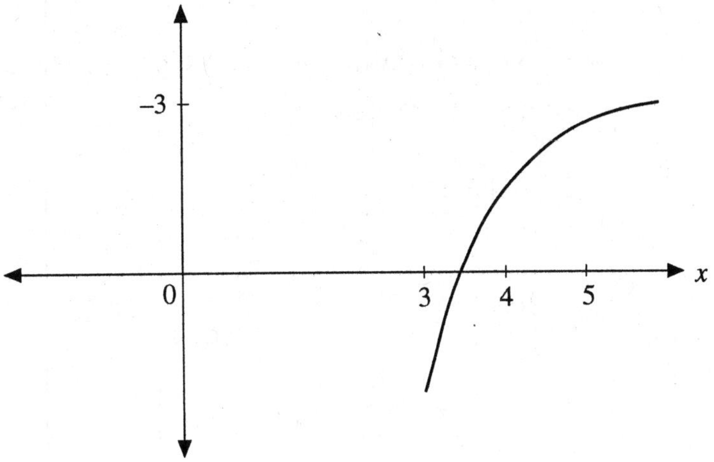

By tracing the x coordinate to $x = 5$, $f(5)$ can be found to equal 2.64 .

(c) Use your calculator directly and perform *der* 1 (ln X^2 – X – 6, X, –3), which should give –1.67 .

4.

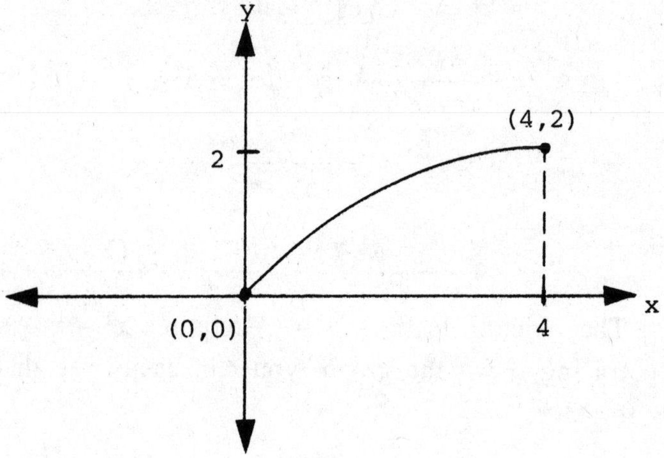

(a)

$$A = \int_0^4 y\,dx = \int_0^4 \sqrt{x}\,dx$$

$$= \frac{2}{3}x^{\frac{3}{2}}\Big|_0^4 = \frac{16}{3}$$

(b)

$$V = \pi\int_0^4 y^2 dx = \pi\int_0^4 x\,dx$$

$$= \frac{\pi}{2}x^2\Big|_0^4 = 8\pi$$

5. (a) For $y = 0, \sin x_0 = -e^0 = -1$, so $x_0 = 2n\pi - \frac{\pi}{2}$, an infinite number of solutions.

(b) setting $n = 0$, $x_0 = -\frac{\pi}{2}$.

(c) Differentiate implicitly:

$$y + xy' + \cos x + e^y y' = 0,$$

$$y' = \frac{y + \cos x}{x + e^y}. \text{ At } \left(-\frac{\pi}{2}, 0\right), y' = 0$$

(d) Since $y' = -\dfrac{y + \cos x}{x + e^y}$,

$$y'' = -\frac{(y' - \sin x)(x + e^y) - (y + \cos x)(1 + y\acute{e}^y)}{(x + e^y)^2}$$

and at $\left(-\frac{\pi}{2}, 0\right)$,

$$y'' = -\frac{\left(0 - \sin\left(\frac{-\pi}{2}\right)\right)\left(1 - \frac{\pi}{2}\right) - \left(\cos\frac{-\pi}{2}\right)(1)}{\left(1 - \pi/2^2\right)}$$

$$= \frac{\pi/2 - 1}{(1 - \pi/2)^2} = \frac{-1}{1 - \pi/2}$$

6. (a) $v(t) = 2t + \cos t + c$. Since $v_0 = 0, c = -1$

$v(t) = 2t + \cos t - 1$

(b) $x(t) = t^2 + \sin t - t + d$. Since $x_0 = 0, d = 0$

$x(t) = t^2 - t + \sin t$

(c) Since $|\sin t| \leq 1$, boundedness depends only on $t^2 - t$, which is unbounded, so $x(t)$ is unbounded.

THE ADVANCED PLACEMENT EXAMINATION IN

CALCULUS BC

TEST III

ADVANCED PLACEMENT CALCULUS BC EXAM III

SECTION I

PART A

Time: 45 minutes
25 questions

DIRECTIONS: Each of the following problems is followed by five choices. Solve each problem, select the best choice, and blacken the correct space on your answer sheet.

NOTE:

Unless otherwise specified, the domain of function *f* is assumed to be the set of all real numbers *x* for which *f*(*x*) is a real number.

1. $\frac{d}{dx}\left(x^2 + 3xe^{2x}\right)$ at $x = 1$ is approximately:

(A) 54.489

(B) 46.334

(C) 68.502

(D) 24.167

(E) None of the above

2. Find $y(2)$ if $y(0) = 1$ and $y'(x) = 2x + 3$.

(A) 11
(B) 10
(C) 9
(D) 8
(E) 7

3. $\int_0^4 \frac{dx}{(x-1)^{2/3}}$ is approximately

(A) 1.327
(B) 7.326
(C) 3
(D) 4.326
(E) None of the above

4. If $x^2y^2 + 2x - y = 0$, $y'(1) =$

(A) -4
(B) 2
(C) 0
(D) Can not be determined
(E) Does not exist

5. The maximum value of $2x + y$ on the circle $x^2 + y^2 = 4$ is

(A) 4

(B) $2\sqrt{5}$

(C) $3\sqrt{3}$

(D) 5

(E) 6

6. $\int_0^1 \frac{dx}{\sqrt{4 - x^2}}$

Sin⁻¹

(A) 2.221

(B) 1.111

(C) 1.481

(D) 0.741

(E) None of the above

7. How many relative or absolute maxima does $x - \cos x$ have on the interval $(-2\pi, 2\pi)$?

(A) 1

(B) 2

(C) 3

(D) 4

(E) 5

8. If the motion of a particle on the x -axis has acceleration $\frac{d^2x}{dt^2} = t^2 - 2t$, and it is stationary at 1 when $t = 1$, then $12x(t) =$

(A) $t^4 + 4t^3$

(B) $t^4 - 4t^3 + 8t + 7$

(C) $4t^4 + 8t^3$

(D) $t^4 - 4t^3 + 15t^2$

(E) $t^4 - 2t^3 + 3t^2 - 4t + 14$

9. $\lim_{x \to 2} \frac{e^x - e^2}{x - 2} =$

(A) 0

(B) 2.718

(C) 7.389

(D) 0.368

(E) None of the above

10. $\sum_{n=0}^{\infty} 2^{-n} x^n$ converges for x in

(A) $[-2, 2]$

(B) $[-2, 2)$

(C) $(-2, 2]$ (D) $(-2, 2)$

(E) Cannot be determined

11. $\int_{-1}^{1} \frac{dx}{x^2 - 4x + 4} =$

(A) $\frac{2}{3}$ (D) 1

(B) $\frac{1}{3}$ (E) ∞

(C) 0

12. A square is inscribed in a circle. How fast is the area of the square changing when the area of the circle is increasing one square inch per minute?

(A) $\frac{1}{2}$ in^2 min (D) $\frac{\pi}{2}$ in^2/min

(B) 1 in^2/min (E) Cannot be determined

(C) $\frac{2}{\pi}$ in^2 min

13. If $xy = x + y$, what is y' when x is -1?

(A) $\frac{1}{2}$

(B) $-\frac{1}{4}$

(E) $\frac{1}{4}$

(D) $-\frac{1}{2}$

(E) Cannot be determined

14. $\lim\limits_{x \to 1} \dfrac{\tan^{-1} x - \tan^{-1} 1}{x - 1} =$

(A) -1

(B) $-\frac{1}{2}$

(C) 0

(D) $\frac{1}{2}$

(E) 1

15. The maximum value of $x^2 e^x$ on $\left[-3, \frac{1}{2}\right]$ is

(A) $\frac{\sqrt{e}}{4}$

(B) $\frac{4}{e^2}$

(C) $\frac{4}{e}$

(D) $2e^{-\sqrt{2}}$

(E) $9e^{-3}$

16. $\int_0^1 x\sqrt{1 - x^2}\, dx =$

(A) .333

(B) 1.118

(C) 2.236 (D) 3.354

(E) 4.472

17. If $y = 3x^2 \sin x$ and $x = \sqrt{t}$ then $\frac{dy}{dt} =$

(A) $6t \sin \sqrt{t}$

(B) $6t \cos \sqrt{t}$

(C) $3 \sin \sqrt{t} + \frac{3}{2}\sqrt{t} \cos \sqrt{t}$

(D) $\frac{3}{2} \sin \sqrt{t} + 3 \cos \sqrt{t}$

(E) $3(\sqrt{t} \sin \sqrt{t} + \cos \sqrt{t})$

18. The length of arc joining (1,0) to (0,1) on the curve $x = \cos t$, $y = \sin^2 t$ is

(A) $\int_0^1 (1 + x^2)\, dx$

(B) $\int_0^1 \sqrt{1 + x^2}\, dx$

(C) $\int_0^1 (1 + 4x^2)\, dx$

(D) $\int_0^1 \sqrt{1 + 4x^2}\, dx$

(E) None of the above

19. If $\frac{1}{1-x} = \sum_{n=0}^{\infty} x^n$, what is $\sum_{n=0}^{\infty} nx^n$?

(A) $\frac{2x}{1-x}$

(B) $\frac{x}{1-x}$

(C) $\frac{nx}{1-x}$

(D) $\frac{1}{(1-x)^2}$

(E) $\frac{x}{(1-x)^2}$

20. $\frac{d}{dy}\left(y^2 \ln\left(\frac{1}{y^2}\right)\right) =$

(A) $-2y \ln(y^2) - 2y$

(B) $-4y \ln y - 2y$

(C) $2y \ln \frac{1}{ey^2}$

(D) $-2y(1 + 2\ln y)$

(E) All of the above

21. $\lim_{h \to 0} \frac{\sqrt{1+2h} - 1}{h} =$

(A) 2

(B) 1

(C) $\frac{1}{2}$

(D) 0

(E) Does not exist

22. If a is a positive real number, $\sum_{n=1}^{\infty} \frac{\sqrt[n]{a}}{n}$ converges for

(A) Any $a > 0$

(B) $0 < a < 1$ only

(C) $a = 1$ only

(D) $a > 1$ only

(E) No a

23. A particle moves in the plane according to $x = t \cos t$, $y = t \sin t$. Which of the following vectors is orthogonal to the acceleration vector at $t = \pi$?

(A) $(1, \pi)$

(B) $(2, -\pi)$

(C) $(2, \pi)$

(D) $(\pi, 2)$

(E) $(\pi, 1)$

24. The area between $y = x^2$ and $y = 1 - x^2$ is

(A) $\frac{2\sqrt{2}}{3}$

(B) $\frac{\sqrt{2}}{3}$

(C) $\frac{1}{\sqrt{2}}$

(D) $\sqrt{2}$

(E) $2\sqrt{2}$

25. Let $f(x) = \int_0^x \left(t - t^2\right) dt$ for $x \geq 0$. The maximum value of f is

(A) 0

(B) 1

(C) –1

(D) $\frac{1}{6}$

(E) $\frac{1}{3}$

SECTION I

PART B

Time: 45 minutes
15 questions

DIRECTIONS: Calculators may be used for this section of the test. Each of the following problems is followed by five choices. Solve each problem, select the best choice, and blacken the correct space on your answer sheet.

NOTES:

1. Unless otherwise specified, answers can be given in unsimplified form.
2. The domain of function *f* is assumed to be the set of all real numbers *x* for which *f*(*x*) is a real number.

26. If $y^2 = x + y^3$, $y' =$

(A) $1+3y^2$

(B) $\dfrac{1}{2y-3y^2}$

(C) $\dfrac{2x}{3-y^2}$

(D) $\dfrac{1}{2y\left(1+y^2\right)}$

(E) $\dfrac{1}{2y\left(1+3y^2\right)}$

27. A particle moves along a straight line. Its velocity is

$$V(t) = \begin{cases} t^2 & \text{for} \quad 0 \le t \le 2 \\ t+2 & \text{for} \quad t \ge 2 \end{cases}$$

The distance travelled by the particle in the interval $1 \le t \le 3$ is

(A) 3

(B) 7.1

(C) 4.3

(D) 5

(E) 6.8

28. The volume generated by revolving $y = x^3(-1 \le x \le 1)$ around the y-axis is

(A) π

(B) 2π

(C) $\frac{6\pi}{5}$

(D) $\frac{2\pi}{5}$

(E) $\frac{4\pi}{5}$

29. Let $f(x) = x + \frac{1}{x^{1.6}}$. Then, $\int_{0.1}^{2} f(x)$ equals

(A) 3.64

(B) 4.99

(C) 7.53

(D) 5.1

(E) 11.2

30. If $f''(x_0)$ exists, find $\lim_{h \to 0} \frac{f(x_0 + h) - f(x_0 - h)}{h}$

(A) $f''(x_0)$

(B) $2f'(x_0)$

(C) $2f''(x_0)$

(D) $f'(x_0)$

(E) May not exist

31. If $8 + 2x + x^2 = 6x^3$, one solution for x is

(A) 1.143

(B) 2.25

(C) –17.2

(D) 5.78

(E) 12.3

32. If $y' = x^2 + y,\ y(0) = 0$ then $y(1) =$

(A) $2e$

(B) $2e - 5$

(C) $e + 1$

(D) $e - 4$

(E) $3e$

33. Let $f(x) = \dfrac{\sin x \cos x}{\cos 9x \tan 2x}$. $f'(0.5)$ equals

(A) 3.8

(B) –2.5

(C) –49.5

(D) 70.1

(E) –5

34. The curves $y = \frac{x^2}{2}$ and $y = 1 - \frac{x^2}{2}$ intersect in the first quadrant. The angle at which they intersect is

(A) 30° (D) 90°

(B) 45° (E) 0°

(C) 60°

35. Let $f(x) = \frac{x}{\sqrt{4 - x^2}}$. The minimum of $f'(x)$ is

(A) 0.5 (D) –0.5

(B) 1 (E) 2

(C) –1

36. If $y = \int_0^{x^2} e^{t^2}\, dt$, $y''(0) =$

(A) 0 (D) 3

(B) 1 (E) 4

(C) 2

37. $\int_2^4 \frac{dx}{x^2-1} =$

(A) $\ln \frac{3}{\sqrt{5}}$

(B) $\ln 3$

(C) $\ln 5 - \ln 3$

(D) $\ln \sqrt{\frac{5}{3}}$

(E) $\ln \sqrt{5}$

38. $\lim\limits_{x \to \frac{\pi}{4}} \frac{\tan x - 1}{\sin x - \cos x} =$

(A) 1

(B) $\sqrt{2}$

(C) 2

(D) $2\sqrt{2}$

(E) Does not exist

39. If $\tan^{-1} x = \sum_{n=0}^{\infty} \frac{(-1)^n x^{2n+1}}{2n+1}$ then $\sum_{n=0}^{\infty} \frac{(-1)^n}{3^n(2n+1)}$ is

(A) $\frac{\pi}{2}$

(B) $\frac{\pi}{4}$

(C) $\frac{\pi}{\sqrt{3}}$

(D) $\frac{\pi}{6}$

(E) $\frac{\pi}{2\sqrt{3}}$

40. $\lim_{h \to 0} \frac{\sqrt{1+h} + \sqrt{1-h} - 2}{h^2} =$

(A) 0

(B) $\frac{1}{2}$

(C) $\frac{1}{4}$

(D) $-\frac{1}{4}$

(E) Does not exist

ADVANCED PLACEMENT CALCULUS BC EXAM III

SECTION II

Time: 1 hour and 30 minutes
6 questions†

DIRECTIONS: Show all your work. Grading is based on the methods used to solve the problems as well as the accuracy of your final answers. Please make sure all procedures are clearly shown.

NOTES:

1. ln x denotes the natural logarithm of x (that is, logarithm to the base e).

2. Unless otherwise specified, the domain of function f is assumed to be the set of all real numbers x for which $f(x)$ is a real number.

†The practice tests in this book incorporate Section II free-response solutions that approximate the content breakdown you will encounter on the AP exam. The overall timing and formatting of the practice tests mirror the actual test; examinees should note, however, that this section is split into two parts on the AP exam. Furthermore, prospective examinees should pay attention to restrictions on calculator use. For details, consult current official College Board materials in print or on the Web.

1. A greenhouse is shaped like a semicircle of radius 10 feet. A 12-foot-long ladder is leaning against it :

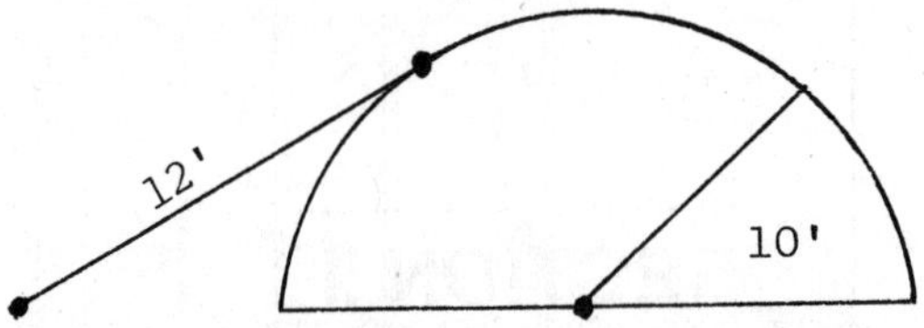

(a) How near may the foot of the ladder be to the greenhouse before the other end stops touching the greenhouse?

(b) Starting from the position of part (a), the lower end is pulled out at b feet/sec. Find equations for the position of the upper end at time t.

(c) How fast is the high end dropping when the foot is 11 feet out ?

2. A particle is traveling in the xy plane subject to an acceleration $(\cos 2t , \sin t)$.

(a) If its initial velocity is $(0,-1)$, find its velocity.

(b) If it starts at the point $(1,0)$, find its position at time t.

(c) Is the motion bounded?

(d) Graph the trajectory.

3. Let $f(x) = \dfrac{\dfrac{3}{x^2}}{\dfrac{2}{x^2} + \dfrac{105}{x}}$.

(a) Find $f'(0)$.

(b) What happens at $x = -0.019$?

(c) Find $\int_0^2 f(x)$.

4. Consider the differential equation $y'' + y' = x$.

(a) Write $p = y'$ and solve the resulting first order equation.

(b) Replace p by y' and solve the resulting first order equation.

(c) Find the solution that has $y(0) = y'(0) = 0$.

5. A boy is standing 50 feet from the end of a swimming pool when he sees a girl 25 feet along the end:
He can swim 3 ft/second and run 5 ft/sec.

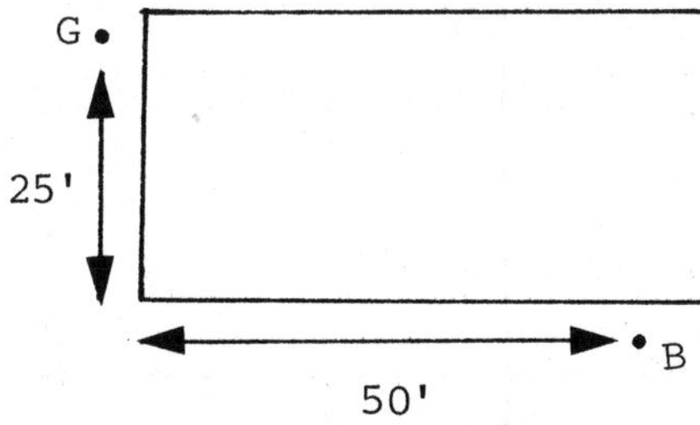

How far should he run along the edge before he starts swimming toward her in order to reach her most quickly?

(a) If he runs x feet, set up an equation for time consumed.

(b) Differentiate with respect to x and equate to zero.

(c) Solve for the optimum x.

(d) What is the least time?

6. **If $xe^y + y \cos x = 1$ defines y as a function of x,**

(a) Find $y(0)$.

(b) Find $y'(0)$.

(c) Find $y''(0)$.

(d) Sketch near $x = 0$.

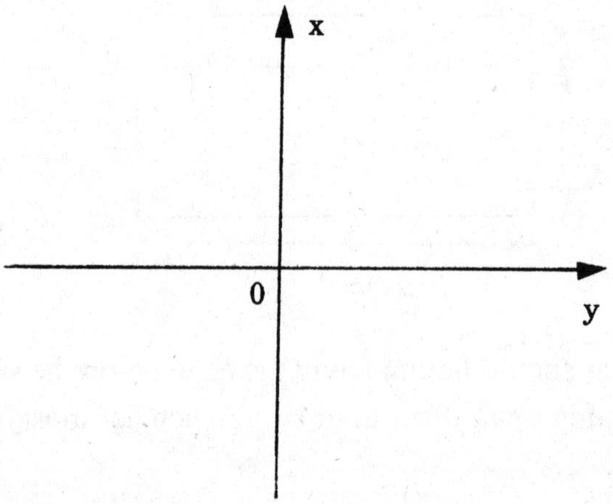

ADVANCED PLACEMENT CALCULUS BC EXAM III

ANSWER KEY

SECTION I

1.	C	21.	B
2.	A	22.	E
3.	B	23.	C
4.	E	24.	A
5.	B	25.	D
6.	D	26.	B
7.	A	27.	E
8.	B	28.	C
9.	C	29.	C
10.	D	30.	B
11.	A	31.	A
12.	C	32.	B
13.	B	33.	C
14.	D	34.	D
15.	B	35.	A
16.	A	36.	C
17.	C	37.	A
18.	D	38.	B
19.	E	39.	E
20.	E	40.	D

SECTION II

See Detailed Explanations of Answers.

ADVANCED PLACEMENT CALCULUS BC EXAM III

SECTION I

DETAILED EXPLANATIONS OF ANSWERS

1. (C)

$$\frac{d}{dx}\left(x^2 + 3xe^{2x}\right) = 2x + \frac{d}{dx}(3x)e^{2x}$$

$$3x\frac{d}{dx}(e^{2x}) = 2x + 3e^{2x} + 6xe^{2x} =$$

$$\left.\frac{d}{dx}\right|_1 = 2 + 3e^{2\times 1} + 6 \times 1e^{2\times 1} = 2 + 3e^2 + 6e^2 = 68.502$$

2. (A)

$y(x) = \int_0^x (2t + 3)dt = x^2 + 3x + c$. Since

$y(0) = 1, c = 1.$

$y(x) = x^2 + 3x + 1$ and $y(2) = 4 + 6 + 1 = 11$

3. (B)
Since the function $f(x) = \dfrac{1}{(x-1)^{2/3}}$ becomes infinite at $x = 1$, which lies between the limits of integration, we must split the integral into two parts and take limits.

$$\int_0^4 \frac{dx}{(x-1)^{2/3}} = \lim_{a \to 1^-} \int_0^a \frac{dx}{(x-1)^{2/3}} + \lim_{b \to 1^+} \int_b^4 \frac{dx}{(x-1)^{2/3}}$$

$$= \lim_{a \to 1^-} 3(x-1)^{\frac{1}{3}} \Big|_0^a + \lim_{b \to 1^+} 3(x-1)^{\frac{1}{3}} \Big|_b^4$$

$$= \lim_{a \to 1^-} 3(a-1)^{\frac{1}{3}} - 3(0-1)^{\frac{1}{3}}$$

$$+ 3(4-1)^{\frac{1}{3}} - \lim_{b \to 1^+} 3(b-1)^{\frac{1}{3}}$$

$$= 0 - 3(-1) + 3 \cdot \sqrt[3]{3} - 0 = 3\sqrt[3]{3} + 3 = 7.326$$

4. (E)
$2xy^2 + 2x^2yy' + 2 - y' = 0$ so $y' = \dfrac{2xy^2 + 2}{1 - 2x^2y}$.

Attempting to determine $y'(1)$, $y^2 + 2 - y = 0$

so $y(1) = \dfrac{1}{2} \pm \dfrac{1}{2}\sqrt{1-8}$ by the quadratic formula.

But this is imaginary. (Of course, one could have determined that $y(1)$ cannot exist without finding y').

5. (B)

On the circle $y = \pm\sqrt{4 - x^2}$, so

$$\frac{d}{dx}(2x + y) = 2 + y' = 2 \pm \frac{x}{\sqrt{4 - x^2}} = 0$$

implies $2\sqrt{4 - x^2} - x = 0$, $4(4 - x^2) = x^2$,

$16 = 5x^2$, $x = \pm\frac{4}{\sqrt{5}}$.

At $-\frac{4}{\sqrt{5}}$ the object function is negative, so the maximum is

$$= \frac{8}{\sqrt{5}} + \sqrt{4 - \frac{16}{5}} = \frac{8}{\sqrt{5}} + \frac{2}{\sqrt{5}} = \frac{10}{\sqrt{5}} = 2\sqrt{5}.$$

6. (D)

For $a = 2$

$$\sqrt{2}\int_0^1 \frac{dx}{\sqrt{a^2 - x^2}} = \sqrt{2}\int_0^1 \frac{dx}{\sqrt{4 - x^2}}$$

$$= \sqrt{2}\sin^{-1}\frac{x}{a}\Big|_0^1 = \sqrt{2}\sin^{-1}\frac{x}{2}\Big|_0^1$$

$$= \sqrt{2}\sin^{-1} - \sqrt{2}\sin^{-1}0 = \frac{\sqrt{2}\pi}{6} = 0.741$$

7. (A)

$y' = 1 + \sin x = 0$ at $x = -\frac{\pi}{2}$ and $\frac{3\pi}{2}$.

$y'' = \cos x = 0$ so the second derivative test fails.

However, notice that $y'(x) \geq 0$ for all x, so y is monotone increasing. Thus the only max is at 2π.

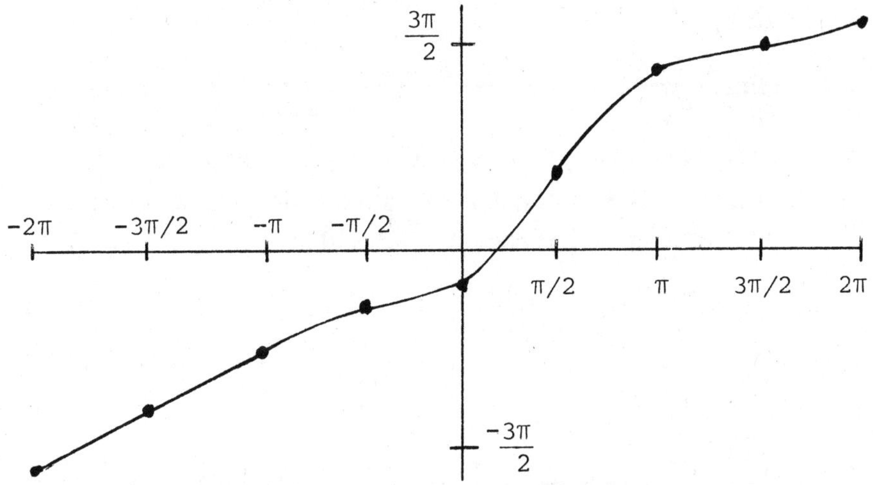

8. (B)

$\frac{dx}{dt} = \frac{1}{3}t^3 - t^2 + c$ and $\frac{dx}{dt}(1) = 0$ so $c = \frac{2}{3}$.

$x(t) = \frac{1}{12}t^4 - \frac{1}{3}t^3 + \frac{2}{3}t + d$ and $x(1) = 1$ so

$d = 1 - \frac{1}{12} + \frac{1}{3} - \frac{2}{3} = \frac{2}{3} - \frac{1}{12} = \frac{7}{12}$

[Notice $\underline{12}\,x(t)$]

9. (C)

The limit is simply $\frac{d}{dx}(e^x)\Big|_{x=2} = e^x\Big|_{x=2} = e^2$

$= 7.389$

10. (D)

$$\lim_{n \to \infty} \frac{a_n}{a_{n+1}} = \lim_{n \to \infty} \frac{2^{-n}}{2^{-(n+1)}} = \lim_{n \to \infty} 2 = 2,$$ so the

radius of convergence is 2. Thus the convergence set is one of A, B, C, or D. Checking the endpoints, it diverges at $x = \pm 2$: at $+2$ it becomes $\sum 1$ and at -2 it is $\sum (-1)^n$.

11. (A)

$$\int_{-1}^{1} \frac{dx}{(x-2)^2} = \left.\frac{-1}{x-2}\right|_{-1}^{1} = \frac{-1}{-1} - \frac{-1}{-3} = 1 - \frac{1}{3} = \frac{2}{3}$$

12. (C)

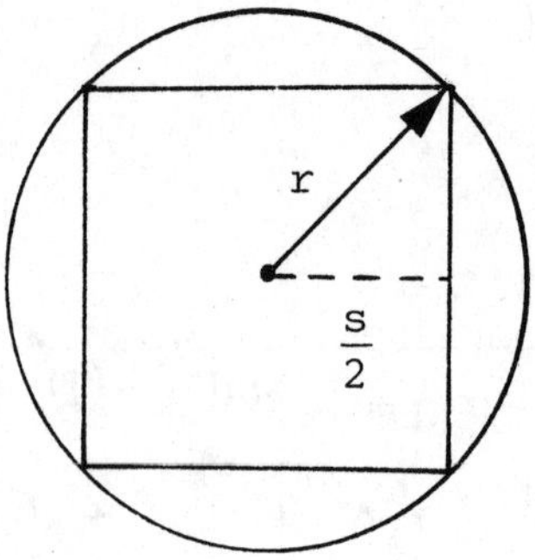

The side of the square, s, is $\sqrt{2}\,r$. The areas are $A = \pi r^2$ and $A_s = 2r^2$. Thus $\frac{d}{dt}(A_s) = 4r\frac{dr}{dt}$. Since

$$\frac{d}{dt}(A_0) = 1 = 2\pi r\frac{dr}{dt}, \quad \frac{dr}{dt} = \frac{1}{2\pi r}.$$

so $\frac{d}{dt}(A_s) = 4r \cdot \frac{1}{2\pi r} = \frac{2}{\pi}$.

13. (B)

When x is -1, $-y = y - 1$ so $y = \frac{1}{2}$.

Now $y + xy' = 1 + y'$ so

$$y' = \frac{y - 1}{1 - x} = \frac{-1/2}{2} = -\frac{1}{4}$$

14. (D)

One way of solving this problem is $\frac{d}{dx}(\tan^{-1} x)\Big|_{x=1} = \frac{1}{2}$.

Another way is by using L ' Hôpital's Rule :

$$\lim_{x \to 0} \frac{\frac{1}{1+x^2}}{1} = \frac{1}{2}.$$

15. (B)

Taking derivatives, $2xe^x + x^2e^x = 0$ implies $2x + x^2 = 0$ implies $x = 0$ or -2. Since both are in the interval, use second derivative $2e^x + 4xe^x + x^2e^x = e^x(2 + 4x + x^2)$, which is > 0 at 0 and < 0 at -2.

Since $f\left(\frac{1}{2}\right) = \frac{\sqrt{e}}{4} < \frac{1}{2}$ and $f(-2) = \frac{4}{e^2} > \frac{1}{2}$,

$\therefore$ the maximum value is $\frac{4}{e^2}$.

16. (A)

$\int_0^1 x\sqrt{1-x^2}\,dx$

$u = 1-x^2 \quad du = -2xdx$

this becomes $-\frac{1}{2}\int\sqrt{u}\ du = -\frac{1}{2}\left(\frac{2}{3}\right)\left(u^{\frac{3}{2}}\right)$

which is equivalent to $-\frac{1}{3}(1-x^2)^{\frac{3}{2}}\Big|_0^1$

$0-\left(-\frac{1}{3}\right)=\frac{1}{3}$ or .333

17. (C)

$y' = 6x\sin x + 3x^2\cos x$

$= 6\sqrt{t}\sin\sqrt{t} + 3t\cos\sqrt{t}$, and

$$\frac{dy}{dt} = \frac{dy}{dx}\cdot\frac{dx}{dt} = \frac{dy}{dx}\cdot\frac{1}{2\sqrt{t}}$$

$$= 3\sin\sqrt{t} + \frac{3\sqrt{t}}{2}\cos\sqrt{t}$$

18. (D)

Eliminate t: $y = \sin^2 t = 1 - \cos^2 t = 1 - x^2$.

Thus, $s = \int_0^1 \sqrt{1+y'^2}\,dx = \int_0^1 \sqrt{1+4x^2}\,dx.$

19. (E)

$$\frac{d}{dx}\left(\sum_{n=0}^{\infty} x^n\right) = \sum_{n=0}^{\infty} nx^{n-1}, \text{ so}$$

$$\sum_{n=0}^{\infty} nx^n = x\frac{d}{dx}\left(\frac{1}{1-x}\right) = \frac{x}{(1-x)^2}$$

20. (E)

$$\frac{d}{dy}\left(y^2 \ln\left(\frac{1}{y^2}\right)\right) = \frac{d}{dy}(-y^2 \ln y^2)$$

$$= -2y \ln y^2 - 2y = -4y \ln y - 2y$$

$$= 2y(-1 - 2\ln y) = 2y \ln\frac{1}{ey^2}.$$

21. (B)

Multiply and divide by 2 :

$$2 \cdot \lim_{h \to 0} \frac{\sqrt{1+2h} - 1}{2h} = 2 \lim_{t \to 0} \frac{\sqrt{1+t} - 1}{t}$$

$$= 2 \frac{d}{dx}\sqrt{x}\,\Big|_{x=1} = 2 \cdot \frac{1}{2\sqrt{x}}\Big|_{x=1} = 1$$

22. (E)

For $a > 0$, $\lim_{n \to \infty} a^{\frac{1}{n}} = \lim_{n \to \infty} e^{\frac{1}{n}\ln a} = e^{\lim_{n \to \infty} \frac{\ln a}{n}} = e^0 = 1$,

so by the limit comparison test $\left(\lim_{n \to \infty} \frac{\frac{1}{n}}{\frac{\sqrt[n]{a}}{n}} = 1\right)$

it diverges for any a.

23. (C)

The velocity vector is $(\cos t - t\sin t, \sin t + t\cos t)$,
The acceleration vector is $(-2\sin t - t\cos t, 2\cos t - t\sin t)$. At $t = \pi, a = (\pi, -2)$, so an orthogonal vector is $(2, \pi)$.

24. (A)

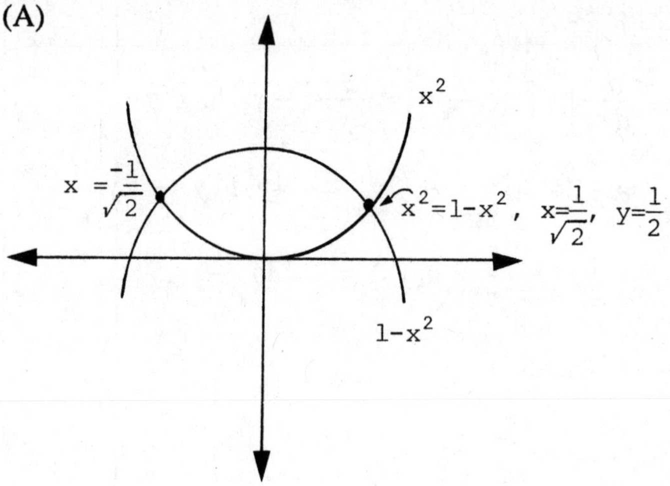

$$x^2 = 1 - x^2,\ x = \frac{1}{\sqrt{2}},\ y = \frac{1}{2}.$$

$$\int_{\frac{-1}{\sqrt{2}}}^{\frac{1}{2}} (1 - x^2 - x^2)dx = \left(x - \frac{2}{3}x^3\right)\Bigg|_{-\frac{1}{\sqrt{2}}}^{\frac{1}{\sqrt{2}}} = \frac{2\sqrt{2}}{3}.$$

25. (D)

$$\frac{d}{dx}\int_0^x (t - t^2)dt = x - x^2 = 0 \text{ at } x = 0, 1.$$

$$\frac{d^2}{dx^2} = -2x < 0 \text{ at } x = 1. \text{ Thus } x = 1 \text{ is a max,}$$

$$\int_0^1 (t - t^2)dt = \frac{1}{2} - \frac{1}{3} = \frac{1}{6}.$$

26. (B)

$$2yy' = 1 + 3y^2y', \quad y' = \frac{1}{2y - 3y^2}.$$

27. (E)

The graph of $V(t)$ is

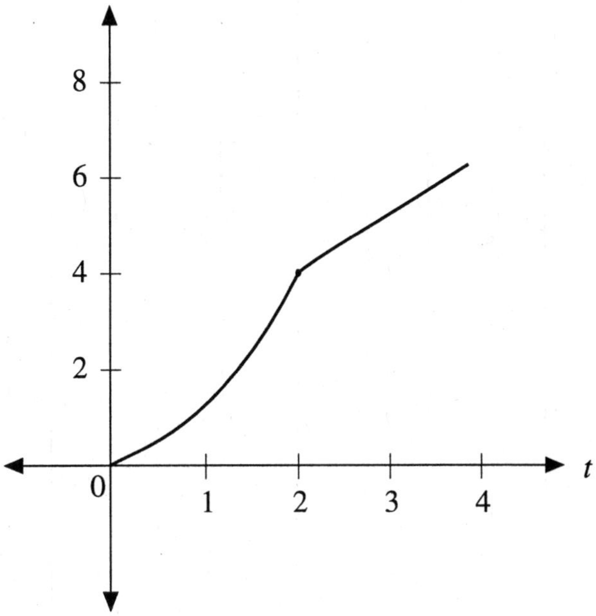

The distance travelled between $t = 1$ and $t = 2$ is

fnInt (X^2, X, 1, 2) = 2.3 .

The distance travelled between $t = 2$ and $t = 3$ is

fnInt (X + 2, X, 2, 3) = 4.5 .

Hence, from $t = 1$ to $t = 3$, the particle travelled

$2.3 + 4.5 = 6.8$.

28. (C)

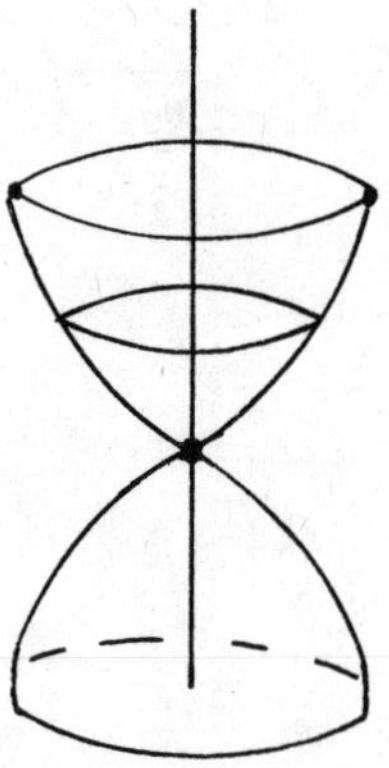

$V = 2 \cdot$ top half

$$= 2\int_0^1 \pi x^2 dy = 2\pi\int_0^1 y^{\frac{2}{3}} dy = \frac{6\pi}{5} y^{\frac{5}{3}}\Big|_0^1$$

$$= \frac{6\pi}{5}$$

29. (C)

Use your calculator to solve this problem:

$fnInt\left(X + \frac{1}{X\text{^}1.6},\ X,\ 0.1,\ 2\right)$, which should give 7.53 .

30. (B)

The $f''(x_0)$ assumption is stronger than necessary.

$$\lim_{h\to 0} \frac{f(x_0 + h) - f(x_0 - h)}{h}$$

$$= \lim_{h\to 0} \frac{f(x_0 + h) - f(x_0)}{h} + \lim_{h\to 0} \frac{f(x_0) - f(x_0 - h)}{h}$$

$= f'(x_0) + f'(x_0)$

$= 2f'(x_0)$

31. (A)

Let $f(x) = 8 + 2x - x^2$ and $g(x) = 6x^3$. Draw the graphs of $f(x)$ and $g(x)$.

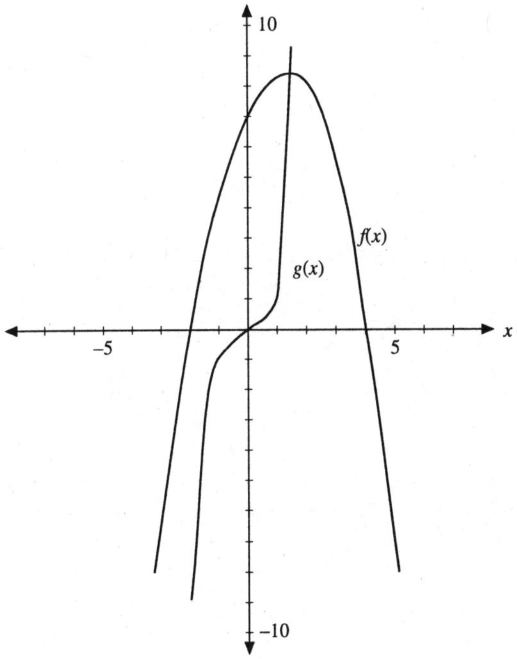

One solution is between 1 and 2 on the x-axis. Reset the window to [1,2] · [8,10]. This solution can be found to be 1.143.

32. (B)

$y' - y = x^2$, so, multiplying by e^x,

$d(ye^{-x}) = x^2e^{-x}dx$. Thus, $ye^{-x} \int x^2e^{-x}dx =$

$-2xe^{-x} - 2e^{-x} + k,\ y = ke^x - x^2 - 2x - 2$.

Since $y(0) = 0$, $0 = k - 2$, so $k = 2$,

$y = 2e^x - x^2 - 2x - 2$,

$y(1) = 2e - 1 - 2 - 2 = 2e - 5$.

33. (C)

Use your calculator to solve this problem. For example,

$$der1\left(\frac{\sin x \cos x}{\cos 9x \tan 2x},\ x,\ 0.5\right).$$

–49.5 will be given as the answer.

34. (D)

Setting $\frac{x^2}{2} = 1 - \frac{x^2}{2}$, $x = 1$ so $y = \frac{1}{2}$

$y_1' = x = 1,\ y_2' = -x = -1$

so $\theta = 45° - (-45°) = 90°$.

35. (A)

Draw the graph of $f(x)$ and $f'(x)$.

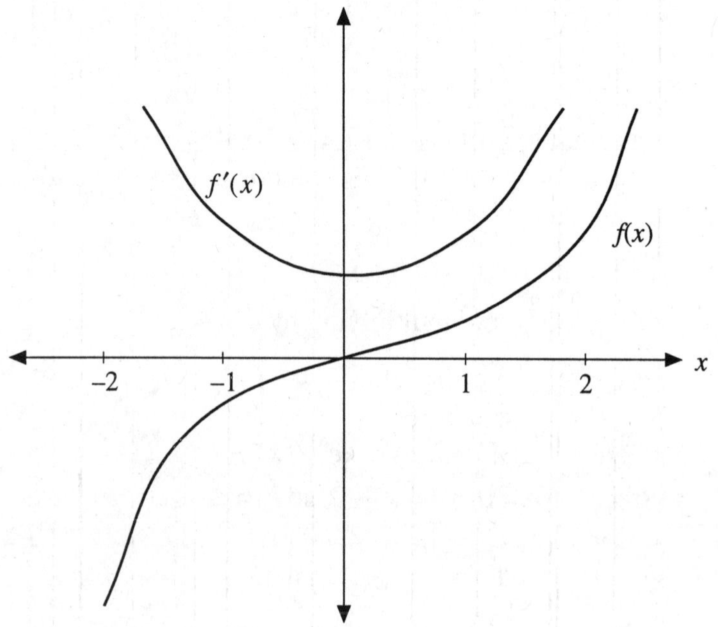

Obviously, the minimum occurs at $x = 0$. Set the window to [– 2,2] · [–1,1] and trace the x variable to $x = 0$. The minimum is $f'(0) = 0.5$.

36. (C)

By Leibniz's Rule $y = 2xe^{x^2}$, so $y'' = 2e^{x^2} + 4x^2e^{x^2}$.

Thus, $y''(0) = 2$.

37. (A)

$$\int_2^4 \frac{d}{x^2-1} = \int_2^4 \frac{\frac{1}{2}}{x-1} + \frac{-\frac{1}{2}}{x+1} dx$$

$$= \left(\frac{1}{2}\ln|x-1| - \frac{1}{2}\ln|x+1|\right)\Big|_2^4$$

$$= \ln\sqrt{\frac{|x-1|}{|x+1|}}\Bigg|_2^4 = \ln\sqrt{\frac{3}{5}} - \ln\sqrt{\frac{1}{3}}$$

$$= \frac{1}{2}\ln\frac{1}{5} + \ln 3 = \ln\frac{3}{\sqrt{5}}$$

38. (B)

Use L'Hôpital's Rule :

$$\lim_{x \to \frac{\pi}{4}} \frac{\sec^2}{\cos x + \sin x} = \frac{2}{2/\sqrt{2}}.$$

39. (E)

The second series is obtained from the first series by setting $x = \frac{1}{\sqrt{3}}$ and multiplying the whole series by $\sqrt{3}$. Thus we have $\sqrt{3}\tan^{-1}\frac{1}{\sqrt{3}} = \sqrt{3}\cdot\frac{\pi}{6} = \frac{\pi}{2\sqrt{3}}$.

40. (D)

Using L'Hôpital's Rule once, we obtain

$$\lim_{h\to 0}\frac{\frac{1}{2\sqrt{1+h}} - \frac{1}{2\sqrt{1-h}}}{2h}$$

$$= \frac{1}{4}\left\{\lim_{h\to 0}\frac{\frac{1}{\sqrt{1+h}} - 1}{h} + \lim_{h\to 0}\frac{1 - \frac{1}{\sqrt{1-h}}}{h}\right\}$$

$$= \frac{1}{4}\left[2\frac{d}{dx}\left(\frac{1}{\sqrt{x}}\right)\right]\Big|_{x=1}$$

$$= \left[\frac{1}{2}\right]\left[-\frac{1}{2}x^{\frac{-3}{2}}\right]\Big|_{x=1} = \left(\frac{1}{2}\right)\left(\frac{-1}{2}\right) = -\frac{1}{4}$$

(Alternately, this is a second divided difference for f'' with $f = \sqrt{x}$ at $x = 1$).

ADVANCED PLACEMENT CALCULUS BC EXAM III

SECTION II

DETAILED EXPLANATIONS OF ANSWERS

1.

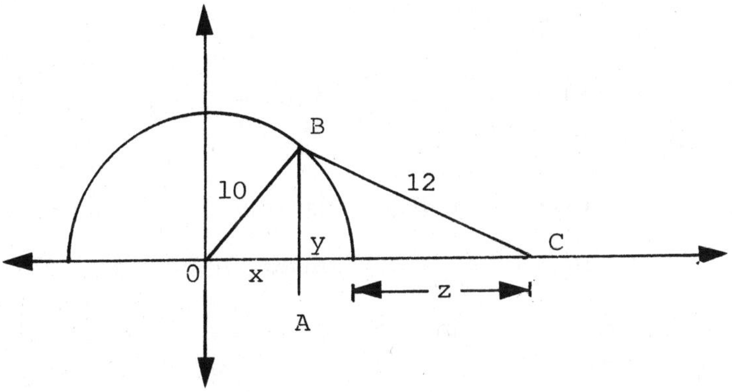

$x^2 + y^2 = 100$, $(z+10-x)^2 + y^2 = 144$ are the basic relations. Also, squaring out, $(z+10)^2 - 2x(z+10) = 44$

(a) The minimum z occurs at tangency :

ΔOAB is similar to ΔBAC . Thus $\frac{x}{10} = \frac{y}{12}, \frac{x}{y} = \frac{5}{6}.$

Since $x^2 + y^2 = 100, x^2 + \frac{36}{25}x^2 = 100, x = \frac{50}{\sqrt{61}}$

and $y = \frac{60}{\sqrt{61}}$ Also $\frac{x}{y} = \frac{y}{z + 10 - x'}$ so

$\frac{5}{6} = \frac{60/\sqrt{61}}{10 + z - 50/\sqrt{61}} = \frac{60}{10\sqrt{61} - 50 + \sqrt{61}z}$, :

$z = 2\sqrt{61} - 10.$

(b) Since $z(t) = 2\sqrt{61} - 10 + bt$, :

$z + 10 = 2\sqrt{61} + bt$ and setting $y^2 = 100 - x^2$

yields $(2\sqrt{61} + bt - x)^2 + 100 - x^2 = 144,$

$x^2 - 2x(2\sqrt{61} + bt) + (2\sqrt{61} + bt)^2 - x^2 = 44,$

$$2x = \frac{(2\sqrt{61} + bt)^2 - 44}{2\sqrt{61} + bt} x$$

$= \sqrt{61} + \frac{b}{2}t - \frac{22}{2\sqrt{61} + bt}$, and $y = \sqrt{100 - x^2}.$

(c) Rather than differentiate the complicated expression for y, use the chain rule and do it implicitly :

$2x\frac{dx}{dt} + 2y\frac{dy}{dt} = 0, \frac{dy}{dt} = -\frac{x}{y}\frac{dx}{dt}.$

Also $2(z + 10)\frac{dz}{dt} - 2\frac{dx}{dt}(z + 10) - 2x\frac{dz}{dt} = 0.$

Since $z = 11$ and $\frac{dz}{dt} = b$, $42b - 42\frac{dx}{dt} - 2xb = 0.$

Thus $\frac{dx}{dt} = \frac{42 - 2x}{42}b$. But when $z = 11$,

$$x = \frac{(21)^2 - 44}{42} = \frac{397}{42},$$

so $\dfrac{dx}{dt} = \left(1 - \dfrac{794}{(42)^2}\right)b = \dfrac{970}{1764}b$.

$x^2 + y^2 = 100$ so $y = \dfrac{1}{42}\sqrt{(420)^2 - (397)^2}$,

$$\frac{x}{y} = \frac{397}{\sqrt{(420)^2 - (397)^2}},$$

$$\frac{dy}{dt} = -\frac{970}{1764} \cdot \frac{397}{\sqrt{(420)^2 - (397)^2}}b.$$

(Approximately $1.6b$ ft/sec)

2. (a) Integrating once, one gets a velocity of $\left(\frac{1}{2}\sin 2t, -\cos t\right) + (a, b.)$ Since the initial velocity is $(0, -1)$, $a = b = 0$, and $v = \left(\frac{1}{2}\sin 2t, -\cos t\right)$.

(b) Integrating again

$r(t) = \left(-\frac{1}{4}\cos 2t, -\sin t\right) + (c, d)$

Since $r(0) = (1, 0)$, $c = \frac{5}{4}$ and $d = 0$.

Thus $x(t) = \frac{5}{4} - \frac{1}{4}\cos 2t$, $y(t) = -\sin t$.

(c) Both x and y are bounded, so the motion is bounded.

(d) To graph, eliminate t:

$$y^2 = \sin^2 t = \frac{1 - \cos 2t}{2} = 2x - 2$$

so $x = \frac{1}{2}y^2 + 1.$

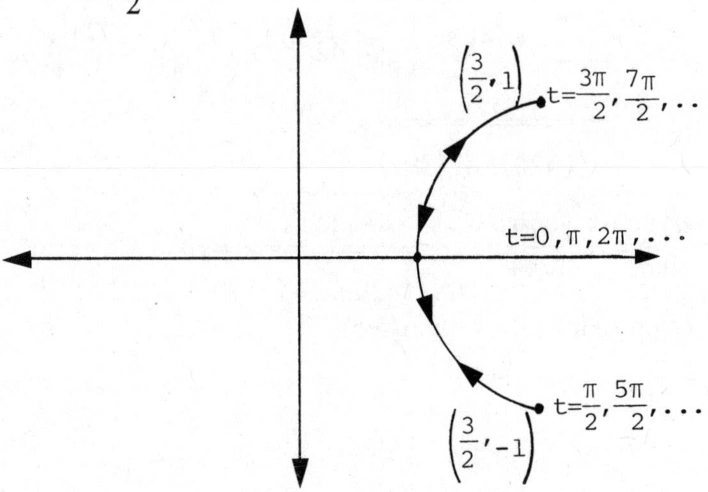

Thus the particle bounces back and forth.

3. (a) Using the first derivative function,

$der1\left(\frac{3}{2 + 105x}, \ x, \ 0\right)$, $f'(0) = -78.75$ can be found.

(b) Draw the graph $f(x)$ for $-1 < x < 1$.

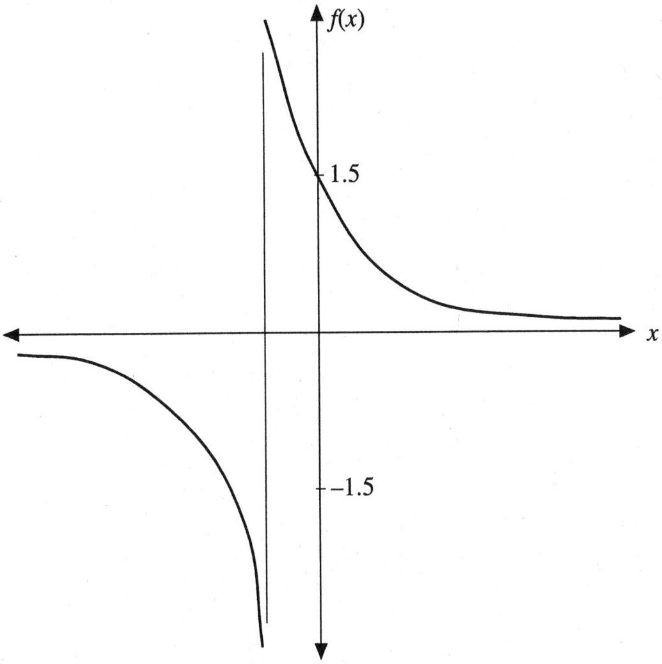

At $x = -0.019$, $f(x)$ jumps from an extremely large negative value to an extremely large positive value. So, $f(x)$ at $x = -0.019$ has no value.

(c) Using the calculator to $\int_0^2 f(x)$ by

$$fnInt\left(\frac{3}{2+105x},\ x,\ 0,\ 2\right),$$

you can get $\int_0^2 f(x)dx = 0.1332$.

4. (a) If $p = y'$, $y'' = p'$, and $p' + p = x$. This is a first order linear equation. Multiplying by e^x, $d(pe^x) = xe^x dx$, and integrating once, we get

$pe^x = (x - 1)e^x + c$, $p = x - 1 + ce^{-x}$.

(b) Writing $p = y' = x - 1 + ce^{-x}$ and integrating once, $y = \frac{x^2}{2} - ce^{-x} + d$.

(c) If $y(0) = 0$, $0 = -c + d$. If $y'(0) = 0$, $c - 1 = 0$.

Thus $c = 1, d = 1$, $y = \frac{x^2}{2} - x - ce^{-x} + 1$.

(This technique is called reduction of order.)

5. (a) Using distance = rate x time, we get

$$T = \frac{x}{5} + \frac{\sqrt{625 + (50 - x)^2}}{3}$$

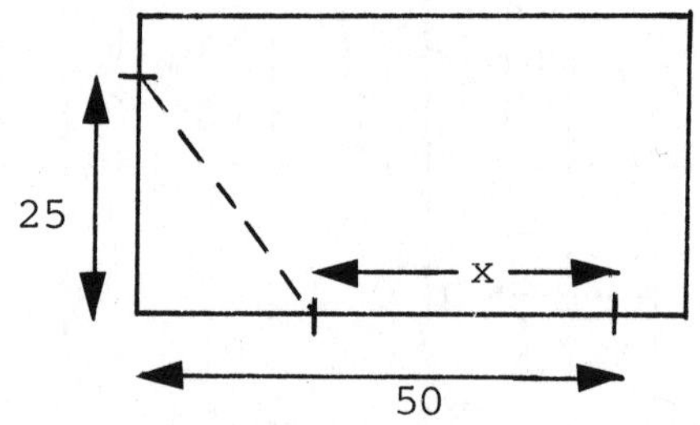

(b) $\frac{dT}{dx} = \frac{1}{5} + \frac{1}{3} \cdot \frac{1}{2}\left(625 + (50 - x)^2\right)^{-1/2}$

$\cdot\ 2(x - 50) = 0.$

(c) Thus $3 + \dfrac{5(x - 50)}{\sqrt{625 + (50 - x)^2}} = 0,$

$*3\sqrt{625 + (50 - x)^2} = 5(50 - x),$

$9\left(625 + (50 - x)^2\right) = 25(50 - x)^2,$

$9 \cdot 625 = 16(50 - x)^2,$

$3 \cdot 25 = 4(50 - x),$

$50 - x = \dfrac{75}{4},$

$x = \dfrac{125}{4} \cong 31$ feet.

(d) $T = \dfrac{125}{20} + \dfrac{1}{3}\left(\dfrac{5}{3}\right)(50 - x)$ (Using *)

$= \dfrac{25}{4} + \dfrac{5}{9} \cdot \dfrac{75}{4} = \dfrac{14}{9} \cdot \dfrac{74}{4} = \dfrac{50}{3}$ sec.

$\left(T''\left(\dfrac{125}{4}\right) > 0\right.$ so it is a minimum.)

6. (a) Setting $x = 0, y = 1$.

(b) Differentiate (≠) implicitly :
$(*) e^{y} + xy'e^{y} \cos x - y \sin x = 0$
and setting $x = 0, y = 1, e + y' = 0, y'(0) = -e$.

(c) Differentiate (*) implicitly :
$y'e^{y} + y'e^{y} + xy'^{2}e^{y} + xy'' \cos x - y' \sin x -$

$y' \sin x - y \cos x = 0.$

Setting $x = 0, y = 1$, and $y' = -e$,

$-e^{2} - e^{2} + y'' - 1 = 0,$
$y''(0) = 1 + 2e^{2}$

(d)

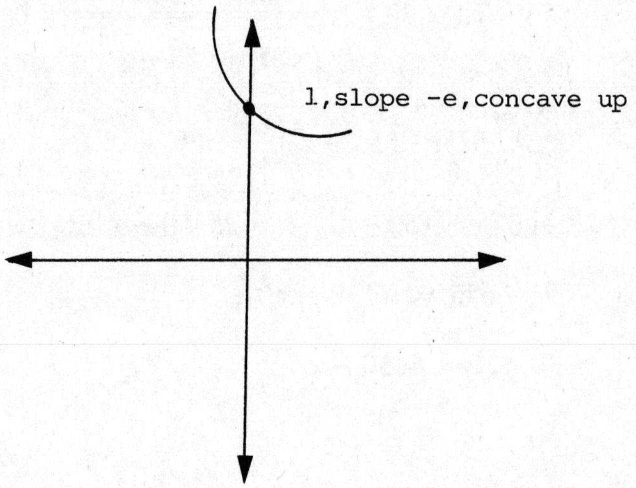

THE ADVANCED PLACEMENT EXAMINATION IN

CALCULUS BC

TEST IV

ADVANCED PLACEMENT CALCULUS BC EXAM IV

SECTION I

PART A

Time: 45 minutes
25 questions

DIRECTIONS: Each of the following problems is followed by five choices. Solve each problem, select the best choice, and blacken the correct space on your answer sheet.

NOTE:

Unless otherwise specified, the domain of function *f* is assumed to be the set of all real numbers *x* for which *f*(*x*) is a real number.

1. The area of the region between the graph of $y = 5x^4 - 4x$ and the x-axis from $x = 1$ to $x = 2$ is

(A) 19 (D) 79

(B) 23 (E) 81

(C) 25

2. At what value of x does $f(x) = 2x^5 - 5x^4 - 10x^3 + 8$ have a relative maximum ?

(A) -3

(B) -2

(C) 0

(D) 2

(E) -1

3. $\int_1^2 \frac{x^2 + 1}{x^3 + 3x + 1} dx =$

(A) 0.231

(B) 0.406

(C) 0.366

(D) 0.535

(E) 1.609

4. If $y = x \sin(x + y)$, then $\frac{dy}{dx} =$

(A) $\sin(x + y) + x \cos(x + y)$

(B) $\sin(x + y) - x \cos(x + y)$

(C) $\frac{\sin(x + y) + x \cos(x + y)}{1 + x \cos(x + y)}$

(D) $\frac{\sin(x + y) - x \cos(x + y)}{1 + x \cos(x + y)}$

(E) $\frac{\sin(x + y) + x \cos(x + y)}{1 - x \cos(x + y)}$

5.

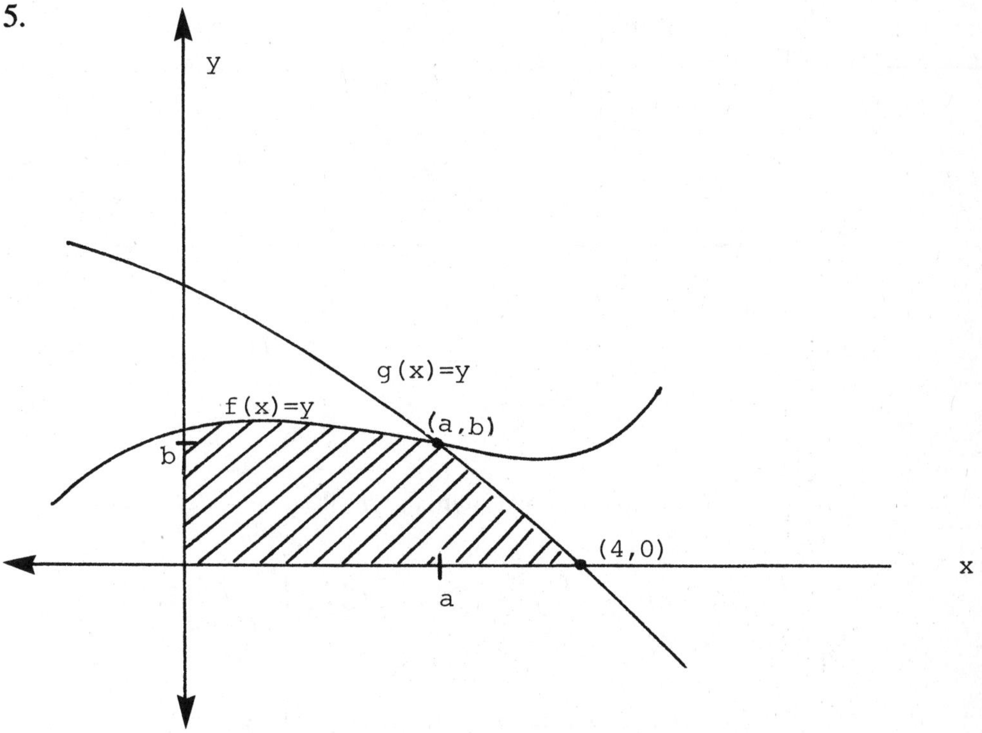

The curves $y = f(x)$ and $y = g(x)$ shown in the figure above intersect at the point (a, b). The area of the shaded region, bounded by these curves and the coordinate axes, is given by :

(A) $\int_0^a (f(x) - g(x))dx$

(B) $\int_0^a (g(x) - f(x))dx$

(C) $\int_0^a f(x)dx - \int_a^4 g(x)dx$

(D) $\int_0^a f(x)dx + \int_a^4 g(x)dx$

(E) $\int_0^4 g(x)dx - \int_0^a f(x)dx$

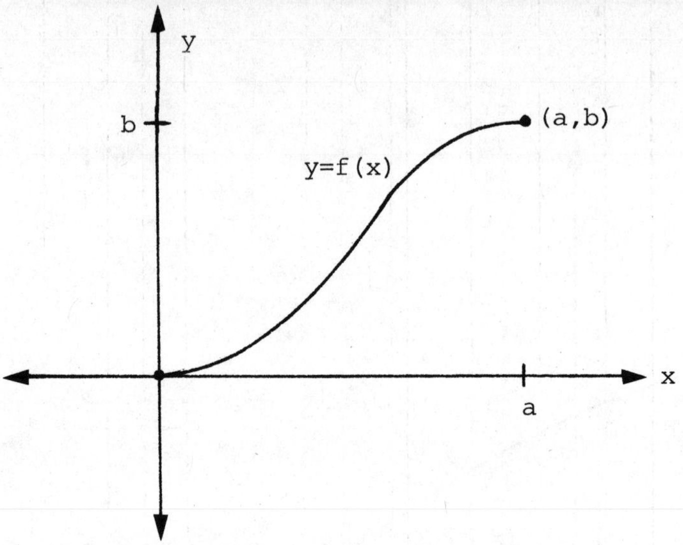

6. If f has the graph shown above, then $\int_0^b f^{-1}(x)\,dx =$

(A) $ab - \int_0^a f(x)\,dx$

(B) $\dfrac{1}{\int_0^b f(x)\,dx}$

(C) $\dfrac{1}{\int_0^a f(x)\,dx}$

(D) $\int_0^b \dfrac{1}{f(x)}\,dx$

(E) $\int_0^a \dfrac{1}{f(x)}\,dx$

7. $\int \dfrac{1}{9+x^2}\,dx =$

(A) $\text{Arctan}\,\dfrac{x}{3} + C$

(B) $3\,\text{Arctan}\,\dfrac{x}{3} + C$

(C) $\dfrac{1}{3}\,\text{Arctan}\,\dfrac{x}{3} + C$

(D) $3\,\text{Arctan}\,3x + C$

(E) $\dfrac{1}{3}\,\text{Arctan}\,3x + C$

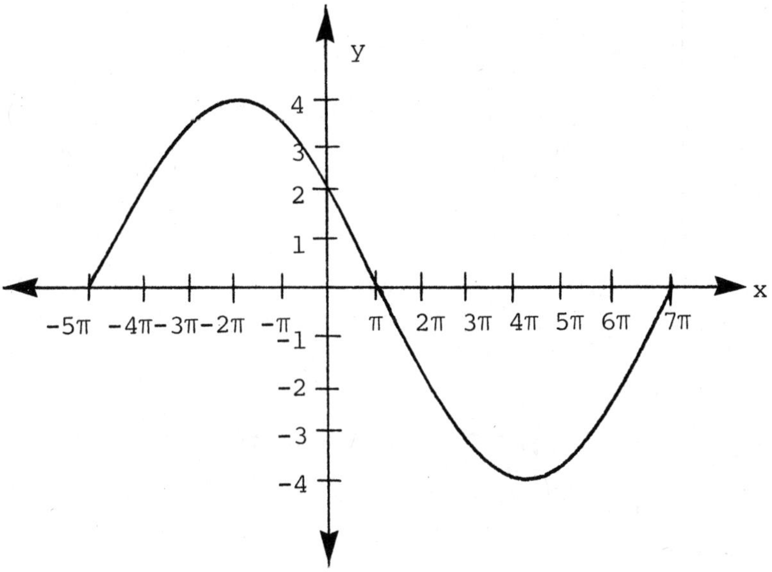

8. The curve shown above is the graph of :

(A) $y = 4\sin(6x + 5\pi)$ (D) $y = 4\sin\dfrac{x - 5\pi}{6}$

(B) $y = 4\sin 6(x + 5\pi)$ (E) $y = 4\sin\left(\dfrac{x}{6} - 5\pi\right)$

(C) $y = 4\sin\dfrac{x + 5\pi}{6}$

9. $\int (x^3 + 1)\sqrt{x}\,dx =$

(A) $\left(\frac{1}{3}x^3 + x\right)\cdot \frac{2}{3}x^{\frac{3}{2}} + C$

(B) $\frac{2}{9}x^{\frac{9}{2}} + \frac{2}{3}x^{\frac{3}{2}} + C$

(C) $\frac{2}{5}x^{\frac{5}{2}} + \frac{2}{3}x^{\frac{3}{2}} + C$

(D) $3x^2 \cdot \frac{1}{2\sqrt{x}} + C$

(E) $\frac{7}{2}x^{\frac{5}{2}} + \frac{1}{2}x^{-\frac{1}{2}} + C$

10. If $f(x) = \sum_{n=0}^{\infty} \frac{(-1)^n}{n!} x^{2n}$ for all real x, then $f''(0) =$

(A) 0

(B) 1

(C) $\frac{1}{2}$

(D) 2

(E) -2

11. $\frac{d}{dx} \ln\left(\frac{1+x^2}{1-x^2}\right)$ at $x = 2.5$ is approximately:

(A) -0.191

(B) 0.952

(C) 0.027

(D) -0.263

(E) 0.270

12. $\int \frac{dx}{x^2 + x} =$

(A) $\ln|x^2 + x| + C$

(B) $\ln\left|\frac{x}{x+1}\right| + C$

(C) $\ln\left|\frac{x+1}{x}\right| + C$

(D) $\ln\left|\frac{1}{x^2 + x}\right| + C$

(E) $2\ln|x^2 + x| + C$

13. Let $f(x) = \sqrt{x - 1}$ for $x \geq 1$. What are the possible x-values, usually denoted by c in the statement of the Mean Value Theorem, at which f' attains its mean value over the interval $1 \leq x \leq 5$?

(A) 1

(B) 2

(C) 4

(D) 1 and 2

(E) 1 and 4

14. Which of the following series converge?

I. $1 + \frac{1}{2} + \frac{1}{3} + \ldots + \frac{1}{n} + \ldots$

II. $1 - \frac{1}{2} + \frac{1}{3} - \ldots + \frac{(-1)^n}{n} + \ldots$

III. $1 - \frac{1}{\sqrt{2}} + \frac{1}{\sqrt{3}} - \ldots + \frac{(-1)^n}{\sqrt{n}} + \ldots$

(A) I only

(B) II only

(C) I and II only

(D) II and III only

(E) I, II and III

15. If the velocity of a particle moving along the x - axis is $v(t) = 3t^2 - 5$ and if the particle is at $x = 9$ when $t = 1$, then its position function $x(t)$ is :

(A) $6t + 3$

(B) $t^3 - 5t$

(C) $3t^2 + 6$

(D) $t^3 - 5t + 9$

(E) $t^3 - 5t + 13$

16. If f is the function given by : $f(x) = \begin{cases} 0, & \text{if } x \le 0 \\ x, & \text{if } x \ge 0, \end{cases}$

which of the following statements are true?

I. $\lim_{x \to 0} f(x) = 0$

II. f is continuous at $x = 0$

III. f is differentiable at $x = 0$

(A) I only

(B) II only

(C) I and II only

(D) I and III only

(E) I, II, and III

17. If $f(x) = x^2 \ln(x^3)$, then $f'(x) =$

(A) $3x + \ln x^3$

(D) $2x$

(B) $3x(1 + \ln x^2)$

(E) $2x \ln(3x^2)$

(C) $\frac{1}{x}$

18. $\int \cos(5x - 2)dx =$

(A) $\frac{1}{5}\sin(5x - 2) + C$

(B) $5\sin(5x - 2) + C$

(C) $-\frac{1}{5}\sin(5x - 2) + C$

(D) $-5\sin(5x - 2) + C$

(E) $\sin(5x - 2) + C$

19. $\lim_{x \to 0^+} e^{x^2 + \ln x} =$

(A) 0

(B) 1

(C) e

(D) e^2

(E) e^e

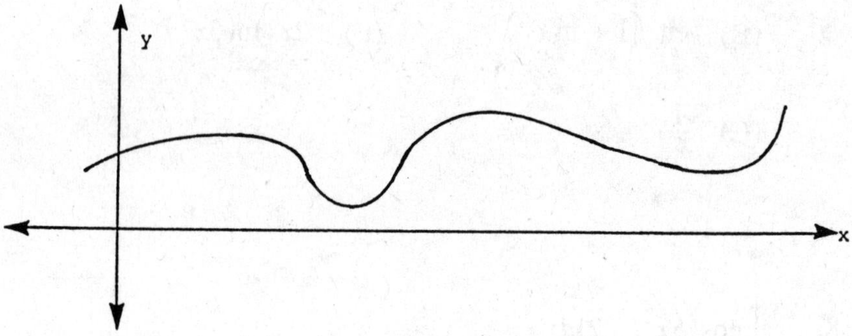

20. How many inflection points does the curve shown above have ?

(A) 0

(B) 1

(C) 2

(D) 3

(E) 4

21. If $\int f(x)e^{-x}dx = -f(x)e^{-x} + \int 2x\, e^{-x}dx$, then $f(x)$ could be :

(A) e^x

(B) $-e^{-x}$

(C) x^2

(D) $-x^2$

(E) $2x$

22. Let V be the volume of the region bounded between two expanding concentric spheres. At time $t = 0$ the spheres have radii 6 cm and 40 cm. The radius of the smaller sphere increases at 8cm/sec while the radius of the larger sphere increases at 2cm/sec. The volume V will be maximal at $t =$

(A) $\frac{1}{2}$

(B) 1

(C) 2

(D) $\frac{3}{2}$

(E) 3

23. $\lim_{h \to 0} \frac{1}{h} \int_0^h \sqrt[3]{1 + x^2}\,dx$ is

(A) 0

(B) 1

(C) 2

(D) $\sqrt[3]{9}$

(E) nonexistent

24. The total area of the region enclosed by the polar graph of $r = \cos 3\theta$ is

(A) 0.262

(B) 0.524

(C) 0.785

(D) 1.047

(E) 2.437

25. A particle moves along the x-axis so that its position at time t is given by $x(t) = \left(1 + t^2\right)e^{-t}$.
For what values of t will the particle be at rest ?

(A) No values

(B) 0 only

(C) $\frac{1}{2}$ only

(D) 1 only

(E) 2 only

SECTION I

PART B

Time: 45 minutes
15 questions

DIRECTIONS: Calculators may be used for this section of the test. Each of the following problems is followed by five choices. Solve each problem, select the best choice, and blacken the correct space on your answer sheet.

NOTES:

1. Unless otherwise specified, answers can be given in unsimplified form.
2. The domain of function *f* is assumed to be the set of all real numbers *x* for which *f*(*x*) is a real number.

26. If $y = x^{2^x}$, for $x > 0$, then $\left.\frac{dy}{dx}\right|_{x=2}$ is

(A) 32.000 (D) 17.374

(B) 22.181 (E) 62.749

(C) 15.374

27. The area enclosed by $f(x) = x^3 + x^2$ and $g(x) = \ln(x + 1)$ for $x \geq 0$ is

(A) 0.0513 (D) 2.89

(B) 0.01 (E) 7.8

(C) 2.5

28. If $f(x)$ is continuous on the interval $[a, b]$ and if $\int_a^x f(t)\,dt = 0$ for all x in $[a, b]$, then which of the following must be true ?

I. f is constant on $[a, b]$

II. $f(x) \geq 0$ for all x in $[a, b]$

III. $f(x) = 0$ for all x in $[a, b]$

(A) I only

(B) II only

(C) I and II only

(D) I, II, and III

(E) None of the above

29. The area in the first quadrant that is enclosed by $y = \sin 3x \cos x$ and the x-axis from $x = 0$ to the first x-intercept on the positive side is

(A) 1

(B) 0.56

(C) 0.78

(D) 2.5

(E) 1.5

30. If $x = t^3 - 3t$ and $y = \left(t^2 + 1\right)^2$, then at $t = 2$, $\frac{dy}{dx}$ is

(A) 40

(B) 9

(C) $\frac{40}{9}$

(D) $\frac{9}{40}$

(E) 0

31. $6\int_{-1}^{1} \frac{x^3 + 1}{x + 1} dx =$

(A) 4

(B) 2

(C) 12

(D) 8

(E) 16

32. An equation of the line normal to the graph of $y = x^4 - 3x^2 + 1$ at the point where $x = 1$ is:

(A) $2x - y + 3 = 0$

(B) $x - 2y + 3 = 0$

(C) $2x - y - 3 = 0$

(D) $x - 2y - 3 = 0$

(E) $x - 2y = 0$

33. Let $f(x) = 256x^{-\frac{1}{2}} + 64x^{\frac{1}{2}} + 3x^{\frac{2}{3}}$. $f'(64)$ equals

(A) 4.25

(B) 8.75

(C) 0.75

(D) 10.25

(E) 5.78

34. Which of the following gives the area of the surface generated by revolving about the x-axis the arc of $y = x^3 - x$ from $x = 0$ to $x = 2$?

(A) $2\pi\int_0^2 x\sqrt{9x^4 - 6x^2 + 2}\,dx$

(B) $2\pi\int_0^2 \left(x^3 - x\right)\sqrt{9x^4 - 6x^2 + 2}\,dx$

(C) $2\pi\int_0^2 x\sqrt{9x^4 - 6x^2}\,dx$

(D) $2\pi\int_0^2 \left(x^3 - x\right)\sqrt{9x^4 - 6x^2}\,dx$

(E) $2\pi\int_0^2 \left(x^3 - x\right)\sqrt{9x^4 - 6x^2 + 1}\,dx$

35. The smallest value of $y = x^2 (1 - x^{-1})$ is

(A) 0

(B) –0.25

(C) 0.25

(D) –1

(E) 1

36. Which integral has the same value as $\int_0^{\infty} \frac{x^2}{\left(9+x^2\right)^{\frac{5}{2}}} dx$?

(A) $\frac{1}{9}\int_0^{\frac{\pi}{2}} \sin^2\theta \cos\theta \, d\theta$

(B) $\frac{1}{27}\int_0^{\frac{\pi}{2}} \sin^2\theta \cos^3\theta \, d\theta$

(C) $\frac{1}{9}\int_0^{\infty} \frac{\sin^2\theta}{\cos^3\theta} d\theta$

(D) $\frac{1}{27}\int_0^{\infty} \frac{\sin^2\theta}{\cos^2\theta} d\theta$

(E) $\frac{1}{9}\int_0^{\frac{\pi}{2}} \frac{\cos\theta}{\sin^4\theta} d\theta$

37. The general solution to the differential equation $\frac{dy}{dx} = 1 + y^2$ is

(A) $y = Ce^{-x^2}$

(B) $y = Ce^{-2x}$

(C) $y = \sin(x + C)$

(D) $y = \tan(x + C)$

(E) $y = x + \frac{1}{3}x^3 + C$

38. $\lim_{x \to \infty} \sqrt[x]{1 + x^2}$ is

(A) 0

(B) 1

(C) 2

(D) e

(E) nonexistent

39. Where does the graph of $y = x\int_0^x e^{-t^2}\,dt$ have inflection points?

(A) Only at $x = 0$

(B) Only at $x = 1$

(C) Only at $x = 0$ and $x = 1$

(D) Only at $x = -1$ and $x = 1$

(E) Nowhere

40. The substitution $u = \ln x$ transforms the integral

$\int_1^e \frac{1-\ln x}{x^2} dx$ into

(A) $\int_0^1 (1-u)\,du$

(B) $\int_0^1 (1-u)e^u\,du$

(C) $\int_0^1 (1-u)e^{-u}\,du$

(D) $\int_1^e (1-u)\,du$

(E) $\int_1^e (1-u)e^{-u}\,du$

ADVANCED PLACEMENT CALCULUS BC EXAM IV

SECTION II

Time: 1 hour and 30 minutes
6 questions†

DIRECTIONS: Show all your work. Grading is based on the methods used to solve the problems as well as the accuracy of your final answers. Please make sure all procedures are clearly shown.

NOTES:

1. In x denotes the natural logarithm of x (that is, logarithm to the base e).

2. Unless otherwise specified, the domain of function f is assumed to be the set of all real numbers x for which $f(x)$ is a real number.

† The practice tests in this book incorporate Section II free-response solutions that approximate the content breakdown you will encounter on the AP exam. The overall timing and formatting of the practice tests mirror the actual test; examinees should note, however, that this section is split into two parts on the AP exam. Furthermore, prospective examinees should pay attention to restrictions on calculator use. For details, consult current official College Board materials in print or on the Web.

1. A particle moves on the $x - \frac{1}{n}$ axis so that its acceleration at time t is given by $a = 12t^2 - 16$ for $t \geq 0$.
At $t = 0$, the velocity is $v = 0$ and the position is $x = 3$.

(a) Write an expression for the velocity v as a function of t.

(b) Write an expression for the position x as a function of t.

(c) For what values of $t \geq 0$ is the particle moving to the right ?

(d) Find the total distance traveled by the particle from $t = 0$ to $t = 3$.

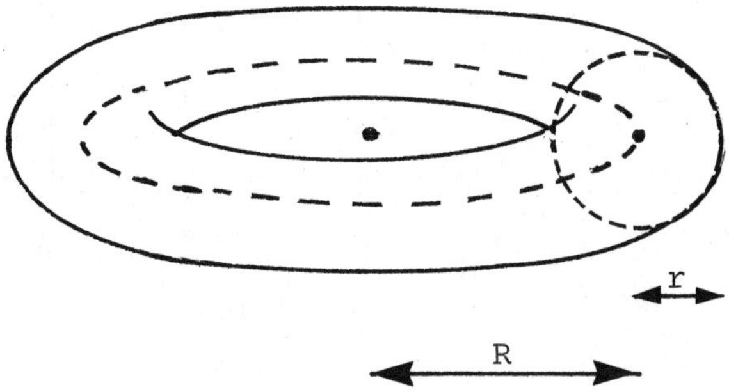

2. The inner tube shown above is in the shape of a torus (do-nut-shape) with large radius R and small radius r. Air is being pumped into the inner tube at a constant rate of $4\pi^2 cm^3$ /min. Assume that R remains constant at 20 in. while r increases.

(a) Express r as a function of time t, where t is the number of minutes after the time when r was 10 inches.

(b) How fast is r increasing when $r = 16$ inches ?

(c) When will $r = R$?

(The volume of a torus with large radius R and small radius r is $X = 2\pi^2 R r^2$.)

3. Given $f(x) = 2x^2 - 2x + 5$ and $g(x) = x^2 + 2x + 4$.

(a) Find the values of x where $f(x) = g(x)$.

(b) If $f'(a) = g'(a)$, find a.

(c) Use the results from (a) to find $\int_a^b (g(x) - f(x))\,dx$, where a and b are where $f(x) = g(x)$.

4. According to Newton's Law of Cooling, the rate at which a hot body cools is proportional to the difference in temperature between the body and its surrounding environment.

(a) Let T_0 be the temperature of a hot body at time $t = 0$, and let T_∞ be the (constant) temperature of the surrounding environment. Express Newton's Law of Cooling as a differential equation,whose solution would give the body's temperature T as a function of time t.

(b) Solve the differential equation.

(c) Suppose a body is heated to $100°C$ and is then allowed to cool in air whose temperature is kept at $10°C$. If it takes 50 minutes for the body to cool to 60°C how much longer will it take to cool to 40°C?

5. Consider the polar graph of the equation $r = 1 + 2\cos 3\theta$.

(a) Sketch the polar graph :

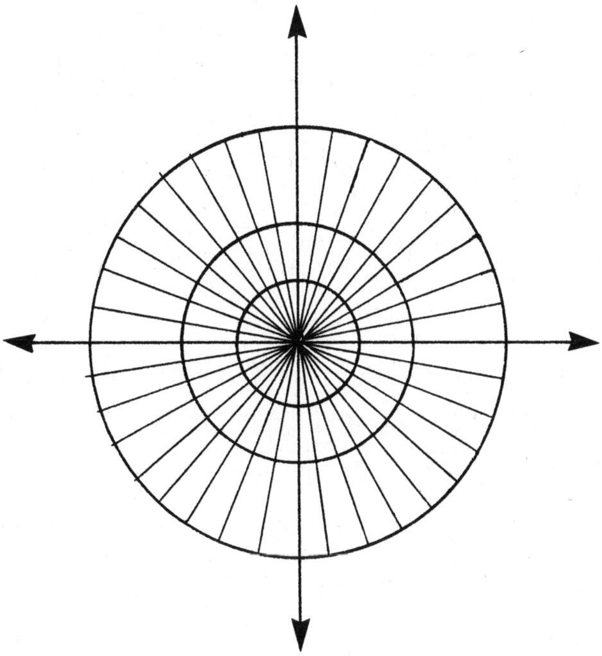

(b) The graph partitions the disk $r \leq 3$ into 9 pieces. Find the area of each piece.

6. Let f be a function that is defined and twice differentiable for all $x > 0$ and has the following properties :

(i) $f(1) = 2$

(ii) $\lim_{x \to 0^+} f(x) = +\infty$

(iii) $\lim_{x \to +\infty} f(x) = 1$

(iv) $f'(1) = -1$

(v) $f'(x) < 0$ for all $x > 0$.

(vi) $f''(x) > 0$ for all $x > 0$.

Let g be the function defined by $g(x) = f\left(\frac{1}{x}\right)$

(a) Find $g(1)$.

(b) Find $\lim_{x \to 0^+} g(x)$.

(c) Find $g'(1)$.

(d) Using the information found in parts (a), (b), and (c), sketch a possible graph of g.

ADVANCED PLACEMENT CALCULUS BC EXAM IV

ANSWER KEY

SECTION I

1.	C	21.	C
2.	E	22.	C
3.	C	23.	B
4.	E	24.	C
5.	D	25.	D
6.	A	26.	E
7.	C	27.	A
8.	C	28.	D
9.	B	29.	B
10.	E	30.	C
11.	D	31.	E
12.	B	32.	D
13.	B	33.	A
14.	D	34.	B
15.	E	35.	B
16.	C	36.	A
17.	B	37.	D
18.	A	38.	B
19.	A	39.	D
20.	D	40.	C

SECTION II

See Detailed Explanations of Answers.

ADVANCED PLACEMENT CALCULUS BC EXAM IV

SECTION I

DETAILED EXPLANATIONS OF ANSWERS

1. (C)

The area is the integral :

$$A = \int_1^2 (5x^4 - 4x)dx$$

Use the Fundamental Theorem of Calculus to evaluate the integral :

$$A = \int_1^2 (5x^4 - 4x)dx$$

$$= (x^5 - 2x^2)\Big|_1^2$$

$$= \left[(2)^5 - 2(2)^2\right] - \left[(1)^5 - 2(1)^2\right]$$

$$= [32 - 8] - [1 - 2]$$

$$= 25$$

2. (E)

The relative maximum occurs at a critical point of the function. Since the function is a polynomial, its critical points occur where its derivative is zero.

The derivative is : $f'(x) = 10x^4 - 20x^3 - 30x^2$.

Factoring : $f'(x) = 10x^2(x - 3)(x + 1)$.

This is zero at $x = 0$, $x = 3$, and $x = -1$

To see which of these is a relative maximum, use The Second Derivative Test.

The second derivative is : $f''(x) = 40x^3 - 60x^2 - 60x$.

Its values at the critical points are :

$f''(0) = 0$

$f''(3) = 360$

$f''(-1) = -40$

At a relative maximum, the second derivative must be negative (because the graph must be concave downward there). Hence, the only relative maximum is at $x = -1$.

3. (C)

Let $u = x^3 + 3x + 1$

Then $du = 3x^2dx + 3dx = 3(x^2 + 1)dx$ so the integrand is :

$$\frac{x^2 + 1}{x^3 + 3x + 1}dx = \frac{1}{3} \cdot \frac{3(x^2 + 1)dx}{x^3 + 3x + 1} = \frac{1}{3} \cdot \frac{du}{u}$$

Also, if $x = 1$ then $u = (1)^3 + 3(1) + 1 = 5$,

and, if $x = 2$ then $u = (2)^3 + 3(2) + 1 = 15$.

$$\int_1^2 \frac{x^2 + 1}{x^3 + 3x + 1}dx = \int_5^{15} \frac{1}{3}\frac{du}{u}$$

$$= \frac{1}{3} \ln|u| \Big|_5^{15}$$
$$= \frac{1}{3} \ln 15 - \frac{1}{3} \ln 5$$
$$= \frac{1}{3} (\ln 15 - \ln 5)$$
$$= \frac{1}{3} \left(\ln \frac{15}{5} \right)$$
$$= \frac{1}{3} \ln 3 = 0.366$$

4. (E)

Since the given equation cannot be solved explicitly for y, the method of implicit differentiation must be used :

$$y = x \sin(x + y)$$
$$\frac{dy}{dx} = \left(\frac{d}{dx}x\right) \cdot (\sin(x+y)) + (x) \cdot \left(\frac{d}{dx}\sin(x+y)\right)$$
$$= 1 \cdot \sin(x+y) + x \cdot \cos(x+y) \cdot \frac{d}{dx}(x+y)$$
$$= \sin(x+y) + x\cos(x+y) \cdot \left(1 + \frac{dy}{dx}\right)$$
$$= \sin(x+y) + x\cos(x+y) + x\cos(x+y) \cdot \frac{dy}{dx}$$

Solve this equation for $\frac{dy}{dx}$:

$$\frac{dy}{dx} - x\cos(x+y) \cdot \frac{dy}{dx}$$
$$= \sin(x+y) + x\cos(x+y)$$

$$(1 - x\cos(x+y)) \cdot \frac{dy}{dx}$$
$$= \sin(x+y) + x\cos(x+y)$$

$$\frac{dy}{dx} = \frac{\sin(x+y) + x\cos(x+y)}{1 - x\cos(x+y)}$$

5. (D)

The area of a region bounded above by the graph of a function and below by the x-axis is the integral of the function. Since the given region is bounded above by two functions, its area is the sum of the integrals of the two functions.

Let A_1 be the area of the region bounded by f, and let A_2 be the area of the region bounded by g :

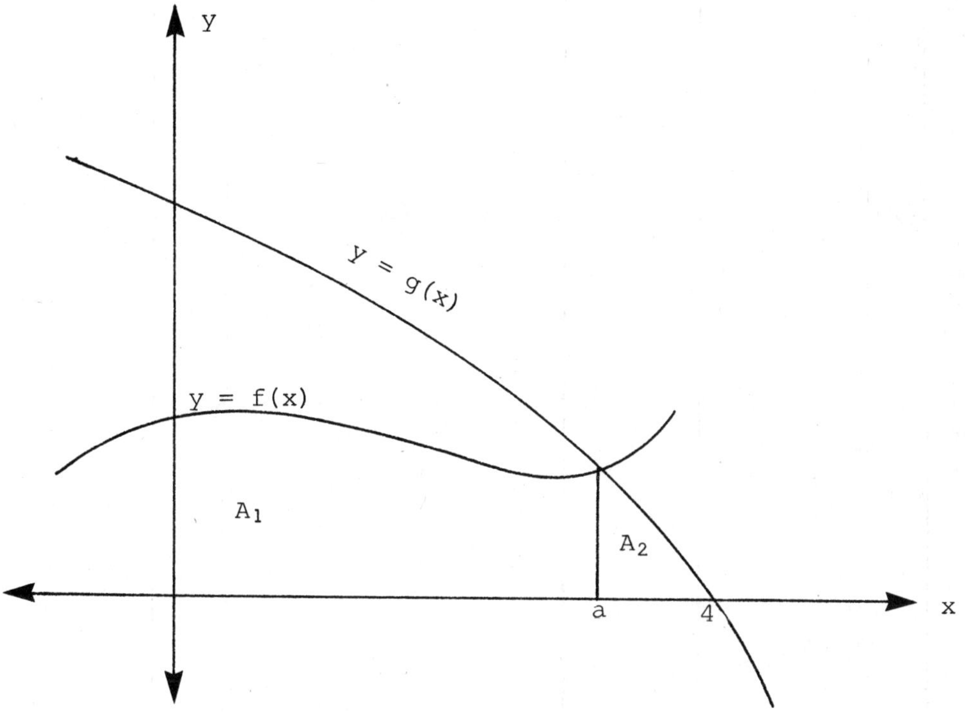

The total area is their sum :

$$A = A_1 + A_2$$

$$= \int_0^a f(x)\,dx + \int_a^4 g(x)\,dx$$

6. (A)

The graph of the inverse function f^{-1} is obtained from the graph of f by reflecting across the line $y = x$: [45°-line] :

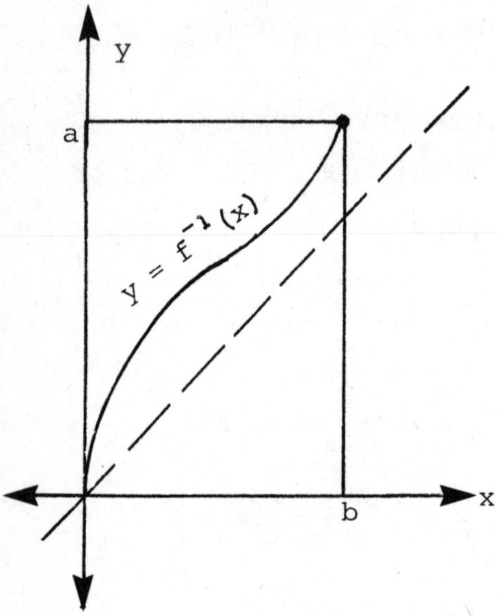

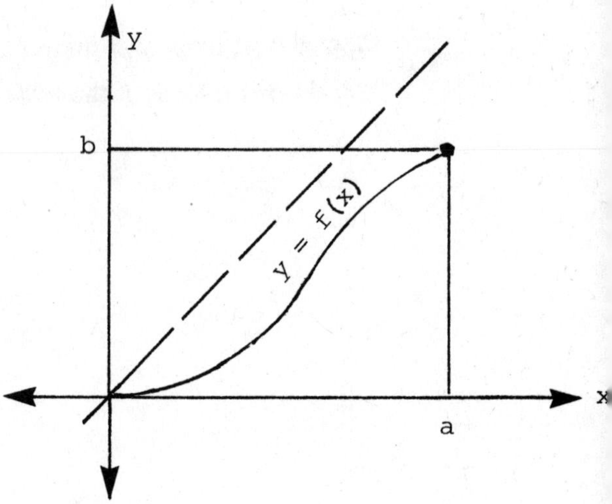

In both pictures, the curve divides a rectangle into two pieces :

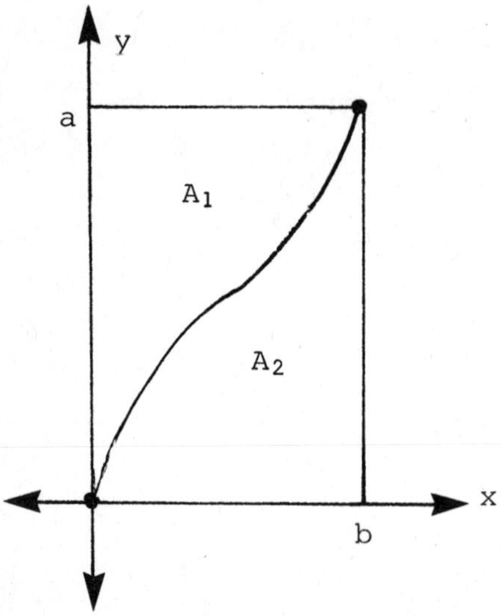

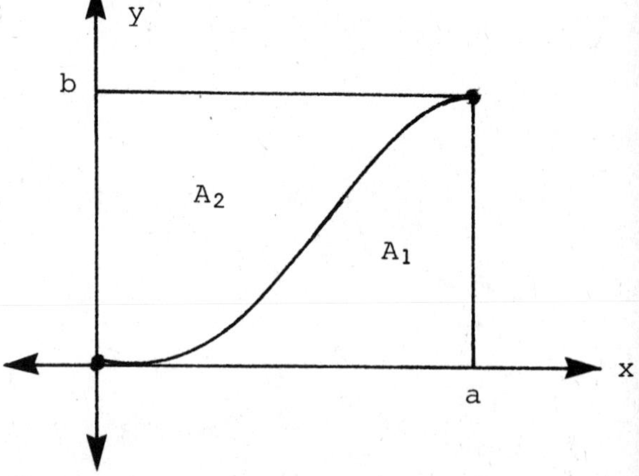

The areas of these two pieces are :

$$A_1 = \int_0^a f(x)dx$$

$$A_2 = \int_0^b f^{-1}(x)dx$$

The sum of these two areas equals the area of the rectangle whose side lengths are a and b :

$$A_1 + A_2 = a \cdot b$$

Thus : $A_2 = ab - A_1$

i.e. $\int_0^b f^{-1}(x)dx = ab - \int_0^a f(x)dx$

7. (C)

The quickest way to pick the correct answer from those given is to check their derivatives :

$$\frac{d}{dx} \text{Arctan} \frac{x}{3} = \frac{1}{1+\left(\frac{x}{3}\right)^2} \cdot \frac{d}{dx}\left(\frac{x}{3}\right)$$

$$= \frac{1}{1+\frac{x^2}{9}} \cdot \frac{1}{3}$$

$$= \frac{1}{3+\frac{x^2}{3}}$$

$$= 3\left(\frac{1}{9+x^2}\right)$$

So : $\frac{1}{3} \cdot \frac{d}{dx} \text{Arctan} \frac{x}{3} = \frac{1}{9+x^2}$

Thus $\frac{1}{3}\text{Arctan}\,\frac{x}{3}$ is an antiderivative of $\frac{1}{9+x^2}$,
so :

$$\int \frac{1}{9+x^2}\,dx = \frac{1}{3}\text{Arctan}\,\frac{x}{3} + C\,.$$

8. (C)

The curve shows that $y = 2$ when $x = 0$. Check each equation for this value :

(A) $y = 4\sin(6(0) + 5\pi) = 4\sin 5\pi = 0$

(B) $y = 4\sin 6(0 + 5\pi) = 4\sin 30\pi = 0$

(C) $y = 4\sin\frac{0 + 5\pi}{6} = 4\sin\frac{5\pi}{6} = 4\cdot\frac{1}{2} = 2$

(D) $y = 4\sin\frac{0 - 5\pi}{6} = 4\sin\left(\frac{-5\pi}{6}\right) = 4\left(-\frac{1}{2}\right) = -2$

(E) $y = 4\sin\left(\frac{0}{6} - 5\pi\right) = 4\sin(-5\pi) = 0$

9. (B)

$$\int (x^3 + 1)\sqrt{x}\,dx = \int (x^3 + 1)x^{\frac{1}{2}}dx$$

$$= \int \left(x^3 \cdot x^{\frac{1}{2}} + x^{\frac{1}{2}}\right)dx$$

$$= \int \left(x^{\frac{7}{2}} + x^{\frac{1}{2}}\right)dx$$

$$= \frac{2}{9}x^{\frac{9}{2}} + \frac{2}{3}x^{\frac{3}{2}} + C$$

10. (E)

First, identify the first few terms of the series :

$$f(x) = \sum_{n=0}^{\infty} \frac{(-1)^n}{n!} x^{2n}$$

$$= \frac{(-1)^0}{0!} x^0 + \frac{(-1)^1}{1!} x^2 + \frac{(-1)^2}{2!} x^4 + \ldots$$

$$= 1 - x^2 + \frac{1}{2} x^4 - \ldots$$

Then differentiate the series termwise :

$$f'(x) = 0 - 2x + \frac{1}{2} \cdot 4x^3 - \ldots$$

$$= -2x + 2x^3 - \ldots$$

$$f''(x) = -2 + 6x^2 - \ldots$$

Then substitute $x = 0$:

$$f''(0) = -2 + 6(0)^2 - \ldots$$

$$= -2 + 0 - \ldots$$

$$= -2$$

11. (D)

First, simplify the function :

$$\ln\left(\frac{1+x^2}{1-x^2}\right) = \ln(1+x^2) - \ln(1-x^2)$$

Then differentiate and simplify :

$$\frac{d}{dx}\ln\left(\frac{1+x^2}{1-x^2}\right) = \frac{d}{dx}\ln(1+x^2) - \frac{d}{dx}\ln(1-x^2)$$

$$\left.\frac{d}{dx}\right|_{2.5} = \frac{4(2.5)}{1-(2.5)^4} = 0.263$$

12. (B)

The simplest way to find the correct answer is to differentiate each of the five given answers :

(A) $$\frac{d}{dx}\ln\left|x^2+x\right| = \frac{1}{x^2+x}\cdot\frac{d}{dx}(x^2+x)$$

$$= \frac{1}{x^2+x}\cdot(2x+1)$$

(B) $$\frac{d}{dx}\ln\left|\frac{x}{x+1}\right| = \frac{d}{dx}\ln|x| - \frac{d}{dx}|x+1|$$

$$= \frac{1}{x} - \frac{1}{x+1}$$

$$= \frac{(x+1)-(x)}{x(x+1)}$$

$$= \frac{1}{x^2 + x}$$

Since $\frac{1}{x^2 + x}$ is the derivative of the function given in (B), that must be the antiderivative $\int \frac{1}{x^2 + x} dx$.

One could also factor the denominator and use partial fractions :

$$\int \frac{dx}{x^2 + x} = \int \frac{dx}{x(x+1)}$$

Write $\frac{A}{x} + \frac{B}{x+1} = 1$

$$Ax + A + Bx = 1, \quad A = 1, \quad A + B = 0, \quad B = -1$$

$$\int \frac{dx}{x} - \int \frac{dx}{x+1} = \ln|x| - \ln|x+1| + C$$

$$= \ln\left|\frac{x}{x+1}\right| + C.$$

13. (B)

The Mean Value Theorem states that the equation

$$f'(c) = \frac{f(b) - f(a)}{b - a}$$

holds for some c between a and b. Here $a = 1$ and $b = 5$ are given and $f(x) = \sqrt{x - 1}$.The right- hand side of the equation is :

$$\frac{f(b) - f(a)}{b - a} = \frac{f(5) - f(1)}{5 - 1}$$

$$= \frac{\sqrt{5-1} - \sqrt{1-1}}{4}$$

$$= \frac{\sqrt{4} - \sqrt{0}}{4} = \frac{2-0}{4}$$

$$= \frac{1}{2}$$

This is the mean value of the derivative function f' over the interval $1 \leq x \leq 5$.
The derivative function is :

$$f'(x) = \frac{d}{dx}\sqrt{x-1}$$

$$= \frac{1}{2\sqrt{x-1}}$$

Hence f' attains its mean value at any c for which

$$\frac{1}{2\sqrt{c-1}} = \frac{1}{2}$$

Solve this equation for c :
Cross multiply : $2 = 2\sqrt{c-1}$
Divide by 2 : $1 = \sqrt{c-1}$
Square both sides : $1 = c - 1$
Add 1 to both sides : $c = 2$

14. (D)
Series I is the Harmonic Series which diverges.
Both series II and III converge by the Alternating Series Test. This states that the alternating series

$$a_1 - a_2 + a_3 - \ldots + (-1)^n a_n + \ldots$$

converges if the sequence $a_1, a_2, a_3, \ldots, a_n, \ldots$ decreases to zero.

Both sequences $1, \frac{1}{2}, \frac{1}{3}, \ldots \frac{1}{n}, \ldots$ and

$1, \frac{1}{\sqrt{2}}, \frac{1}{\sqrt{3}}, \ldots, \frac{1}{\sqrt{n}}, \ldots$ decreases to zero,

so both alternating series converge.

15. (E)

The position function $x(t)$ is the antiderivative of the velocity function $v(t)$:

$$x(t) = \int v(t)dt$$

$$= \int (3t^2 - 5)dt$$

$$= t^3 - 5t + C$$

To evaluate the constant C, substitute the given values $x = 9$ and $t = 1$:

$$x = t^3 - 5t + C$$

$$9 = (1)^3 - 5(1) + C$$

$$= 1 - 5 + C$$

$$= c - 4$$

Solve for C : $C = 13$

Then replace C with this value in the general equation :

$$x(t) = t^3 - 5t + C$$

$$= t^3 - 5t + 13$$

16. (C)

The graph of the function is :

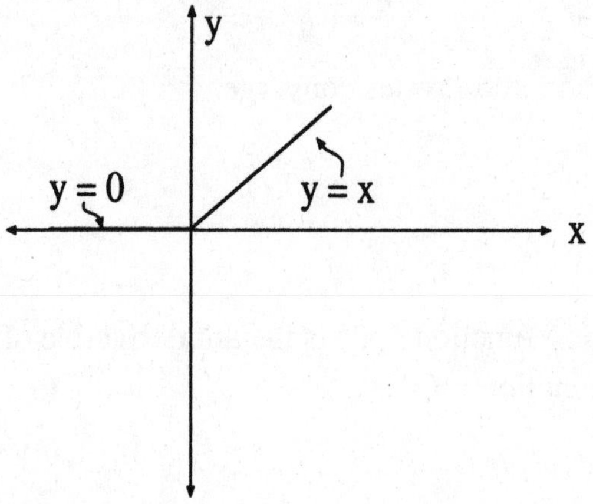

Clearly, the function is continuous at $x = 0$, (and all other x-values). Therefore, $\lim_{x \to 0} = f(x) = f(0) = 0$.

But f is not differentiable at $x = 0$ because $f'x = 0$ for $x \leq 0$ while $f'(x) = 1$ for $x \geq 0$,
i.e., $f'(0^-) = 0$ and $f'(0^+) = 1$.
(If $f'(0)$ exists then $f'(0^-)$ and $f'(0^+)$ must be equal.)
The graph shows that f has a "corner" where $x = 0$. If f were differentiable at $x = 0$, then its graph would be smooth there.

17. (B)

First simplify the function :

$f(x) = x^2 \ln x^3$

$= 3x^2 \ln x$

Then apply the Product Rule :

$$f'(x) = 6x \cdot \ln x + 3x^2 \cdot \frac{1}{x}$$

$= 6x \cdot \ln x + 3x$

$= 3x + 6x \ln x$

$= 3x \ (1 + 2 \ln x)$

$= 3x \ (1 + \ln x^2)$

18. (A)

All five answers involve $\sin(5x - 2)$, so check its derivative :

$$\frac{d}{dx} \sin(5x - 2) = \cos(5x - 2) \cdot \frac{d}{dx}(5x - 2)$$

$= \cos(5x - 2) \cdot 5$

Thus : $\frac{d}{dx} \frac{1}{5} \sin(5x - 2) = \cos(5x - 2)$

so : $\frac{1}{5} \sin(5x - 2) = \int \cos(5x - 2) dx$

19. (A)

First simplify the function :

$e^{x^2 + \ln x} = e^{x^2} \cdot e^{\ln x}$

$= e^{x^2} \cdot x$

$= x \cdot e^{x^2}$

Then : $\lim_{x \to 0^+} e^{x^2 + \ln x} = \lim_{x \to 0^+} x \, e^{x^2}$

$= 0 \cdot e^{0^2}$

$= 0 \cdot 1 = 0$

20. (D)

An inflection point is where the graph switches from concave up to concave down or vice-versa. This occurs at the three points marked :

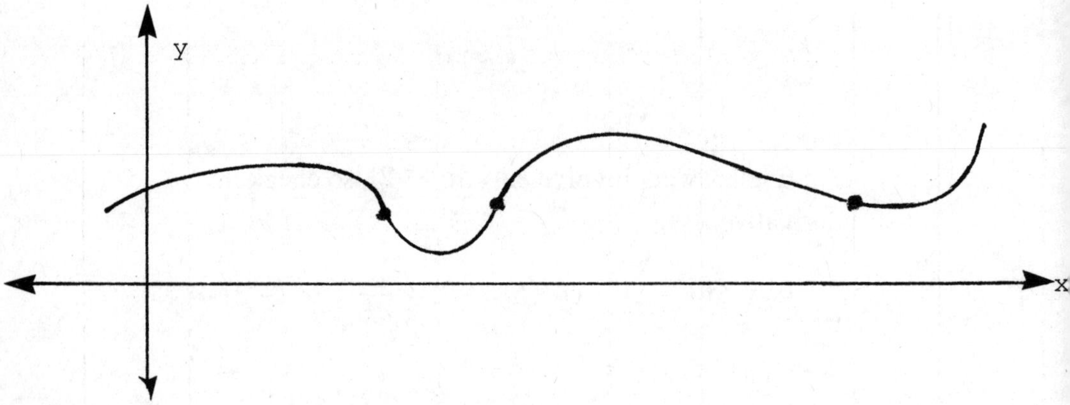

21. (C)

The given equation fits the Integration By Parts Formula :

$$\int u\, dv = uv - \int v\, du$$

where $u = f(x)$
and $v = -e^{-x}$

Here : $\int u dv = \int f(x) e^{-x} dx$

$$uv = -f(x) e^{-x}$$

$$\int v du = -\int 2x\, e^{-x} dx$$

so $du = 2x$
and $u = x^2$

22. (C)

Since the radii of the spheres are increasing at constant rates, they may easily be expressed as linear functions of time t. The radius of the smaller sphere is $6 + 8t$ and the radius of the larger sphere is $40 + 2t$.

The volume of a sphere is $\frac{4}{3}\pi r^3$ where r is its radius. Thus,

the volume of the smaller sphere is $\frac{4}{3}\pi(6 + 8t)^3$ and the

volume of the larger sphere is $\frac{4}{3}\pi(40 + 2t)^3$.

Thus : $V = \frac{4}{3}\pi(6 + 8t)^3 - \frac{4}{3}\pi(40 + 2t)^3$.

This function is maximal when its derivative is 0 :

$$0 = \frac{dV}{dt} = 4\pi(6 + 8t)^2 \cdot 8 - 4\pi(40 + 2t)^2 \cdot 2^2$$

$$8\pi(40 + 2t)^2 = 32\pi(6 + 8t)^2$$

$$(40 + 2t)^2 = 4(6 + 8t)^2$$

$$40 + 2t = 2(6 + 8t)$$

$$= 12 + 16t$$

$$28 = 14t$$

$$t = 2$$

23. (B)

The limit fits the form

$$\lim_{n \to 0} \frac{F(h) - F(0)}{h} = F'(0)$$

where

$$F(t) = \int_0^t \sqrt[3]{1+x^2}\,dx$$

so that

$$F(h) = \int_0^h \sqrt[3]{1+x^2}\,dx$$

and

$$F(0) = \int_0^0 \sqrt[3]{1+x^2}\,dx = 0$$

By the Fundamental Theorem of Calculus :

$$F'(t) = \frac{d}{dt}\int_0^t \sqrt[3]{1+x^2}\,dx$$

$$= \sqrt[3]{1+t^2}$$

Thus

$$F'(0) = \sqrt[3]{1+0^2} = 1.$$

24. (C)

The formula for the area of a region bounded by a polar graph is $A = \frac{1}{2}\int_{\alpha}^{\beta} r^2 d\,\theta.$

The given polar graph is a three-petal rose. Half of one petal is enclosed by $0 \le \theta \le \frac{\pi}{6}$:

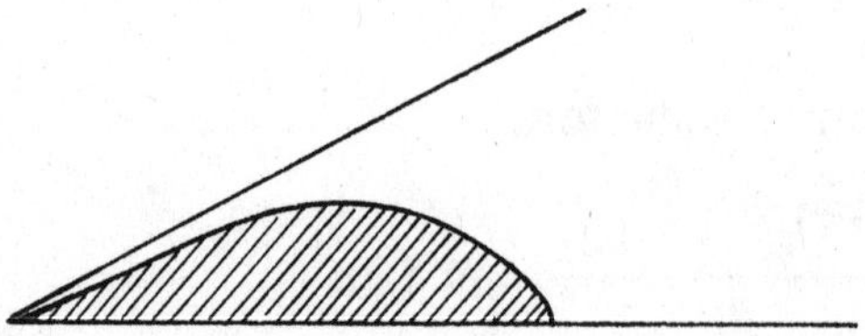

Hence the total area is 6 times the area of this piece :

$$A = 6\left(\frac{1}{2}\int_0^{\frac{\pi}{6}} (\cos 3\theta)^2\, d\theta\right)$$

$$= 3\int_0^{\frac{\pi}{6}} \cos^2 3\theta\, d\theta$$

$$= 3\int_0^{\frac{\pi}{6}} \left(\frac{1}{2} + \frac{1}{2}\cos 6\theta\right) d\theta$$

$$= 3\left[\frac{1}{2}\theta + \frac{1}{12}\sin 6\theta\right]\Bigg|_0^{\frac{\pi}{6}}$$

$$= 3\left[\left(\frac{1}{2}\cdot\frac{\pi}{6} + \frac{1}{12}\sin 6\cdot\frac{\pi}{6}\right) - \left(\frac{1}{2}\cdot 0 + \frac{1}{12}\sin 6\cdot 0\right)\right]$$

$$= 3\left[\left(\frac{\pi}{12} + 0\right) - (0+0)\right]$$

$$= \frac{\pi}{4} = 0.785$$

25. (D)

The particle is at rest when its velocity is zero. The velocity function is the derivative of the position function :

$$v(t) = \frac{d}{dt}x(t)$$

$$= \frac{d}{dt}(1+t^2)e^{-t}$$

$$= 2te^{-t} + (1+t^2)(-e^{-t})$$

$$= (2t - 1 - t^2)e^{-t}$$

$$= -(1-t)^2 e^{-t}$$

Set this equal to 0 and solve for t :

$$-(1-t)^2 e^{-t} = 0$$

$$(1-t)^2 = 0$$

$$1-t = 0$$

$$t = 1$$

26. (E)

Use logarithmic differentiation. First, take the natural logarithm of both sides and simplify :

$$y = x^{2^x}$$

$$\ln y = \ln x^{2^x} = 2^x \ln x$$

Then differentiate both sides :

$$\frac{d}{dx}(ln\, y) = \frac{d}{dx}\left(2^x\, ln\, x\right)$$

$$\frac{1}{y}\cdot\frac{dy}{dx} = \left(2^x\, ln\, 2\right)\cdot ln\, x \;+\; 2^x\cdot\left(\frac{1}{x}\right)$$

Finally, solve for

$$\frac{dy}{dx} = y\left[\left(2^x\, ln\,2\, ln\, x\right) + \frac{2^x}{x}\right]$$

$$= \left(x^{2^x}\right)\left[\left(2^x\, ln\,2\, ln\, x\right) + \frac{2^x}{x}\right]$$

$$= x^{2^x}\left(2^x\right)\left[ln\,2\, ln\, x + \frac{1}{x}\right]$$

$$= x^{2^x}\left(2^x\right)\left[\frac{x\, ln\,2\, ln\, x + 1}{x}\right]$$

$$= \left(x^{2^x - 1}\right) 2^x\left(x\, ln\,2\, ln\, x + 1\right)$$

$$\left.\frac{dy}{dx}\right|_2 = \left(2^{2^2-1}\right)\,(2^2)(2ln2ln2+1)$$

$$=(2^3)(2^2)(2ln2ln\,2+1)$$

$$=(2^5)(1.961) = 62.749$$

27. (A)

Draw graphs of $f(x)$ and $g(x)$.

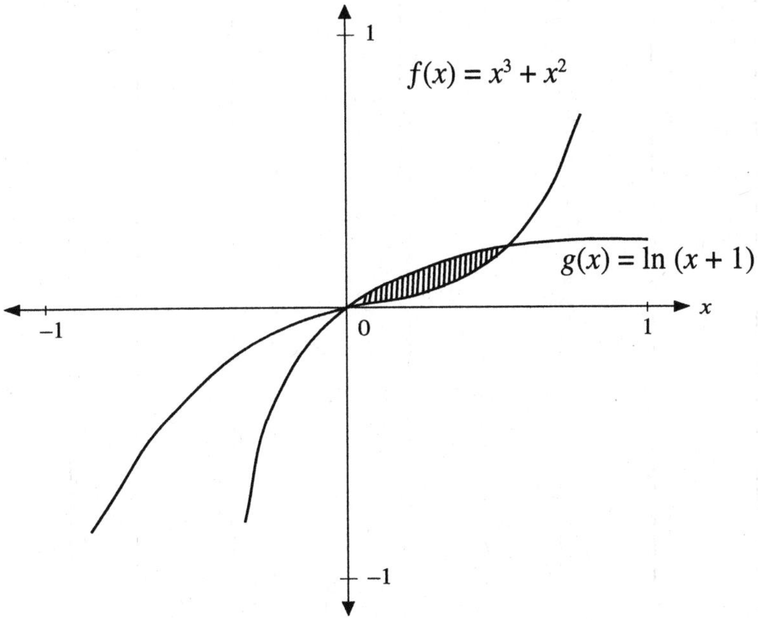

Reset the viewing window to [0,1] · [0,1] and trace to the intersection point of $f(x)$ and $g(x)$, which should turn out to be $x = 0.5238$, $y = 0.0418$.

The area enclosed is the integral $\int_0^{0.5238} \ln(x+1) - (x^3 + x^2)$, using your calculator, which can be easily computed. The answer is 0.0513 .

28. (D)

Let $F(x) = \int_a^x f(t)dt$. Then by the Fundamental Theorem of Calculus, $F'(x) = f(x)$. But $F(x) = 0$ for all x in $[a, b]$, so $F'(x) = 0$ for all x in $[a, b]$; i.e. $f(x) = 0$ for all x in $[a, b]$.

29. (B)

Draw the graph of $y = \sin 3x \cos x$.

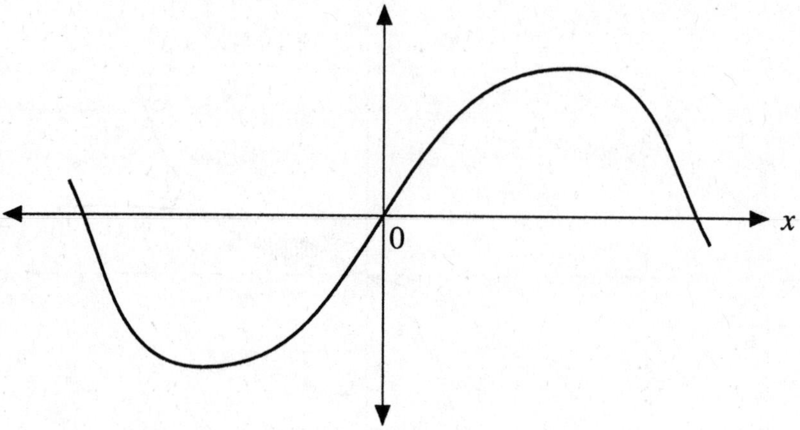

Tracing the first value of x when $y = 0$ gives the x-intercept 1.03 .

Then the area is the integral $\int_0^{1.03} \sin 3x \cos x$ or *fnInt* (sin 3x cos x, x, 0, 1.03) which equals 0.56 .

30. (C)

First find the derivatives of the two functions and evaluate them at $t = 2$:

$$x = t^3 - 3t \quad \Rightarrow \frac{dx}{dt} = 3t^2 - 3$$

$$\Rightarrow = \frac{dx}{dt}\Big|_{t=2} = 3(2)^2 - 3 = 9$$

$$y = \left(t^2 + 1\right)^2 \quad \Rightarrow \frac{dy}{dt} = 2\left(t^2 + 1\right) \cdot 2t$$

$$\Rightarrow \frac{dy}{dt}\Big|_{t=2} = 2\left((2)^2 + 1\right) \cdot 2(2) = 40$$

Then use the fact that

$$\frac{dy}{dx} = \frac{\left(\frac{dy}{dt}\right)}{\left(\frac{dx}{dt}\right)}:$$

$$\frac{dy}{dx}\bigg|_{t=2} = \frac{\frac{dy}{dt}\Big|_{t=2}}{\frac{dx}{dt}\Big|_{t=2}} = \frac{40}{9}$$

31. (E)

Using your calculator,

$fnInt\left(6\frac{x\wedge 3+1}{x+1},\ x,\ -1,\ 1\right)$, which gives 16.

32. (D)

The normal line is the line that is perpendicular to the curve at the given point. Its equation is $y = y_0 + m(x - x_0)$ where (x_0, y_0) is the given point and m is the slope. At the point where $x = 1$,

$$y = x^4 - 3x^2 + 1$$

$$= (1)^4 - 3(1)^2 + 1$$

$$= -1$$

Thus, $(x_0, y_0) = (1, -1)$.

The slope m of the normal line is the negative reciprocal of the slope of the tangent line, which is the value of the derivative at the given point ;

i.e. $m = \dfrac{-1}{\left.\dfrac{dy}{dx}\right|_{x=1}}$

Since $\dfrac{dy}{dx} = \dfrac{d}{dx}\left(x^4 - 3x^2 + 1\right)$

$= 4x^3 - 6x,$

$m = \dfrac{-1}{\left.\left(4x^3 - 6x\right)\right|_{x=1}}$

$= \dfrac{-1}{(4-6)}$

$= \dfrac{-1}{-2}$

$= \dfrac{1}{2}$

Thus, the equation of the normal line is :

$y = y_0 + m(x - x_0)$

$y = -1 + \dfrac{1}{2}(x-1)$

$2y = -2 + (x-1)$

$2y = x - 3$

$x - 2y - 3 = 0$

33. (A)
You can directly solve this problem by using the calculator. For example,

der 1 (256 *X*^ (–0.5) + 64 *X*^0.5 + 3*X*^$\left(\dfrac{2}{3}\right)$, *X*, 64)

should give 4.25 .

34. (B)

The formula for the area of a surface of revolution is :

$$S = 2\pi \int_a^b y\sqrt{1+\left(\frac{dy}{dx}\right)^2}\,dx$$

Here $y = x^3 - x$

so $\frac{dy}{dx} = 3x^2 - 1$

$$\left(\frac{dy}{dx}\right)^2 = \left(3x^2 - 1\right)^2$$

$$= 9x^4 - 6x^2 + 1$$

Then $y\sqrt{1+\left(\frac{dy}{dx}\right)^2} = \left(x^3 - x\right)\sqrt{1+\left(9x^4 - 6x^2 + 1\right)}$

$$= \left(x^3 - x\right)\sqrt{9x^4 - 6x^2 + 2}$$

so $S = 2\pi \int_0^2 \left(x^3 - x\right)\sqrt{9x^4 - 6x^2 + 2}\,dx$.

35. (B)

Draw the graph of $y = x^2\,(1 - x^{-1})$.

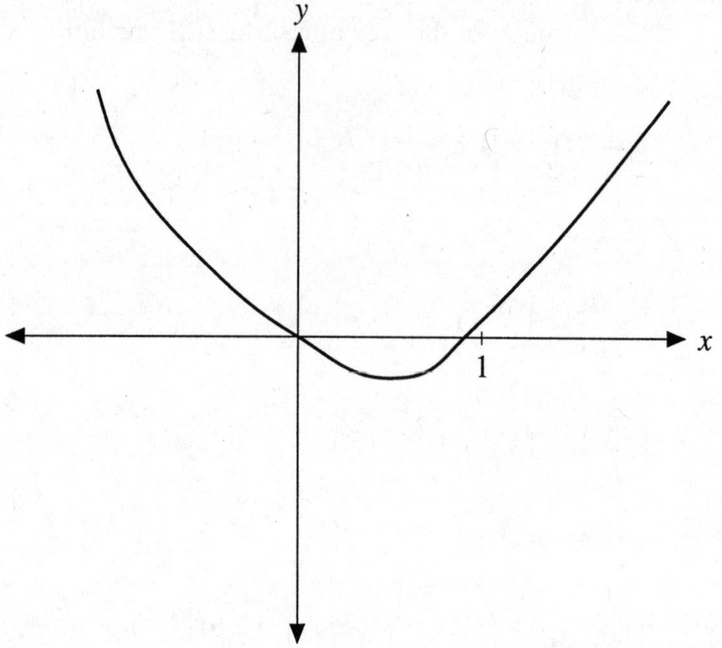

Set the viewing window to [0,1] · [–1,1]. By tracing y to the lowest value, you can get $y = -0.25$.

36. (A)

The correct substitution is dictated by the radical $\left(9+x^2\right)^{\frac{5}{2}}$. The form $9 + x^2$ requires the substitution

$x = 3\tan\theta$

$dx = 3\sec^2\theta\, d\theta$

Then $9 + x^2 = 9 + (3\tan\theta)^2$

$9 + 9\tan^2\theta = 9\sec^2\theta$

so $\left(9+x^2\right)^{\frac{5}{2}} = \left(9\sec^2\theta\right)^{\frac{5}{2}} = 243\sec^5\theta$

Thus $\int \frac{x^2}{\left(9+x^2\right)^{\frac{5}{2}}} dx = \int \frac{(3\tan\theta)^2}{243\sec^5\theta}\left(3\sec^2\theta\, d\theta\right)$

$= \int \frac{27\tan^2\theta\sec^2\theta}{243\sec^5\theta} d\theta$

$= \int \frac{\tan^2\theta}{9\sec^3\theta} d\theta$

$= \frac{1}{9}\int \sin^2\theta\cos\theta\, d\theta$

Finally, convert the limits :

$x = 0 \Rightarrow \theta = \arctan\frac{x}{3} = \arctan 0 = 0$

$x = \infty \Rightarrow \theta = \arctan\frac{x}{3} = \arctan\infty = \frac{\pi}{2}$

Hence, $\int_0^{\infty} \frac{x^2}{\left(9+x^2\right)^{\frac{5}{2}}} dx = \frac{1}{9}\int_0^{\frac{\pi}{2}} \sin^2\theta\cos\theta\, d\theta$

37. (D)

The simplest way to find the right answer is to differentiate each of the five answers :

(A) $\frac{dy}{dx} = -2xce^{-x^2} \neq 1+y^2 = 1+c^2e^{-2x^2}$

(B) $\frac{dy}{dx} = -2ce^{-x^2} \neq 1+y^2 = 1+c^2e^{-4x}$

(C) $\frac{dy}{dx} = \cos(x+c) \neq 1+y^2 = 1+\sin^2(x+c)$

(D) $\frac{dy}{dx} = \sec^2(x+c) = 1+y^2 = 1+\tan^2(x+c)$

(E) $\frac{dy}{dx} = 1 + x^2 \neq 1 + y^2 = 1 + \left(x + \frac{1}{3}x^3 + c \right)^2$

38. (B)

Since the given expression has the variable x in both its base and exponent, logarithms must be used :

$$y = \sqrt[x]{1 + x^2} = \left(1 + x^2\right)^{\frac{1}{x}}$$

$$\ln y = \ln\left(1 + x^2\right)^{\frac{1}{x}} = \frac{1}{x}\ln\left(1 + x^2\right)$$

$$\ln y = \frac{\ln\left(1 + x^2\right)}{x}$$

Now the expression on the left yields the indeterminant form

$\frac{\infty}{\infty}$ as $x \to \infty$, so L' Hôpital's Rule may be used :

$$\lim_{x \to \infty} \ln y = \lim_{x \to \infty} \frac{\ln\left(1 + x^2\right)}{x}$$

$$= \lim_{x \to \infty} \frac{\frac{d}{dx}\ln\left(1 + x^2\right)}{\frac{d}{dx}x}$$

$$= \lim_{x \to \infty} \frac{\left(\frac{2x}{1 + x^2}\right)}{1}$$

$$= \lim_{x \to \infty} \frac{2x}{1 + x^2}$$

$$= \lim_{x \to \infty} \frac{2}{\frac{1}{x} + x}$$

$$= \frac{2}{0+\infty} = \frac{2}{\infty} = 0$$

Thus $\lim\limits_{x\to\infty} \ln y = 0$

so $\ln\left(\lim\limits_{x\to\infty} y\right) = \lim\limits_{x\to\infty} (\ln y) = 0$

so $\lim\limits_{x\to\infty} y = e^{\ln\left(\lim\limits_{x\to\infty}\right)} = e^0 = 1.$

39. (D)

Let $g(x) = \int_0^x e^{-t^2}\,dt$. Then : $y = x\int_0^x e^{-t^2}\,dt = x \cdot g(x)$

$$\frac{dy}{dx} = g(x) + xg'(x)$$

$$\frac{d^2y}{dx^2} = g'(x) + g'(x) + x \cdot g''(x)$$

$$= 2g'(x) + x \cdot g''(x)$$

By the Fundamental Theorem of Calculus,

$$g'(x) = \frac{d}{dx}\int_0^x e^{-t^2}\,dt = e^{-x^2}$$

so $g''(x) = -2xe^{-x^2}$

Thus, $\frac{d^2y}{dx^2} = 2g'(x) + xg''(x)$

$$= 2\left(e^{-x^2}\right) + x\left(-2xe^{-x^2}\right)$$

$$= \left(2 - 2x^2\right)e^{-x^2}$$

The graph has inflection points only where $\frac{d^2y}{dx^2} = 0$

$$\frac{d^2y}{dx^2} = \left(2 - 2x^2\right)e^{-x^2} = 0$$

$$2 - 2x^2 = 0$$

$$x^2 = 1$$

$$x = \pm 1.$$

40. (C)

If $u = \ln x$ then $x = e^u$ and $dx = e^u du$.

Thus $\int \frac{1 - \ln x}{x^2} dx = \int \frac{1 - u}{\left(e^u\right)^2}\left(e^u du\right)$

$= \int (1 - u)e^{-u} du.$

Transforming the limits of integration :

$x = e \Rightarrow u = \ln x = \ln e = 1$

$x = 1 \Rightarrow u = \ln x = \ln 1 = 0$

Thus: $\int_1^e \frac{1 - \ln x}{x^2} dx = \int_0^1 (1 - u)e^{-u} du.$

ADVANCED PLACEMENT CALCULUS BC EXAM IV

SECTION II

DETAILED EXPLANATIONS OF ANSWERS

1. (a)

The velocity is the antiderivative of the acceleration :

$$V = \int a\, dt$$

$$= \int \left(12t^2 - 16\right)dt$$

$$= 4t^3 - 16t + v_0$$

Here v_0 is the initial velocity ; i.e. the velocity when $t = 0$. This is given to be $v_0 = 0$.

Thus : $v = 4t^3 - 16t + 0$

i.e., $v = 4t^3 - 16t$

(b) The position function is the antiderivative of the velocity :

$$s = \int v\, dt$$

$$= \int (4t^3 - 16t)\, dt$$

$$= t^4 - 8t^2 + s_0$$

Here s_0 is the initial velocity :
This is given to be $s_0 = 3$.

Thus : $s = t^4 - 8t^2 + 3$

(c)
First find when the velocity is zero :
$v = 4t^3 - 16t = 0$

Factor : $4t\left(t^2 - 4\right) = 0$

$4t(t - 2)(t + 2) = 0$

Solve for t : $t = 0, 2, -2$
For $t \geq 0$, these distinguish the two intervals [0, 2] and $[2, \infty)$
Now check the velocity at some interior point of each interval :

$t = 1 \Rightarrow v = 4t^3 - 16t = 4(1)^3 - 16(1) = -12$

$t = 3 \Rightarrow v = 4t^3 - 16t = 4(3)^3 - 16(3) = 60$

Now, the only time after $t = 0$ that the particle can change direction is at $t = 2$. So, since $v = -12 < 0$ at $t = 1$, v must be negative for all $t \in (0, 2)$.
Similarly, since $v = 60 > 0$ at $t = 3$, v must be positive for all $t \in (2, \infty)$.
Thus, the particle is moving to the left for $0 < t < 2$ and it is moving to the right for $t > 2$.

(d) During $0 \leq t \leq 2$ the particle moves from

$$s = t^4 - 8t^2 + 3 = (0)^4 - 8(0)^2 + 3 = 3$$

to $s = t^4 - 8t^2 + 3 = (2)^4 - 8(2)^2 + 3 = -13$
which is a distance of $3 - (-13) = 16$
During $2 \le t \le 3$ the particle moves from

$$s = t^4 - 8t^2 + 3 = (2)^4 - 8(2)^2 + 3 = -13$$

$$s = t^4 - 8t^2 + 3 = (3)^4 - 8(3)^2 + 3 = 12$$

which is a distance of $12 - (-13) = 25$.
Thus, the total distance travelled during $0 \le t \le 3$ is $16 + 25 = 41$ units.

2. (a)
When $t = 0$, $R = 20$, $r = 10$, and

$s_0 V = 2\pi^2 R r^2 = 2\pi^2\left(20(10)^2\right) = 4000\pi^2.$

Then, since V is increasing linearly at the rate of $4\pi^2$,

$$V = 4000\pi^2 + 4\pi^2 t$$

Now $V = 2\pi^2 R r^2$, and $R = 20$, so:

$$V = 2\pi^2(20)r^2 = 40\pi^2 r^2.$$

Thus: $40\pi^2 r^2 = 4000\pi^2 + 4\pi^2 t$

so: $r^2 = 100 + \frac{1}{10}t$

$$r = \sqrt{100 + \frac{1}{10}t}$$

(b) The rate of increase of r is:

$$\frac{dr}{dt} = \frac{d}{dt}\sqrt{100 + \frac{1}{10}t}$$

$$= \frac{1}{2\sqrt{100 + \frac{1}{10}t}} \cdot \frac{1}{10}$$

$$= \frac{1}{20\sqrt{100 + \frac{1}{10}t}}$$

When $r = 16$, $\sqrt{100 + \frac{1}{10}t} = 16$

so $\frac{dr}{dt} = \frac{1}{20(16)} = \frac{1}{320}$ in/min

(c)

$r = R \Leftrightarrow r = 20$

$\Leftrightarrow \sqrt{100 + \frac{1}{10}t} = 20$

$\Leftrightarrow 100 + \frac{1}{10}t = 400$

$\Leftrightarrow \frac{1}{10}t = 300$

$\Leftrightarrow t =$ 3,000 min. = 50 hrs.

3. (a)
Use a viewing window of [–5,5] · [–5,40] and draw the graphs of $f(x)$ and $g(x)$.

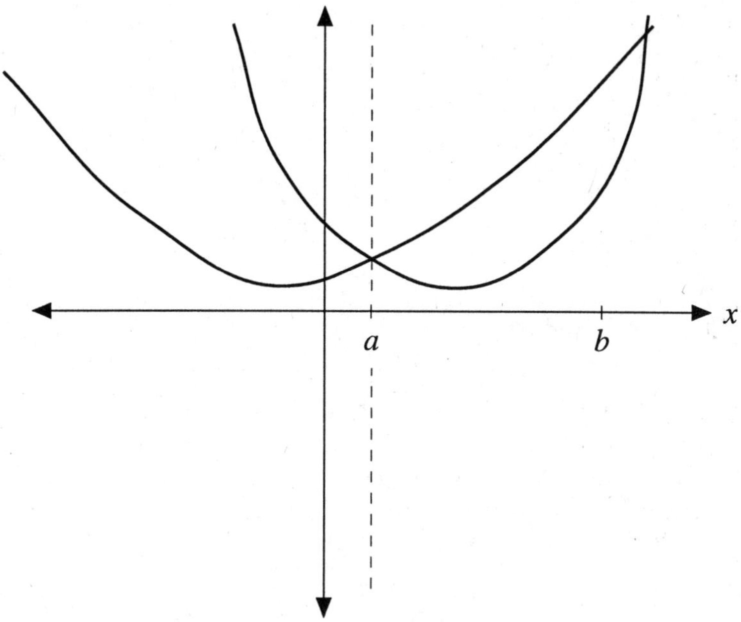

By tracing on the graphs to the intersectional points, you can find $a = 0.2$, $b = 4.81$.

(b) Draw the graphs of $f'(x)$ and $g'(x)$.

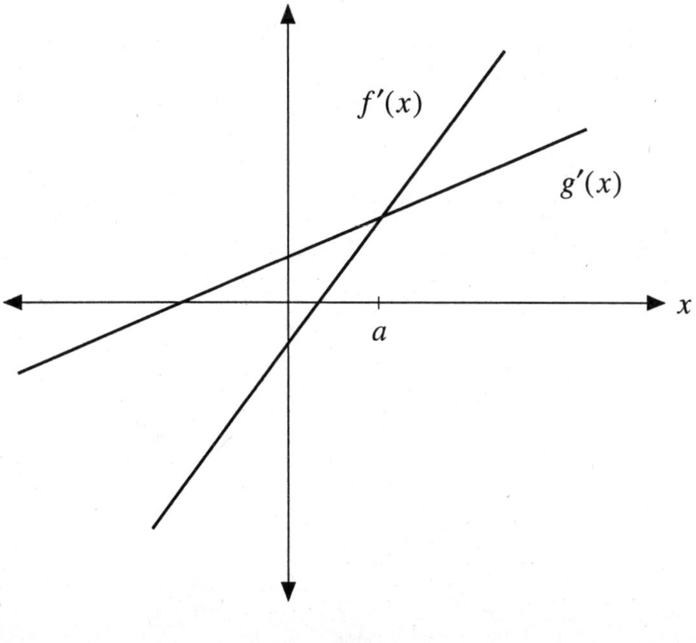

By tracing to where $f'(x) = g'(x)$, you can find $a = 2.57$.

(c) Finding $\int_{0.2}^{4.81} \left((x^2+2x+4)-(2x^2-2x+5)\right)dx$ by using the calculator.

fnInt $(-x\text{^}2 + 4x - 1, x, 0.2, 4.81)$ results in 4.49 .

4. The rate of change of T is its derivative with respect to time: $\frac{dT}{dt}$. If this is proportional to the difference $T - T_\infty$ then there is some constant k for which:

$$\frac{dT}{dt} = k(T - T_\infty)$$

(b) To solve the differential equation, separate the variables :

$$\frac{dT}{T - T_\infty} = k\,dt$$

$$\int \frac{dT}{T - T_{\infty}} = \int k \, dt$$

$$\ln(T - T_{\infty}) = kt + C$$

Evaluate the constant C by using the initial condition : $T = T_0$ when $t = 0$:

$$\ln(T - T_{\infty}) = k(0) + C = C$$

Replace C with this value and simplify :

$$\ln(T - T_{\infty}) = kt + \ln(T_0 - T_{\infty})$$

$$T - T_{\infty} = e^{kt + \ln(T_0 - T_{\infty})}$$

$$= e^{kt} \cdot e^{\ln(T_0 - T_{\infty})}$$

$$= (T_0 - T_{\infty}) e^{kt}$$

$$T = T_{\infty} + (T_0 - T_{\infty}) e^{kt}$$

(c) The given parameters are $T_0 = 100$ and $T_{\infty} = 10$, so :

$$T = 10 + (100 - 10)e^{kt}$$

$$T = 10 + 90e^{kt}$$

Now evaluate the constant k by substituting the given values $T = 60$ and $t = 50$:

$$60 = 10 + 90e^{k(50)}$$

$$90e^{50k} = 60 - 10 = 50$$

$$e^{50k} = \frac{50}{90} = \frac{5}{9}$$

$$50k = \ln\frac{5}{9}$$

$$k = \frac{1}{50}\ln\frac{5}{9}$$

Finally, evaluate t for $T = 40$:

$$T = 10 + 90e^{kt}$$

$$40 = 10 + 90e^{kt}$$

$$90e^{kt} = 40 - 10 = 30$$

$$e^{kt} = \frac{30}{90} = \frac{1}{3}$$

$$kt = \ln\frac{1}{3}$$

$$t = \frac{\ln\frac{1}{3}}{k}$$

$$= \frac{\ln\frac{1}{3}}{\left(\frac{1}{50}\ln\frac{5}{9}\right)}$$

$$= \frac{50\ln\frac{1}{3}}{\ln\frac{5}{9}}$$

$$= \frac{-50\ln 3}{\ln 5 - \ln 9}$$

$$= \frac{50\ln 3}{\ln 9 \ln 5}$$

$$\approx 93.4533$$

i.e., about 1 hour, 33 minutes, 27 seconds.

5. (a)

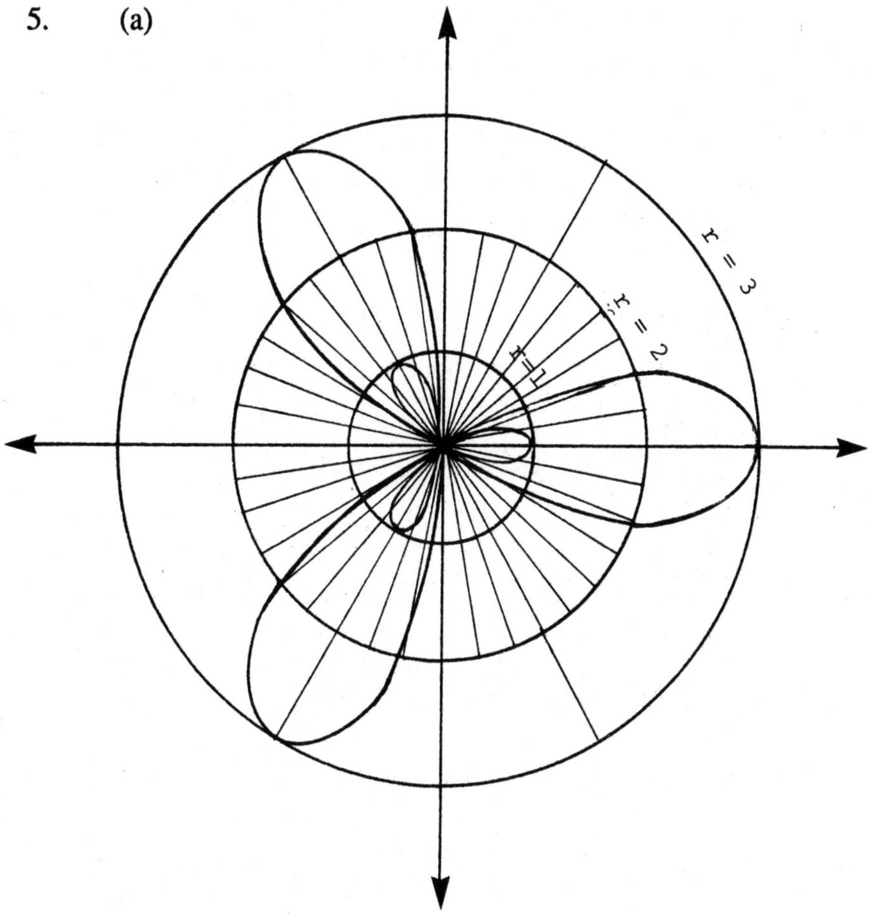

(b) The area formula for polar curves is

$$A = \frac{1}{2}\int_{\alpha}^{\beta} r^2 d\,\theta.$$

The area of one small loop is

$$A_s = \frac{1}{2}\int_{\frac{8\pi}{9}}^{\frac{10\pi}{9}} (1 + 2\cos 3\theta)^2 d\,\theta$$

$$= \frac{1}{2}\int_{\frac{8\pi}{9}}^{\frac{10\pi}{9}} (1 + 4\cos 3\theta + 4\cos^2 3\theta) d\,\theta$$

$$= \frac{1}{2}\int_{\frac{8\pi}{9}}^{\frac{10\pi}{9}} (1 + 4\cos 3\theta + 2 + 2\cos\ 6\,\theta)d\ \theta$$

$$= \int_{\frac{8\pi}{9}}^{\frac{10\pi}{9}} \left(\frac{3}{2} + 2\cos 3\theta + \cos\ 6\theta\right)d\ \theta$$

$$= \frac{3}{2}\theta + \frac{2}{3}\sin 3\theta + \frac{1}{6}\sin 6\theta\Big|_{\frac{8\pi}{9}}^{\frac{10\pi}{9}}$$

$$= \left(\frac{3}{2}\cdot\frac{10\pi}{9} + \frac{2}{3}\sin\frac{10\pi}{3} + \frac{1}{6}\sin\frac{20\pi}{3}\right)$$

$$-\left(\frac{3}{2}\cdot\frac{8\pi}{9} + \frac{2}{3}\sin\frac{8\pi}{3} + \frac{1}{6}\sin\frac{16\pi}{3}\right)$$

$$= \left(\frac{5\pi}{3} + \frac{2}{3}\left(-\frac{\sqrt{3}}{2}\right) + \frac{1}{6}\left(\frac{\sqrt{3}}{2}\right)\right)$$

$$-\left(\frac{4\pi}{3} + \frac{2}{3}\left(\frac{\sqrt{3}}{2}\right) + \frac{1}{6}\left(-\frac{\sqrt{3}}{2}\right)\right)$$

$$= \frac{5\pi}{3} - \frac{\sqrt{3}}{3} + \frac{\sqrt{3}}{12} - \frac{4\pi}{3} - \frac{\sqrt{3}}{3} + \frac{\sqrt{3}}{12}$$

$$= \frac{\pi}{3} - \frac{\sqrt{3}}{2} = \frac{2\pi - 3\sqrt{3}}{6}$$

The total area enclosed by one large loop is

$$A_L = \frac{1}{2}\int_{-\frac{2\pi}{9}}^{\frac{2\pi}{9}} (1 + 2\cos 3\theta)^2 d\ \theta.$$

$$= \frac{3}{2}\theta + \frac{2}{3}\sin 3\theta + \frac{1}{6}\sin 6\theta\Big|_{-\frac{2\pi}{9}}^{\frac{2\pi}{9}}$$

$$=\left(\frac{3}{2}\cdot\frac{2\pi}{9}+\frac{2}{3}\sin\frac{2\pi}{3}+\frac{1}{6}\sin\frac{4\pi}{3}\right)$$

$$-\left(\frac{3}{2}\cdot\left(\frac{2\pi}{9}\right)+\frac{2}{3}\sin\left(-\frac{2\pi}{3}\right)+\frac{1}{6}\sin\left(-\frac{4\pi}{3}\right)\right)$$

$$=\left(\frac{\pi}{3}+\frac{2}{3}\left(\frac{\sqrt{3}}{2}\right)+\frac{1}{6}\left(-\frac{\sqrt{3}}{2}\right)\right)$$

$$-\left(-\frac{\pi}{3}+\frac{2}{3}\left(-\frac{\sqrt{3}}{2}\right)+\frac{1}{6}\left(\frac{\sqrt{3}}{2}\right)\right)$$

$$=\frac{\pi}{3}+\frac{\sqrt{3}}{3}-\frac{\sqrt{3}}{12}+\frac{\pi}{3}+\frac{\sqrt{3}}{3}-\frac{\sqrt{3}}{12}$$

$$=\frac{2\pi}{3}+\frac{\sqrt{3}}{2}=\frac{4\pi+3\sqrt{3}}{6}$$

Each large loop contains a small loop, so the area between a large loop and small loop is :

$$A_B=A_L-A_s$$

$$=\frac{4\pi+3\sqrt{3}}{6}-\frac{2\pi-3\sqrt{3}}{6}$$

$$=\frac{2\pi+6\sqrt{3}}{6}$$

The 3 large loops occupy a total area of :

$$3A_L\ 3\left(\frac{4\pi+3\sqrt{3}}{6}\right)=\frac{4\pi+3\sqrt{3}}{2}.$$

Thus the part of the disk exterior to these loops has a total area of $A_L=\pi r^2-3A_L$

$$=\pi(3)^2-\frac{4\pi+3\sqrt{3}}{2}$$

$$=\frac{14\pi-3\sqrt{3}}{2}$$

This area is divided into 3 congruent pieces, so each of

these has an area of $A_p = \frac{1}{3}A_E$

$\frac{1}{3}\left(\frac{14\pi - 3\sqrt{3}}{2}\right)$

$= \frac{14\pi - 3\sqrt{3}}{6}$

Thus there are 9 pieces,

3 with area $A_s = \frac{2\pi - 3\sqrt{3}}{6}$ each,

3 with area $A_B = \frac{2\pi + 6\sqrt{3}}{6}$ each,

and 3 with area $A_V = \frac{14\pi - 3\sqrt{3}}{6}$ each.

6. (a) Since $g(x) = f\left(\frac{1}{x}\right)$ for all $x > 0$,

$g(1) = f\left(\frac{1}{1}\right) = f(1) = 2.$

(b) $\lim_{x \to 0^+} g(x) = \lim_{x \to 0^+} f\left(\frac{1}{x}\right)$

$= \lim_{\frac{1}{x} \to +\infty} f\left(\frac{1}{x}\right)$, since $\frac{1}{0^+} = +\infty$

$= \lim_{y \to +\infty} f(y)$, substituting $y = \frac{1}{x}$

$= 1$ by (iii)

(c) $g'(x) = \frac{d}{dx} g(x)$

$= \frac{d}{dx} f\left(\frac{1}{x}\right)$

$= f'\left(\frac{1}{x}\right) \cdot \frac{d}{dx}\left(\frac{1}{x}\right)$

$= f'\left(\frac{1}{x}\right) \cdot \left(\frac{-1}{x^2}\right)$

$= -\frac{f'\left(\frac{1}{x}\right)}{x^2}$

so : $g'(1) = -\frac{f'\left(\frac{1}{1}\right)}{1^2}$

$= -f'(1)$

$= -(-1)$, by (iv)

$= 1$

(d) The information given indicates that the graph of f must look like :

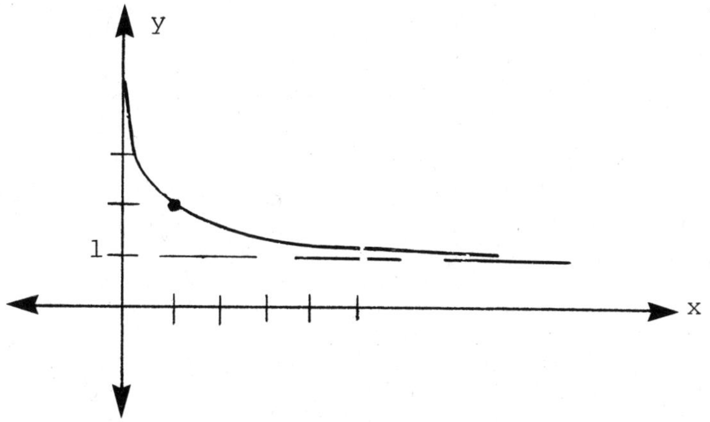

A specific "realization" of the given conditions would be the function $f(x) = 1 + \frac{1}{x}$

(i.e. this example satisfies conditions (i)-(vi)). For this example, the function g would be

$$g(x) = f\left(\frac{1}{x}\right)$$

$$= 1 + \frac{1}{\left(\frac{1}{x}\right)}$$

$$= 1 + x:$$

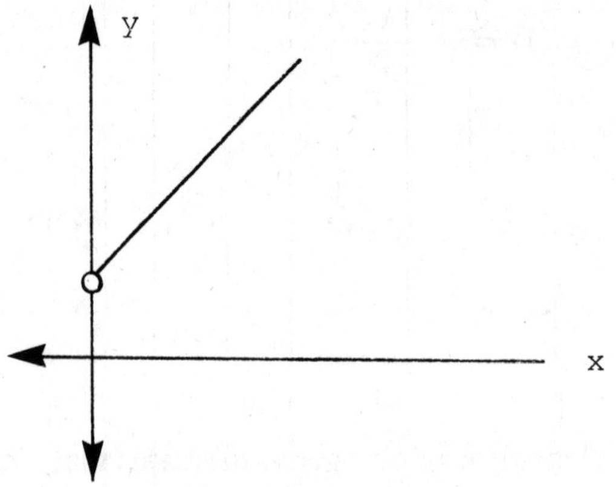

THE ADVANCED PLACEMENT EXAMINATION IN

CALCULUS BC

TEST V

ADVANCED PLACEMENT CALCULUS BC EXAM V

SECTION I

PART A

Time: 45 minutes
25 questions

DIRECTIONS: Each of the following problems is followed by five choices. Solve each problem, select the best choice, and blacken the correct space on your answer sheet.

NOTE:

Unless otherwise specified, the domain of function f is assumed to be the set of all real numbers x for which $f(x)$ is a real number.

1. Data suggests that between the hours of 1:00 P.M. and 3:00 P.M. on Sunday, the speed of traffic along a street is approximately $S(t) = 3t^2 + 10t$ miles per hour, where t is the number of hours past noon. Compute the average speed of the traffic between the hours of 1:00 P.M. and 3:00 P.M.

(A) 70

(B) 66

(C) 33

(D) 44

(E) 22

2. The solution of the equation $(x+1)\frac{dy}{dx} = x\left(y^2+1\right)$ is

(A) $\ln|y+1| = \tan^{-1}x + C$

(B) $\ln|y+1| = x - \tan^{-1}x + C$

(C) $\tan^{-1}y = \ln|x+1| + C$

(D) $\tan^{-1}y = x - \ln|x+1| + C$

(E) None of the above

3. Find $\lim\limits_{x \to \infty} \frac{4x \ln x}{e^{2x}}$.

(A) 0

(B) 1

(C) ∞

(D) 4

(E) -1

4. If f and g are integrable from a to b then

$$\int_a^b [cf(x) + g(x)]dx =$$

(A) $\int_a^b c[f(x) + g(x)]dx$

(B) $c\int_a^b f(x)dx + \int_b^a g(x)dx$

(C) $c\int_a^b f(x)g(x)dx$

(D) $c\int_a^b f(x)dx - \int_b^a g(x)dx$

(E) $c\int_{-\infty}^0 f(x)dx + \int_0^\infty g(x)dx$

5. If $x = t^3 + t^2 + t$ and $y = \ln(6t^3 + 4)$, then $\frac{dy}{dx}$ at $t = 1$ is

(A) $\frac{1}{10}$

(B) $\frac{10}{3}$

(C) $\frac{3}{10}$

(D) $\frac{5}{3}$

(E) $\frac{3}{5}$

6. What are all the values of x for which the series

$$1 + \frac{x^2}{2!} + \frac{x^4}{4!} \cdots + \frac{x^{2n}}{(2n)!} + \cdots \text{converges?}$$

(A) $-1 \leq x \leq 1$

(B) $0 \leq x \leq 1$

(C) $0 < x < 2$

(D) $-1 < x < 1$

(E) All values of x

7. Find $\frac{dy}{dx}$ for $x = 1$, when $y = \frac{u}{u+1}$ and $u = 3x^2 - 1$.

(A) 9

(B) $\frac{1}{9}$

(C) $\frac{2}{3}$

(D) 2

(E) 6

8. Find the area of the region between the graph of $y = 3x^2 + 2x + 5$ and the x-axis from $x = 0$ to $x = 2$.

(A) 22

(B) 21

(C) 17

(D) 5

(E) 0

9. $\int \frac{\sqrt{x^2 - 9}}{x}\,dx =$

(A) $3\sin^{-1}\left(\frac{3}{x}\right) + C$

(B) $3\sqrt{x^2 - 9} + C$

(C) $\sqrt{x^2 - 9} - 3\cos^{-1}\left(\frac{3}{x}\right) + C$

(D) $3\ln\left|x + \sqrt{x^2 - 9}\right|$

(E) $\sqrt{x^2 - 9} + \cos^{-1}\left(\frac{3}{x}\right) + C$

10. Find $\int 5(x^3 + 2x + 7)^4(3x^2 + 2)dx$.

(A) $(x^3 + 2x + 7)^5 + C$

(B) $(x^3 + 2x + 7)^{\frac{5}{4}} + C$

(C) $(3x^2 + 2)^2 + C$

(D) $(-x^4 - 2x^3 - 7x)^4 + C$

(E) $(x^3 + 2x + 7)^5(3x^2 + 2)^2 + C$

11. What is the length of the arc of $y = \frac{x^{\frac{3}{2}}}{3}$ from $x = 0$ to $x = 5$?

(A) $\frac{7}{3}$

(B) $\frac{19}{3}$

(C) $\frac{15}{3}$

(D) 5

(E) $\frac{8}{3}$

12. Find the derivative of $\cos^2\left(\frac{\pi}{2} - \theta\right)$.

(A) $\sin(\pi - 2\theta)$

(B) $-2\cos\left(\frac{\pi}{2} - \theta\right)\sin\left(\frac{\pi}{2} - \theta\right)$

(C) $-\sin(\pi - 2\theta)$

(D) $\cos(\pi - 2\theta)$

(E) $2\cos\left(\frac{\pi}{2} - \theta\right)$

13. The coefficient of x^4 in the Taylor series for e^{2x} about $x = 0$ is

(A) $\frac{1}{24}$

(B) $\frac{1}{2}$

(C) $\frac{3}{4}$

(D) $\frac{2}{3}$

(E) 2

14. Find $\lim_{x \to \infty} \left(1 + \frac{1}{x}\right)^x$.

(A) 1

(B) 0

(C) ∞

(D) 2

(E) e

15. At each point (x, y) on a curve, the slope of the curve is $4x^3y$. If the curve contains the point (0, 5), then its equation is

(A) $y = x^4 + 5$

(B) $y = 5e^{x^4}$

(C) $y = e^{x^4} + 5$

(D) $y = \ln(x + 1) + 5$

(E) $y^2 = x^3 + 5$

16. When $f(x) = \frac{\pi/2}{(\tan x)^{1/2}}$, find $f'\left(\frac{\pi}{4}\right)$.

(A) $-\frac{\pi}{4}$

(B) $-\frac{\pi}{2}$

(C) $\frac{\pi}{4}$

(D) $\frac{\pi}{2}$

(E) 1

17. The region in the first quadrant between the x-axis from $x = 0$ to $x = 3$, and the graph $y = x$, is rotated about the x-axis. The volume of the resulting solid of revolution is given by

(A) $\int_0^3 \pi x^2 dx$

(B) $\int_0^3 2\pi x^2 dx$

(C) $\int_0^3 \pi x \, dx$

(D) $\int_0^6 2\pi y^3 dy$

(E) $\int_0^6 \pi\left(2 + \sqrt{6 + y}\right)^2 dy$

18. If $f(x) = \dfrac{\sqrt[3]{x} + 1}{x - 1}$ then $f'(2)$ is:

(A) 2.000

(B) 0.000

(C) 1.282

(D) 0.828

(E) – 1.282

19. If u is a positive integer, then

$$\lim_{u \to \infty} \frac{1}{u}\left[\left(\frac{2}{u}\right)^2 + \left(\frac{4}{u}\right)^2 + \ldots + \left(\frac{8u}{u}\right)^2\right]$$

can be expressed as

(A) $8\int_0^1 \frac{1}{x^2}dx$

(B) $\int_0^1 \frac{dx}{x^2}$

(C) $\int_0^8 \frac{dx}{x^2}$

(D) $\int_0^8 x^2 dx$

(E) $\frac{1}{2}\int_0^8 x^2 dx$

20. Find the equation of the line normal to $y = 4x^2 + 2x + 9$ at the point where $x = 1$.

(A) $10x + y = -151$

(B) $x + 10y = 151$

(C) $x - y = 9$

(D) $10x - y = -5$

(E) $x - 10y = 151$

21. $\int_{-2}^{2} \frac{-6}{x^4} dx$ is

(A) 0

(B) $\frac{1}{2}$

(C) -2

(D) 2

(E) nonexistent

22. Find $\int x \sin x \, dx$.

(A) $-x \sin x + \cos x + C$

(B) $-x \cos x + \sin x + C$

(C) $-x \cos x + \cos x + C$

(D) $x \cos x - \sin x + C$

(E) $x \cos x + \cos x + C$

23. If the substitution $u = \frac{x}{4}$ is made, the integral

$$\int_0^4 \frac{1}{x\sqrt{4-\left(\frac{x}{4}\right)^2}}\,dx =$$

(A) $\int_0^4 \frac{1}{u\sqrt{4-u^2}}\,du$

(B) $\int_0^1 \frac{1}{u\sqrt{4-u^2}}\,du$

(C) $\int_0^1 \frac{1}{4u\sqrt{4-u^2}}\,du$

(D) $\int_0^4 \frac{1}{4u\sqrt{4-u^2}}\,du$

(E) $\int_0^4 \frac{1}{u\sqrt{4-u^2}}\,du$

24. A particle moves in the xy-plane so that, at any time t its coordinates are $x = \frac{t^3 - 2t^2}{4}$ and $y = t^2 - t$. At $t = 2$, its acceleration vector is

(A) (0, 0)

(B) (1, 2)

(C) (2, 0)

(D) (2, 2)

(E) (–2,–2)

25. Which of the following functions shows that the statement "If a function is continuous at $x = 0$, then it is differentiable at $x = 0$" is FALSE ?

(A) $f(x) = x^2$

(B) $f(x) = x^{\frac{5}{2}}$

(C) $f(x) = x^{-\frac{4}{5}}$

(D) $f(x) = x^{-\frac{5}{4}}$

(E) $f(x) = x^{\frac{1}{2}}$

SECTION I

PART B

Time: 45 minutes
15 questions

DIRECTIONS: Calculators may be used for this section of the test. Each of the following problems is followed by five choices. Solve each problem, select the best choice, and blacken the correct space on your answer sheet.

NOTES:

1. Unless otherwise specified, answers can be given in unsimplified form.
2. The domain of function *f* is assumed to be the set of all real numbers *x* for which *f*(*x*) is a real number.

26. The equation of the line tangent to the curve $x(t) = t^2$, $y(t) = t^3 - 1$ at the point (4, 7) is

(A) $x - 3y = -5$

(B) $3x - y = 5$

(C) $4x - 7y = 0$

(D) $4x + 7y = 12$

(E) $x^2 + y^3 = 1$

27. If $y = \dfrac{2(x-1)^2}{x^2}$, then which of the following must be true?

I. The range is $\{y \mid y \geq 0\}$.

II. The y-intercept is 1.

III. The horizontal asymptote is $y = 2$.

(A) I only

(B) II only

(C) III only

(D) I and II only

(E) I and III only

28. If f and g are twice differentiable functions such that $g(x) = e^x f(x)$ and $g''(x) = e^x h(x) + e^x f(x)$, then $h(x) =$

(A) $f'(x) + f''(x)$

(B) $f'(x) + (f''(x))^2$

(C) $(f'(x) + f''(x))^2$

(D) $2f'(x) + f''(x)$

(E) $f'(x) + 2f''(x)$

29. The slope of the tangent line to the graph $y = \frac{x^2}{\sqrt[3]{3x^2+1}}$ at $x = 1$ is

(A) 0.945

(B) 2.381

(C) 1.890

(D) 1.191

(E) 1.575

30. If $\int f(x)\cos x\,dx = f(x)\sin x + \int 2x^3 \sin x\,dx$, then $f(x)$ could be

(A) $6x^2$

(B) $\frac{-x^4}{2}$

(C) $\frac{x^4}{2}$

(D) $2x^3$

(E) $-6x^2$

31. If $f(x) = \frac{1}{\sin(x+\sqrt{x})}$, calculate $\int_0^1 f(x)$.

(A) 2.57

(B) 10.26

(C) –3.1

(D) 98.1

(E) 1.65

32. $\lim_{x \to \frac{\pi}{2}} (\sec x - \tan x) =$

(A) 1

(B) 0

(C) ln 3

(D) $\frac{\pi}{2}$

(E) nonexistent

33. Let $f(x) = (x^2 - 3)^2$. The local maximum of $f'(x)$ is

(A) 7.99

(B) 5.80

(C) 3.25

(D) –7.99

(E) 6.28

34.

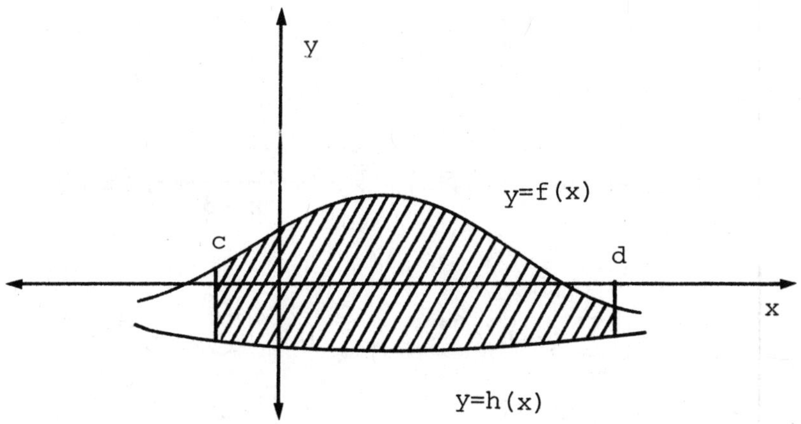

The area enclosed by the curves $y = f(x)$ and $y = h(x)$ and the lines $x = c$ and $x = d$ is given by

(A) $\int_c^d [f(x)-h(x)]dx$

(B) $\int_c^d [f(x)+h(x)]dx$

(C) $\int_c^d [h(x)-f(x)]dx$

(D) $\int_d^c [f(x)+h(x)]dx$

(E) $\int_c^0 [f(x)-h(x)]dx+\int_0^d [f(x)+h(x)]dx$

35. $f(x)=\frac{x^2}{e^x}$ $\int_0^5 \frac{x^2}{e^x}$ is

(A) 2.25

(B) 1.3

(C) 7.1

(D) 1.75

(E) 12.5

36. For $-1<x<1$, if $f(x)=\sum_{n=1}^{\infty}\frac{(-1)^{n+1}x^{5n-3}}{5n-3}$, then $f'(x)=$

(A) $\sum_{n=1}^{\infty}(-1)^{5n}x^{5n}$

(B) $\sum_{n=1}^{\infty}(-1)^{n}x^{5n}$

(C) $\sum_{n=1}^{\infty}(-1)^{n+1}x^{5n}$

(D) $\sum_{n=1}^{\infty}(-1)^{n+1}x^{5n-4}$

(E) $\sum_{n=1}^{\infty}(-1)^{n}x^{5n-4}$

37. $\frac{d}{dx}e^{\sin 2x}$ evaluated at $x = 4°$

(A) 0.000

(B) -3.458

(C) 2.276

(D) -2.276

(E) 5.389

38. $\int \frac{1}{(x+3)(x+4)}dx =$

(A) $\ln\frac{|x+3|}{|x+4|}+C$

(B) $\ln\frac{|x+4|}{|x+3|}+C$

(C) $\ln\frac{|x-4|}{|x-3|}+C$

(D) $(\ln|x+3|)(\ln|x+4|)+C$

(E) $\ln|(x+3)(x+4)|+C$

39. If $f(x) = x^4 - x$, find the value of x that satisfies the Mean Value Theorem on the closed interval [0, 2].

(A) $\sqrt[3]{2}$

(B) $\sqrt[4]{2}$

(C) $\sqrt{2}$

(D) 2

(E) $\frac{1}{2}$

40. If $\frac{dy}{dt} = \frac{1}{2t-1}$ and $y = 1$ when $t = 1$, what is the value of y when $t = 5$?

(A) 1.099

(B) 1.732

(C) 1.386

(D) 0

(E) 2.099

ADVANCED PLACEMENT CALCULUS BC EXAM V

SECTION II

Time: 1 hour and 30 minutes
6 questions†

DIRECTIONS: Show all your work. Grading is based on the methods used to solve the problems as well as the accuracy of your final answers. Please make sure all procedures are clearly shown.

NOTES:

1. ln x denotes the natural logarithm of x (that is, logarithm to the base e).

2. Unless otherwise specified, the domain of function f is assumed to be the set of all real numbers x for which $f(x)$ is a real number.

†The practice tests in this book incorporate Section II free-response solutions that approximate the content breakdown you will encounter on the AP exam. The overall timing and formatting of the practice tests mirror the actual test; examinees should note, however, that this section is split into two parts on the AP exam. Furthermore, prospective examinees should pay attention to restrictions on calculator use. For details, consult current official College Board materials in print or on the Web.

1. Consider the parabola $y^2 = 8x$, and the line $x = 2$.

(a) Find the volume generated by revolving the area bounded by the given parabola and line about the line $x = 2$.

(b) Find the volume generated by revolving the area bounded by the given parabola and line about the y-axis.

(c) Find the volume generated by revolving the area bounded by the parabola, the line, and the x-axis, about the x-axis.

2. A function whose graph is an unbroken curve is said to be continuous. A function that is differentiable must be continuous, although not every continuous function is differentiable.

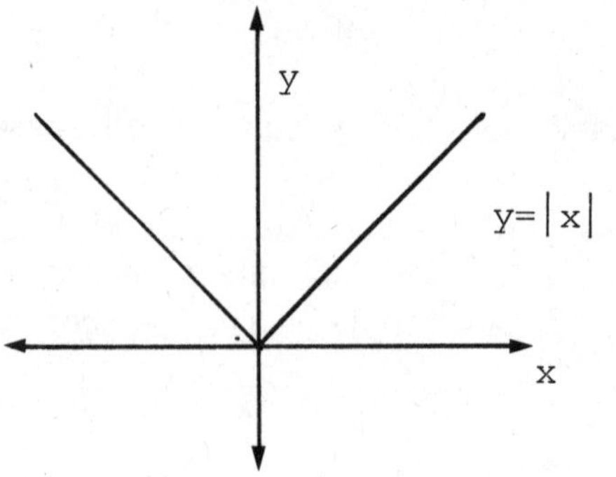

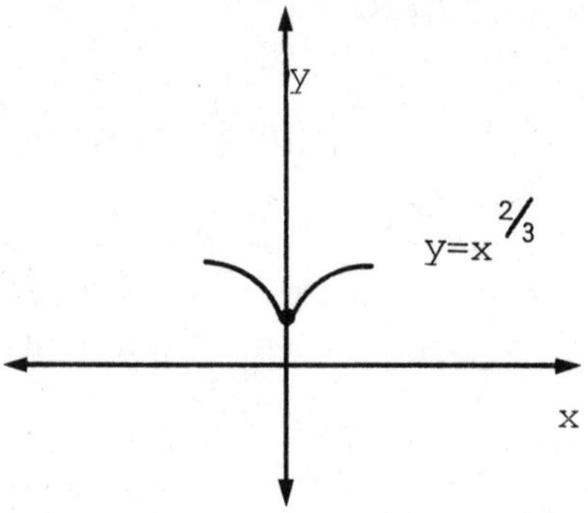

(a) Is the function with graph shown in figure (1) differentiable? Why or why not?

(b) Is the function with graph in figure (2) differentiable? Why or why not?

3. Let $f(x) = \frac{2}{3}x^{\frac{3}{2}}$ and suppose that the line $y = cx + d$ is tangent to $f(x)$ at x_0.

(a) If $x_0 = 2$, find c and d.

(b) If $c = 1$, find x_0 and d.

(c) Find $\int_0^3 \frac{2}{3}x^{\frac{3}{2}}$.

4. The motion of a particle is given by $x = t^2$ and $y = t^3$, where x and y are distance in feet, and t is time in seconds.

(a) Find the speed of the particle when $t = 2$.

(b) Find the direction of the particle when $t = 2$.

5. Consider the ellipse: $x = 9 \cos \theta$
$y = 3 \sin \theta$

(a) Find $f'(x)$.

(b) Find the equation of the line tangent to the ellipse at the point where $\theta = 45°$.

(c) Find the equation of the line normal to the ellipse at $\theta = 45°$.

6. (a) Find the Maclaurin series expansion of e^x.

(b) Find the Taylor series expansion of e^x about $x = a$.

ADVANCED PLACEMENT CALCULUS BC EXAM V

ANSWER KEY

SECTION I

1.	C	21.	E
2.	D	22.	B
3.	A	23.	B
4.	D	24.	D
5.	C	25.	E
6.	E	26.	B
7.	C	27.	E
8.	A	28.	D
9.	C	29.	A
10.	A	30.	B
11.	B	31.	E
12.	A	32.	B
13.	D	33.	A
14.	E	34.	A
15.	B	35.	D
16.	B	36.	D
17.	A	37.	C
18.	E	38.	A
19.	E	39.	A
20.	B	40.	E

SECTION II

See Detailed Explanations of Answers.

ADVANCED PLACEMENT CALCULUS BC EXAM V

SECTION I

DETAILED EXPLANATIONS OF ANSWERS

1. (C)

Average Speed $= \frac{1}{3-1}\int_1^3 (3t^2 + 10t)\,dt = \frac{1}{2}(t^3 + 5t^2)\Big|_1^3$

$= \frac{1}{2}(27 + 45 - 1 - 5) = \frac{1}{2}(66) = 33\ mph$

2. (D)

Change the equation to differential form, then separate the variables and integrate.

$$(x+1)dy = x(y^2+1)dx$$

$$\int \frac{dy}{y^2+1} = \int \frac{xdx}{x+1}$$

Let $u = x + 1, du = dx$

Then $\int \frac{xdx}{x+1} = \int \frac{u-1}{u}du = \int \left(1 - \frac{1}{u}\right)du$

$$= u - \ln|u| + C' =$$

$$= (x+1) - \ln|x+1| + C'$$

$$= x - \ln|x+1| + C$$

$$\Rightarrow \tan^{-1} y = x - \ln|x+1| + C$$

3. (A)

Use L' Hôpital's Rule :

$$\lim_{x\to\infty} \frac{4x \ln x}{e^{2x}} = \lim_{x\to\infty} \frac{4(1+\ln x)}{2e^{2x}} = \lim_{x\to\infty} \frac{2(1+\ln x)}{e^{2x}}$$

This is also of the form ∞/∞.

$$\lim_{x\to\infty} \frac{2(1+\ln x)}{e^{2x}} = \lim_{x\to\infty} \frac{1/x}{e^{2x}} = 0$$

4. (D)

Properties of the definite integral include :

$$\int_a^b cf(x)dx = c\int_a^b f(x)dx, \int_a^b g(x)dx = -\int_b^a g(x)dx$$

and $\int_a^b [f(x) + g(x)]dx = \int_a^b f(x)dx + \int_a^b g(x)dx$

Therefore,

$$\int_a^b [cf(x) + g(x)]dx = c\int_a^b f(x)dx - \int_b^a g(x)dx$$

5. (C)

$g(t) = \ln(6t^3 + 4)$ $\qquad$ $(f) = t^3 + t^2 + t$

$g'(t) = \dfrac{18t}{6t^3 + 4}$ $\qquad$ $f'(t) = 3t^2 + 2t + 1$

$$\frac{dy}{dx} = \frac{18t}{(6t^3 + 4)} \cdot \frac{1}{(3t^2 + 2t + 1)}$$

Substitute $t = 1$: $\left.\dfrac{dy}{dx}\right|_{t=1} = \dfrac{18}{10} \cdot \dfrac{1}{6} = \dfrac{3}{10}$

6. (E)

$$\frac{u_{n+1}}{u_n} = \frac{x^{2n+2}}{(2n+2)!} \cdot \frac{(2n)!}{x^{2n}} = \frac{(2n)!x^2}{(2n+2)!}$$

$$= \frac{x^2}{(2n+1)(2n+2)}$$

$$\lim_{n \to \infty} \frac{1}{(2n+1)(2n+2)} = 0$$

Hence the series converges for all values of x.

7. (C)

$$\frac{dy}{du} = \frac{(u+1)-u}{(u+1)^2} = \frac{1}{(u+1)^2} \qquad \frac{du}{dx} = 6x .$$

when $x = 1$, $u = 3(1)^2 - 1 = 2$

Then $\frac{dy}{du} = \frac{1}{(2+1)^2} = \frac{1}{9}$ and $\frac{du}{dx} = 6(1) = 6$

$$\frac{dy}{dx} = \frac{dy}{du}\frac{du}{dx} = \left(\frac{1}{9}\right)(6) = \frac{2}{3}.$$

One could also substitute directly for u in y yielding

$$y = \frac{3x^2 - 1}{(3x^2-1)+1} = \frac{3x^2-1}{3x^2} = 1 - \frac{1}{3x^2},$$

so $\frac{dy}{dx} = \frac{2}{3x^2} = \frac{2}{3}$ for $x = 1$.

8. (A)

$$\int_0^2 (3x^2 + 2x + 5)dx = [x^3 + x^2 + 5x]_0^2$$

$= 8 + 4 + 10 - 0 = 22$

9. (C)

Use the trigonometric substitution :

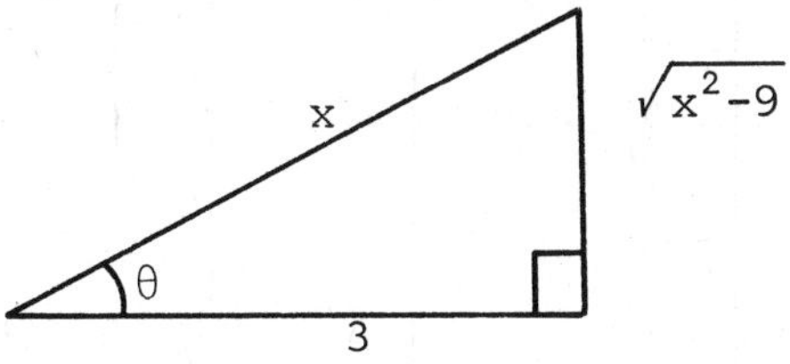

$x = 3\sec\theta \quad dx = (\sec\theta)(\tan\theta)d\theta, \quad \sqrt{x^2-9} = 3\tan\theta$

$$\int \frac{\sqrt{x^2-9}}{x}dx = 3\int \frac{(\tan\theta)(\sec\theta)(\tan\theta)}{\sec\theta}d\theta$$

$$= 3\int \tan^2\theta d\theta$$

$$= 3\int (\sec^2\theta - 1)du$$

$$= 3\tan\theta - 3\theta + C$$

$$= \sqrt{x^2-9} - 3\cos^{-1}\frac{3}{x} + C$$

10. (A)

Notice that $3x^2 + 2$ is the derivative of $x^3 + 2x + 7$.
Let $u = x^3 + 2x + 7$ and $du = (3x + 2)dx$.

So $\int 5u^4 du = u^5 + C$

$$= (x^3 + 2x + 7)^5 + C$$

11. (B)

$$f(x) = \frac{x^{3/2}}{3} \quad f'(x) = \frac{x^{1/2}}{2} \quad [f'(x)]^2 = \frac{x}{4}$$

$$S = \int_a^b \left[1 + f'(x)^2\right]^{1/2} dx = \int_0^5 \left[1 + \frac{x}{4}\right]^{1/2} dx$$

$$= \int_0^5 [4 + x]^{1/2} dx$$

Let $u = 4 + x$, If $x = 5$ then $u = 9$

then $du = dx$. If $x = 0$ then $u = 4$

$$\frac{1}{2}\int_4^9 u^{\frac{1}{2}} du = \frac{1}{2}\left[\frac{2}{3}u^{\frac{3}{2}}\right]_4^9 = \frac{1}{3}(27 - 8) = \frac{19}{3}.$$

12. (A)

$$\frac{d}{d\theta}\cos^2\left(\frac{\pi}{2} - \theta\right) = 2\cos\left(\frac{\pi}{2} - \theta\right)\sin\left(\frac{\pi}{2} - \theta\right)$$

For any angle $\phi, 2\cos\phi\sin\phi = (2\phi)$,

so $2\cos\left(\frac{\pi}{2} - \theta\right)\sin\left(\frac{\pi}{2} - \theta\right) = (\pi - 2\theta)$.

13. (D)

The coefficients for the power series are given by

$a_n = \frac{f^{(n)}(b)}{n!}$, so

$$a_4 = \frac{f^{(4)}(0)}{4!} = \frac{16e^0}{4!} = \frac{4}{6} = \frac{2}{3}$$

14. (E)

Let $y = \left(1 + \frac{1}{x}\right)^x$, Then $\ln y = x \ln\left(1 + \frac{1}{x}\right)$,

and $\lim\limits_{x \to \infty} \ln y = \lim\limits_{x \to \infty} x \ln\left(1 + \frac{1}{x}\right) = \lim\limits_{x \to \infty} \dfrac{\ln\left(1 + \frac{1}{x}\right)}{\frac{1}{x}}$

$$= \lim_{x \to \infty} \frac{\frac{-1/x^2}{1 + 1/x}}{-1/x^2} = \lim_{x \to \infty} \frac{1}{1 + 1/x} = 1$$

Since $\lim\limits_{x \to \infty} \ln y = 1$, then $\lim\limits_{x \to \infty} y = e^1 = e$,

so $\lim\limits_{x \to \infty} \left(1 + \frac{1}{x}\right)^x = e$.

15. (B)

Solve the differential equation $\frac{dy}{dx} = 4x^3y$ by separation of variables.

$$4\int x^3 dx - \int \frac{dy}{y} = C$$

$$x^4 - \ln y = C$$

$$\ln y = x^4 - C$$

$$y = e^{x^4 - C}$$

Let $A = e^{-c}$, then $y = Ae^{x^4}$

Substitute (0, 5) : $5 = Ae^0 = A \cdot 1 = A$,

so $y = 5e^{x^4}$

16. (B)

$$\frac{df(x)}{dx} = \frac{\pi}{2}\left(\frac{-\frac{1}{2}\tan^{-1/2}x \sec^2 x}{\tan x}\right) = \frac{\pi}{2}\left(\frac{-\sec^2 x}{2\tan^{3/2}x}\right)$$

Substitute $\frac{\pi}{4}$ for x : $\frac{\pi}{2}\left(\frac{-2}{2}\right)=\frac{-\pi}{2}$

17. (A)

First find an expression for the cross-section as a function of x; it is a circle of radius y. The cross-sectional area is πy^2. Since the circle touches the line $y = x$, $\pi y^2 = \pi x^2$.

$$\text{Volume} = \int_0^3 \pi x^2 dx$$

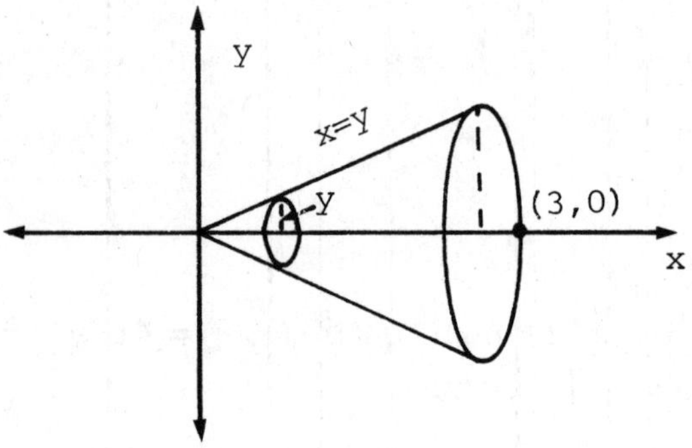

18. (E)

The quotient rule could be used, but the computations are tedious. Another approach is to use the natural logarithm of f.

$$\ln f(x) = \frac{1}{3}\ln(x+1) - \ln(x-1)$$

This method eliminates both the fraction and the cube root. Differentiate both sides.

$$\frac{f'(x)}{f(x)} = \frac{1}{3(x+1)} - \frac{1}{x-1} = \frac{x-1-3x-3}{3(x+1)(x-1)}$$

$$= \frac{-2(x+2)}{3(x+1)(x-1)}$$

Multiply both sides by $f(x)$:

$$\Rightarrow f'(x) = \frac{-2(x+2)}{3(x+1)(x-1)} \cdot \frac{\sqrt[3]{x+1}}{(x-1)}$$

$$= \frac{-2(x+2)}{3(x+1)^{2/3}(x-1)^2}$$

$$= f'(2) = \frac{-2(2+2)}{3(2+1)^{2/3}(2-1)^2} = \frac{-2(4)}{3(3)^{2/3}(1)}$$

$$= \frac{-8}{3(3)^{2/3}} = -1.282$$

Calculator: -8 [÷] 3 [×] 3 [y^x] 0.666 [=] = – 1.282

19. (E)

$$= \lim_{u\to\infty} \frac{1}{u}\left[\left(\frac{2}{u}\right)^2 + \left(\frac{4}{u}\right)^2 + \ldots + \left(\frac{8u}{u}\right)^2\right]$$

$$\lim_{u\to\infty} \frac{4}{u^3}\left(1 + 2^2 + \ldots + (4u)^2\right)$$

The sum of the squares of the first n integers =

$$\sum_{i=1}^{n} i^2 = \frac{n(n+1)(2n+1)}{6}.$$

Let $n = 4u$, then

$$\lim_{u\to\infty} \frac{4}{u^3}\left[\frac{4u(4u+1)(8u+1)}{6}\right]$$

$$= \lim_{u\to\infty} \frac{8}{3}\left(32 + \frac{12}{u} + \frac{1}{u^2}\right) = \frac{256}{3}$$

Also, $\frac{1}{2}\int_0^8 x^2 dx = \frac{x^3}{6}\Big|_0^8 = \frac{256}{3}$

20. (B)

$f(x) = 4x^2 + 2x + 9$, substitute $x = 1$, then $y = 15$

$f'(x) = 8x + 2$

$f'(1) = 10$, so slope of normal line is the negative reciprocal $-\frac{1}{10}$

$(y - 15) = -\frac{1}{10}(x - 1)$

$10y - 150 = -x + 1$

$x + 10y = 151$

21. (E)

The function is not continuous at $x = 0$, therefore the integral is nonexistent (by the Fundamental Theorem of Calculus.)

22. (B)

By integration by parts

$\int u\,dv = uv - \int v\,du$

$u = x \qquad v = -\cos x$

$du = dx \qquad dv = \sin x\, dx$

$\int x \sin x\, dx = -x \cos x - \int -\cos x\, dx$

$= -x \cos x + \sin x + c$

23. (B)

$u = \frac{x}{4}$ $\qquad 4u = x$

$du = \frac{dx}{4}$ $\qquad 4du = dx$

If $x = 4$ then $u = 1$
If $x = 0$ then $u = 0$

Substitute : $\int_0^1 \frac{4}{4u\sqrt{4-u^2}}\,du$

$= \int_0^1 \frac{1}{u\sqrt{4-u^2}}\,du$

24. (D)

$s(t)$ is the position function of a moving point P, with the velocity of P at time t defined to be

$\lim_{h \to 0} \frac{s(t+h) - s(t)}{h}$ and designated $v(t)$.

Thus, for acceleration, velocity and position :

$a(t) = v'(t) = s''(t)$

$x(t) = \frac{t^3 - 2t^2}{4}$, $y(t) = t^2 - t \Rightarrow x'(t) = \frac{3t^2 - 4t}{4}$,

$y'(t) = 2t - 1$

so $x''(t) = (6t - 4)/4$, $y''(t) = 2$

For $t = 2$, $x''(2) = 2$ and $y''(2) = 2$, so $(2, 2)$ is the acceleration vector.

25. (E)

(C) and (D) are not continuous at $x = 0$, so these are not applicable.

(A), (B), and (E) are continuous at $x = 0$. However, (A) and (B) are also differentiable at $x = 0$, $f'(x) = 2x$ or $\frac{5}{2}x^{3/2}$.

(E) is not differentiable at $x = 0$, $f'(x) = \frac{x^{-1/2}}{2}$.

26. (B)

Since the curve passes through (4, 7) only when $t = 2$, there is only one tangent line at (4, 7).

$x(t) = t^2$	$y(t) = t^3 - 1$
$x'(t) = 2t$	$y'(t) = 3t^2$
$x'(2) = 4$	$y'(2) = 12$

The slope of the tangent line is

$$m = y'(2)/x'(2) = \frac{12}{4} \Rightarrow \frac{y - 7}{x - 4} = \frac{12}{4}, \text{ so}$$

$$y - 7 = 3x - 12 \Rightarrow 3x - y = 5.$$

Another way to solve this is to see that

$$y = t^3 - 1 = \left(t^2\right)^{3/2} - 1 = x^{3/2} - 1, \text{ so } y' = \frac{3}{2}x^{1/2}$$

and at the point (4, 7), we have $y' = \frac{3}{2}(4)^{1/2} = 3$, so

$$y - 7 = 3(x - 4) \Rightarrow y = 3x - 5 \text{ or}$$

$$3x - y = 5.$$

27. (E)

Draw the graph of $y = \frac{2(x-1)^2}{x^2}$ on the window [–10,10] · [10,20].

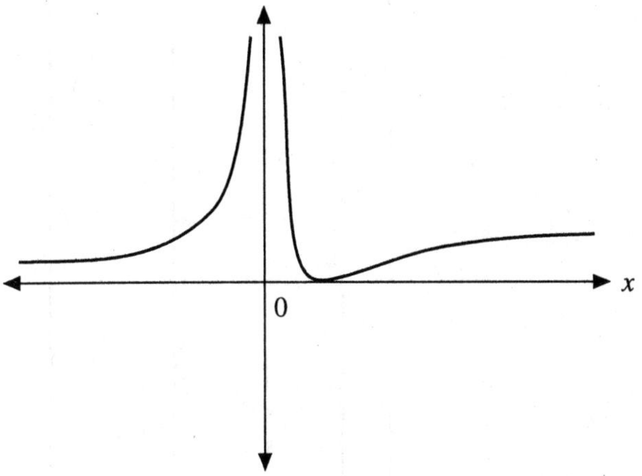

Obviously, $y \geq 0$ for all x; $y \to 2$ as $x \to +\infty$.

28. (D)

We are given that $g(x) = e^x f(x)$ and

$g''(x) = e^x h(x) + e^x f(x)$,

$\Rightarrow g'(x) = e^x f'(x) + e^x f(x)$

$\Rightarrow g''(x) = e^x \left(f(x) + 2f'(x) + f''(x) \right)$, so

$$h(x) = \frac{g''(x)}{e^x} - f(x)$$

$$\Rightarrow h(x) = \frac{e^x}{e^x}\left(\left(f(x) + 2f'(x) + f''(x) \right) - f(x) \right)$$

$$\Rightarrow h(x) = 2f'(x) + f''(x)$$

29. (A)

Use your calculator directly to find $y'_{|x=1}$. For example,

$$der1\left(\frac{X\wedge 2}{(3X\wedge 2+1)\wedge\left(\frac{1}{3}\right)},\ X,\ 1\right)\text{gives } 0.945\ .$$

30. (B)

Integration by parts :

$$\int u\,dv = uv - \int v\,du$$

$u = f(x)$ $\qquad du = f'(x)$

$dv = \cos x\,dx$ $\qquad v = \sin x$

If $f'(x) = -2x^3$ $\qquad f(x) = \frac{-x^4}{2}$

31. (E)

This problem can be solved directly by using your calculator. For example, $fnInt\left(\frac{1}{\sin(x+\sqrt{x})},\ x,\ 0,\ 1\right)$ gives 1.65 .

32. (B)

$$F(x) = \sec x - \tan x$$

$$= \frac{1}{\cos x} - \frac{\sin x}{\cos x} = \frac{1-\sin x}{\cos x}$$

Let $f(x) = 1-\sin x$ and $g(x) = \cos x$

$f'(x) = -\cos x$ $\qquad g'(x) = -\sin x$, so by

L' Hôpital's Rule,

$$\lim_{x\to\frac{\pi}{2}} F(x) = \lim_{x\to\frac{\pi}{2}} \frac{f(x)}{g(x)} = \lim_{x\to\frac{\pi}{2}} \frac{f'(x)}{g'(x)} = \lim_{x\to\frac{\pi}{2}} \frac{-\cos x}{-\sin x}$$

$$= \lim_{x\to\frac{\pi}{2}} \cot x = 0$$

33. (A)

Draw graphs of both $f(x)$ and $f'(x)$.

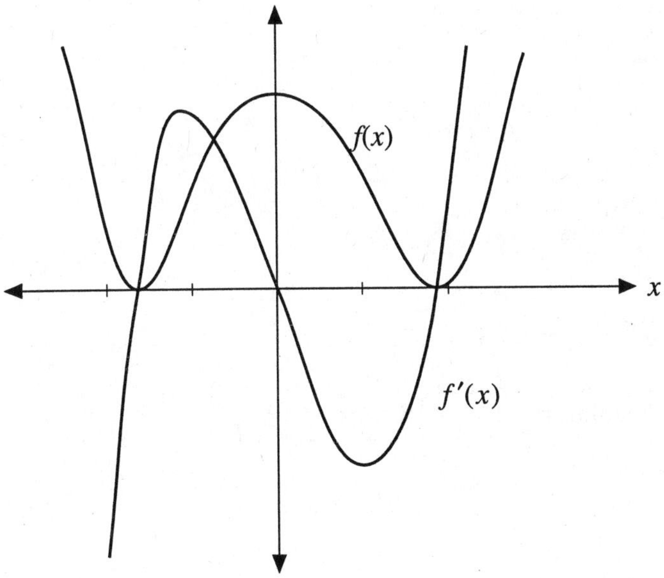

There is only one local minimum. By tracing the graph of $f'(x)$ to the minimum point, you can find $f'_{\max}(x) = 7.99$.

34. (A)

$$\text{Area} = \int_c^d f(x)\,dx - \int_c^d h(x)\,dx = \int_c^d [f(x) - h(x)]\,dx$$

35. (D)

You can solve this problem directly using your calculator.

For example, $fnInt\left(\dfrac{X\wedge 2}{e\wedge X},\ X,\ 0,\ 5\right)$ which would give 1.75.

36. (D)

$\dfrac{d}{dx}\left(\dfrac{x^{5n-3}}{5n-3}\right)=x^{5n-4}$, so differentiating term-by-term gives

$\sum_{n=1}^{\infty}(-1)^{n+1}x^{5n-4}$.

37. (C)

$\dfrac{d}{dx}e^{\sin 2x}=2(\cos 2x)e^{\sin 2x}$

$\left.\dfrac{d}{dx}\right|_4=2(\cos 8)e^{\sin}=2.276$

Calculator: 2 [×] 8 [cos] [×] 1 [e^x] [y^x] 8 [sin] [=] = 2.276

38. (A)

Use partial fractions :

Let $\dfrac{1}{(x+3)(x+4)}=\dfrac{A}{(x+3)}+\dfrac{B}{(x+4)}$

$1=A(x+4)+B(x+3)$

$1=(A+B)x+(4A+3B)$

$0=A+B$

$1=4A+3B$

$\Rightarrow A=1$ and $B=-1$

39. (A)

$f(x) = x^4 - x$ $\qquad$ $f(b) = f(2) = 16 - 2 = 14$

$f'(x_1) = 4x_1^3 - 1$ $\qquad$ $f(a) = f(0) = 0$

$f(b) - f(a) = (b - a)f'(x_1)$

$14 - 0 = (2 - 0)(4x^3 - 1)$

$14 = 8x_1^3 - 2 \Rightarrow 16 = 8x_1^3 \Rightarrow 2 = x_1^3,$

so $x_1 = \sqrt[3]{2}$

40. (E)

$\int dy = \int dt/(2t - 1)$

$y = \frac{1}{2}\ln(2t - 1) + C$

$y = \ln\sqrt{2t - 1} + C.$

To find the value of the constant C, let $y = 1$ and $t = 1$ into the last equation.

Then $1 = \ln\sqrt{1} + C = 0 + C$

$\Rightarrow C = 1$, so

$y = \ln\sqrt{2t - 1} + 1.$

When $t = 5$: $y = \ln\sqrt{9} + 1$

$y = \ln 3 + 1$

Calculator: 3 [ln] [+] 1 [=] = 2.099

ADVANCED PLACEMENT CALCULUS BC EXAM V

SECTION II

DETAILED EXPLANATIONS OF ANSWERS

1. (a)

$$V = \int_{-4}^{4} \pi(2 - x)^2 dy = 2\pi \int_0^4 \left(2 - \frac{y^2}{8}\right)^2 dy$$

$$= \frac{256}{15}\pi$$

(b)

$$V = \int_{-4}^{4} 4\pi dy - \int_{-4}^{4} \pi x^2 dy = 2\pi \int_0^4 (4 - x^2) dy$$

$$= 2\pi \int_0^4 \left(4 - \frac{y^2}{64}\right) dy$$

$$= \frac{128}{5}\pi$$

(c) $V = \int_0^2 \pi y^2 \, dx = \pi \int_0^2 8x \, dx$

$= 16\pi$

2. (a)
Figure (1) is not differentiable. At the point (0, 0), the tangent line cannot be uniquely determined. Therefore, the derivative (slope of the tangent) cannot be defined when $x = 0$.

(b)
Figure (2) is not differentiable. This function, $f(x) = x^{\frac{2}{3}}$, has a verticle tangent when $x = 0$. Since the slope of a verticle line is undefined, this function has no derivative when $x = 0$.

3. (a)
Draw the graphs of $f(x)$ and $f'(x)$.

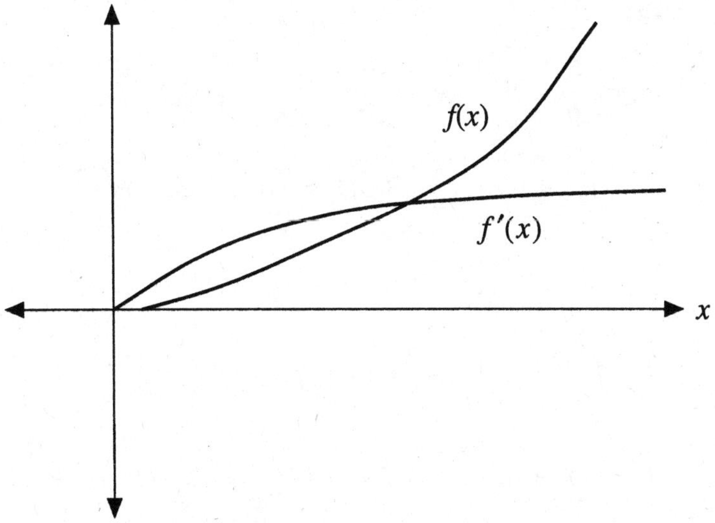

On graph $f'(x)$, by tracing x to $x_0 = 2$, you can find $f'(2) = 1.4$. Then, $c = 1.4$ can make line $y = 1.4x + d$ tangent to $f(x)$ at $x_0 = 2$, if d is found by the following, $\because f(2) = 1.87$.

Hence, $d = y - 1.4x = 1.87 - 1.4x^2 = -0.93$.

(b)

When $c = 1$, we need $f'(x) = 1$, from which $x_0 = 1$ and $f(x_0) = 0.66$. Hence, we can find d by

$d = y - cx = 0.66 - 1 = -0.34$.

(c)

Use your calculator:

fnInt (0.667X^1.5, x, 0, 3), which gives 4.16 .

4. (a)

$$v_x = \frac{dx}{dt} = 2t \qquad v_y = \frac{dy}{dt} = 3t^2$$

$$v = \sqrt{v_x^2 + v_y^2} = \sqrt{4t^2 + 9t^4} = \sqrt{16 + 144} = 4\sqrt{10}$$

(b)

$$\tan\theta = \frac{v_y}{v_x} = \frac{3t^2}{2t} = \frac{3}{2}t = \frac{3}{2}(2) = 3$$

$\theta = \tan^{-1}(3)$.

5. (a)

$x = 9\cos\theta$ $\quad\quad y = 3\sin\theta$

$\frac{dx}{d\theta} = -9\sin\theta$ $\quad\quad \frac{dy}{d\theta} = 3\cos\theta$

$$\frac{dy}{dx} = \frac{dy}{d\theta} \cdot \frac{d\theta}{dx} = \frac{-3\cos\theta}{9\sin\theta} = \frac{-\cos\theta}{3\sin\theta} = \frac{-1}{3}\cot\theta$$

(b)

Slope of the tangent line at $\theta = 45°$:

$-\frac{1}{3}\cot 45° = -\frac{1}{3}$

$x_1 = 9\cos 45° = 9\left(\frac{\sqrt{2}}{2}\right)$, $y_1 = 3\sin 45° = 3\left(\frac{\sqrt{2}}{2}\right)$.

$$\left(y - \frac{3\sqrt{2}}{2}\right) = -\frac{1}{3}\left(x - \frac{9\sqrt{2}}{2}\right)$$

$x + 3y = 9\sqrt{2}$

(c)

$$\left(y - \frac{3\sqrt{2}}{2}\right) = 3\left(x - \frac{9\sqrt{2}}{2}\right)$$

$3x - y = 12\sqrt{2}$

6. (a)

$$f(x) = f(0) + \frac{f'(0)x}{1!} + \frac{f''(0)x^2}{2!} + \ldots$$

$$+ \frac{f^n(0)x^n}{n!} + \ldots$$

$$e^x = 1 + x + \frac{x^2}{2!} + \ldots + \frac{x^n}{n!} + \ldots$$

(b)

$$f(x) = f(a) + \frac{f'(a)(x - a)}{1!} + \ldots$$

$$+ \frac{f^n(a)(x - a)^n}{n!} + \ldots$$

$$e^x = e^a + e^a(x - a) + \frac{e^a(x - a)^2}{2!} + \ldots$$

$$. + \frac{e^a(x - a)^n}{n!} + \ldots$$

THE ADVANCED PLACEMENT EXAMINATION IN

CALCULUS BC

TEST VI

ADVANCED PLACEMENT CALCULUS BC EXAM VI

SECTION I

PART A

Time: 45 minutes
25 questions

DIRECTIONS: Each of the following problems is followed by five choices. Solve each problem, select the best choice, and blacken the correct space on your answer sheet.

NOTE:

Unless otherwise specified, the domain of function f is assumed to be the set of all real numbers x for which $f(x)$ is a real number.

1. The area of the region between the graph of $y = 8x - 8x^3$ and the x-axis from $x = 0$ to $x = 1$ is

   (A) 0
   (B) 2
   (C) 4
   (D) 6
   (E) 8

2. At what value does $f(x) = 4x^5 + 15x^4 + 20x^3 + 10x^2$ have a relative maximum ?

(A) -2

(B) -1

(C) 0

(D) 1

(E) 2

3. $\int_1^3 \frac{2x - 1}{x^2 - x + 4} dx$ is approximately:

(A) 0.916

(B) 1.833

(C) 0.805

(D) 1.097

(E) 1.609

4. A particle moves on the XY-plane so that at any time t its coordinates are $x = t^3 + t$ and $y = t^5 - 2t^2$. At $t = 2$, its acceleration vector is :

(A) (12, 156)

(B) (12, 164)

(C) (6, 156)

(D) (6, 164)

(E) (13, 72)

5. The area of the region bounded by $y = \sin 2x$ and $y = 2\sin x$ for $0 \le x \le \pi$ is:

(A) 0

(B) 2

(C) 4

(D) 5

(E) 6

6. If $f(x) = \dfrac{\sin x}{x^2}$, then $f'(\pi) =$

(A) 0.101

(B) -0.101

(C) 0.065

(D) 1.097

(E) 1.609

7. The length of the arc given by

$x = 4\cos^3 t$

$y = 4\sin^3 t$

$0 \le t \le \dfrac{\pi}{2}$

is :

(A) $\dfrac{\pi}{2}$

(B) $\dfrac{3\pi}{2}$

(C) 3π

(D) 3

(E) 6

8. If f is a function such that $\lim_{x \to 0} \frac{f(x) - f(2)}{x - 2} = 0$

then which of the following must be true?

(I) f is continuous at $x = 2$

(II) f is differentiable at $x = 2$

(III) $f'(2) = 0$

(A) I only

(B) II only

(C) I and II only

(D) II and III only

(E) I, II, and III

9. If $x^2y^2 + 2xy = 8$, then at the point $(1, 2)$ y' is:

(A) -8

(B) -2

(C) 0

(D) 2

(E) 8

10. If $f(x) = \sum_{n=0}^{\infty} \frac{(-1)^n x^{2n+1}}{(2n+1)!}$, then $f'(x) =$

(A) $\sum_{n=0}^{\infty} \frac{(-1)^n x^{2n+1}}{(2n-1)!}$

(B) $\sum_{n=0}^{\infty} \frac{(-1)^n x^{2n}}{(2n)!}$

(C) $\sum_{n=0}^{\infty} (-1)^n x^{2n}$

(D) $\sum_{n=0}^{\infty} \frac{(-1)^n x^{2n}}{(2n-1)!}$

(E) $\sum_{n=0}^{\infty} (-1)^n x^{2n-1}$

11. $\frac{d}{dx}\int_0^{2x} e^{-t^2}\,dt =$

(A) e^{-4x^2}

(B) $2e^{-4x^2}$

(C) $-2xe^{-x^2}$

(D) $-4xe^{-x^2}$

(E) 0

12. $\int \frac{dx}{(x+1)(x-3)} =$

(A) $\ln|(x+1)(x-3)| + C$

(B) $\ln\left|\frac{x-3}{x+1}\right| + C$

(C) $\frac{1}{4}\ln\left|\frac{x-3}{x+1}\right| + C$

(D) $\frac{1}{4}\ln\left|\frac{x+1}{x-3}\right| + C$

(E) $\frac{1}{4}\ln|x-3| - \ln|x+1| + C$

13. If f is continuous on [0 , 1], what does the Mean Value Theorem say about the function $x \cdot f(x)$?

(A) $f'(c) = 0$ for some c between 0 and 1

(B) $c \cdot f'(c) = 0$ for some c between 0 and 1

(C) $1 + f'(c) = c$ for some c between 0 and 1

(D) $f(c) + f'(c) = 1$ for some c between 0 and 1

(E) $f(c) + c \cdot f'(c) = f(1)$ for some c between 0 and 1

14. Which of the following series converge ?

I. $\frac{1}{5} + \frac{1}{10} + \frac{1}{15} + \frac{1}{20} + \ldots + \frac{1}{5n} + \ldots$

II. $\frac{1}{5} + \frac{1}{25} + \frac{1}{125} + \frac{1}{625} + \ldots + \frac{1}{n^5} + \ldots$

III. $\frac{1}{5} - \frac{1}{6} + \frac{1}{10} - \frac{1}{11} + \frac{1}{15} - \frac{1}{16} + \ldots$

$+ \frac{1}{5n} - \frac{1}{1+5n} + \ldots$

(A) I only

(B) II only

(C) III only

(D) I and II only

(E) II and III only

15. Point A moves to the right along the positive x-axis at 7 units per second while point B moves upward along the negative y-axis at 2 units per second. At what rate is the distance between A and B changing when A is at (8, 0) and B is at $(0, -6)$?

(A) $\frac{32}{5}$

(B) 5

(C) $\frac{22}{5}$

(D) $-\frac{22}{5}$

(E) $-\frac{32}{5}$

16. Which of the following functions shows that the statement "If a function is continuous for $0 \leq x < \infty$, then it has an absolute maximum" is <u>false</u>?

(A) $f(x) = \frac{1}{x-1}$

(B) $f(x) = \sqrt{x}$

(C) $f(x) = 1 - x^2$

(D) $f(x) = \sin x$

(E) $f(x) = \tan x$

17. If $f(x) = \dfrac{\ln(1+x^4)}{x}$, then $f'(1) =$

(A) 1.307

(B) 0.693

(C) – 0.193

(D) 0.500

(E) – 0.693

18. Which is largest ?

(A) $\int_0^\pi \sin x \, dx$

(B) $\int_0^\pi \sin 2x \, dx$

(C) $\int_0^\pi 2\sin x \, dx$

(D) $\int_0^\pi (1 + \sin x)\, dx$

(E) $\int_0^\pi \sin^2 x \, dx$

19. If $y = f(\sqrt{x})$ then $\left.\dfrac{d^2y}{dx^2}\right|_{x=4} =$

(A) $f''(2)$

(B) $2f''(2) + \frac{1}{4}f'(2)$

(C) $\frac{1}{2}f''(2) - \frac{1}{16}f'(2)$

(D) $\frac{1}{16}f''(2) - \frac{1}{32}f'(2)$

(E) $\frac{1}{32}f''(2) - \frac{1}{256}f'(2)$

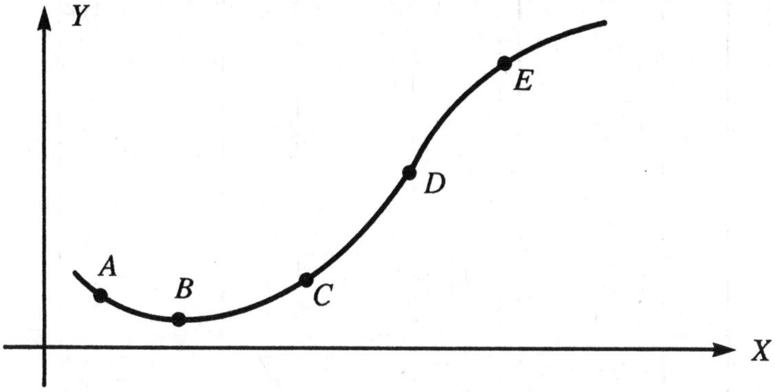

20. At which point on the curve shown above are both $\frac{dy}{dx}$ and $\frac{d^2y}{dx^2}$ positive?

(A) A

(B) B

(C) C

(D) D

(E) E

21. $\int x \cos 2x \, dx =$

(A) $x^2 \sin 2x + C$

(B) $\frac{1}{4}x^2 \sin 2x + C$

(C) $\frac{1}{2}x \sin 2x + \frac{1}{4}\cos 2x + C$

(D) $\frac{1}{2}x \sin 2x - \frac{1}{4}\cos 2x + C$

(E) $\frac{1}{2}(x - 1)\sin 2x + C$

22. If $f(x) = |\sin x|$, then the graph of the derivative f' is :

(A)
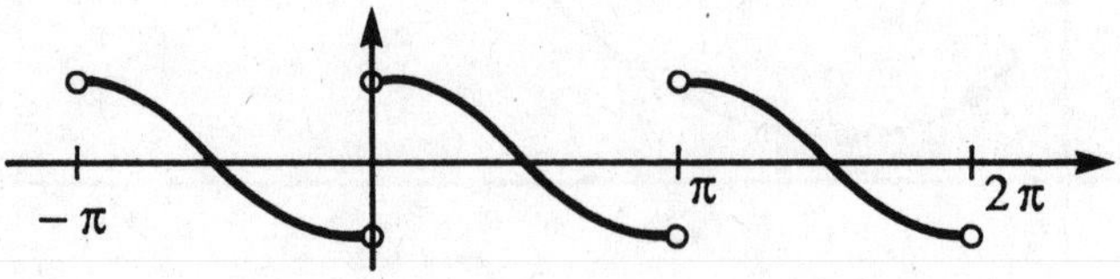

(B)
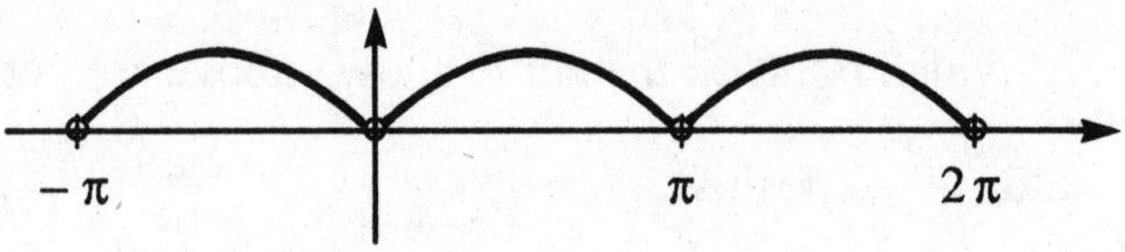

(C)
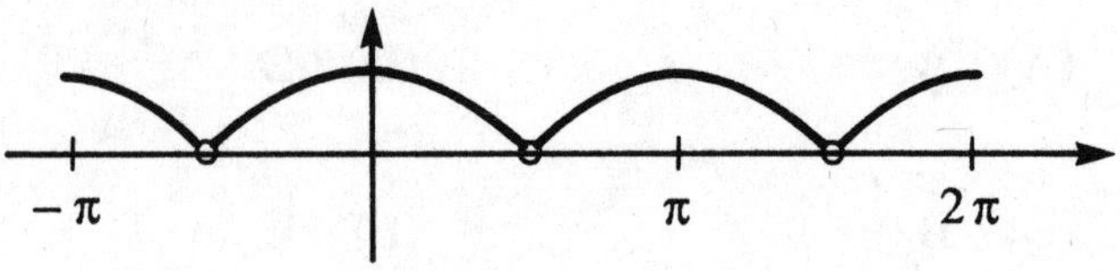

(D)
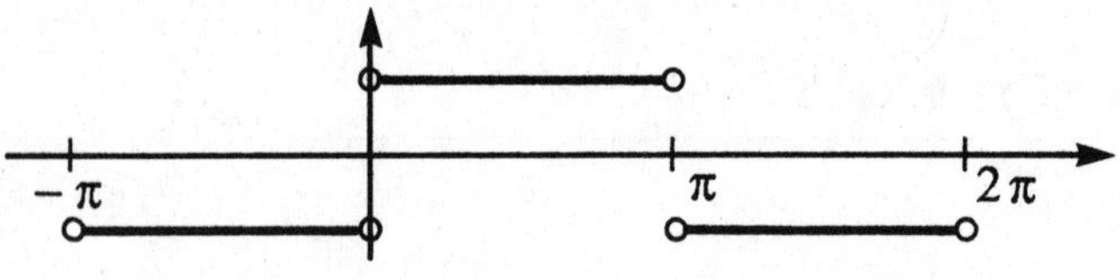

(E)
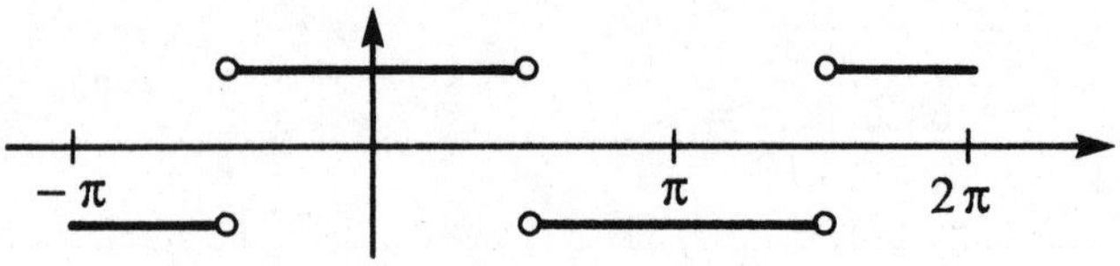

23. A spherical steel ball 64 cm in diameter is coated with a layer of ice which is melting at the rate of 2 cm^3 per minute. If the ice always maintains a uniform thickness, then at what rate is this thickness decreasing when

it is 6 cm thick?

(A) 0.00400

(B) 0.00003

(C) 0.01768

(D) 0.00013

(E) none of the above

24. If $y = f(\sin x)$ and $f'(u) = u\sqrt{1-u^2}$, then, for $0 \le x \le \frac{\pi}{2}$, $\frac{dy}{dx} =$

(A) $\sin^2 x$

(B) $\cos^2 x$

(C) $\sin x \cos x$

(D) $\sin^2 x \cos x$

(E) $\sin x \cos^2 x$

25. Which of the following must be true if f is a continuous function on $[a, b]$?

I. f is differentiable on (a, b)

II. $f(c) = 0$, for some c in (a, b)

III. There exists c and d in $[a, b]$ for which $f(c) \le f(x) \le f(d)$ for all x in $[a, b]$.

(A) I only

(B) II only

(C) III only

(D) I and II only

(E) II and III only

SECTION I

PART B

Time: 45 minutes
15 questions

DIRECTIONS: Calculators may be used for this section of the test. Each of the following problems is followed by five choices. Solve each problem, select the best choice, and blacken the correct space on your answer sheet.

NOTES:

1. Unless otherwise specified, answers can be given in unsimplified form.

2. The domain of function *f* is assumed to be the set of all real numbers *x* for which *f*(*x*) is a real number.

26. What is the minimum slope for the graph of $y = x^3 + 3x^2 + 5x$?

(A) –1

(B) 0

(C) $\frac{1}{3}$

(D) 1

(E) 2

27. Let $f(x) = \sin^2 x \cos^2 2x$. $\int_0^2 f(x)$ equals

(A) 0.715

(B) 1.211

(C) 3.121

(D) 0.015

(E) 4.782

28. If f is a differentiable function on $[a, b]$, and

$0 < f'(x) < \dfrac{f(b) - f(a)}{2}$ for all x in $[a, b]$, and $a > 0$, then

(A) $f(a) > 0$

(B) $f(a) > f(b)$

(C) $f(a) < f(b)$

(D) $a + 2 < b$

(E) $a + 2 > b$

29. $f(x) = \dfrac{2x}{\sqrt{1 - x^4}}$. The minimum of $f'(x)$ is

(A) 1

(B) 0

(C) –1

(D) 2

(E) 3

30. As a particle moves along the line $y = 2x + 7$ its minimum distance from the origin is:

(A) $\dfrac{7}{5}$

(B) $\dfrac{7}{5}\sqrt{5}$

(C) $\dfrac{14}{5}$

(D) $\dfrac{\sqrt{5}}{7}$

(E) $\dfrac{7}{3}\sqrt{5}$

31. Suppose a particle moves on a straight line with a position function of $s(t) = 3t^3 - 11t^2 + 8t$. The highest velocity with which the particle moves in the negative direction is

(A) –5.4

(B) 0

(C) 2.5

(D) –4

(E) 2

32. The rate of change of $\sqrt{1+x^2}$ with respect to $\frac{x}{1+x^2}$ is:

(A) $\frac{\sqrt{1+x^2}}{\left(\frac{x}{1+x}\right)}$

(B) $\frac{x\left(\sqrt{1+x^2}\right)^3}{(1-x)^2}$

(C) $\frac{x\left(\sqrt{1+x^2}\right)^3}{1-x^2}$

(D) $\frac{x^2\left(\sqrt{1+x^2}\right)^3}{1-x}$

(E) $\frac{x^2\sqrt{1+x^2}}{1-x^2}$

33. $\int_0^2 x^x$ is

(A) 3.27

(B) 2.83

(C) 4.21

(D) 3.02

(E) 1.98

34. $\lim_{n\to\infty} \frac{1}{n}\left[\left(\frac{n}{1}\right)^2 + \left(\frac{n}{2}\right)^2 + \ldots + \left(\frac{n}{n}\right)^2\right] =$

(A) $\int_0^1 \frac{dx}{x^2}$

(D) $\int_0^1 x^2 dx$

(B) $\int_0^1 \frac{dx}{x}$

(E) none of the above

(C) $\int_0^1 x dx$

35. Let $f(x) = \frac{e\sqrt{x}}{\sqrt{x}}$. $f'(x) = 0$. Then x equals

(A) 3

(D) 2

(B) 0

(E) 7

(C) 1

36. $\int_{-2}^{2} \frac{4\,dx}{x^2}$ is

(A) $\frac{3}{2}$

(B) $-\frac{3}{2}$

(C) 0

(D) $\frac{15}{16}$

(E) nonexistent

37. The general solution to $\frac{dy}{dx} = y - xe^x$ is

(A) $y = \left(C - \frac{1}{2}x^2\right)e^x$

(B) $y = \frac{1}{2}x^2e^x + C$

(C) $y = \left(C + \frac{1}{2}x^2\right)e^{-x}$

(D) $y = \frac{1}{2}x^2e^{-x} + C$

(E) $y = (C - x)e^{-x}$

38. $\lim_{n\to\infty}\left(\sqrt[3]{n^3 + 5n^2} - n\right) =$

(A) 0

(B) $\frac{3}{5}$

(C) 3

(D) $\frac{5}{3}$

(E) nonexistent

39. The base of a solid is the region enclosed by the graph of $x = 1 - y^2$ and the y -axis. If all plane cross-sections perpendicular to the x-axis are semicircles with diameters parallel to the x -axis, then the volume is :

(A) $\frac{\pi}{8}$

(B) $\frac{\pi}{4}$

(C) $\frac{\pi}{2}$

(D) $\frac{3\pi}{4}$

(E) $\frac{3\pi}{2}$

40. The substitution $x - 1 = \sin\theta$ transforms the integral $\int_1^2 \frac{dx}{x^2 - 2x}$ into :

(A) $\int_0^{\frac{\pi}{2}} \frac{d\theta}{\cos\theta}$

(B) $\int_0^{\frac{\pi}{2}} \frac{d\theta}{\sin\theta}$

(C) $-\int_0^{\frac{\pi}{2}} \frac{d\theta}{\cos\theta}$

(D) $-\int_0^{\frac{\pi}{2}} \frac{d\theta}{\sin\theta}$

(E) $-\int_0^{\frac{\pi}{2}} \frac{d\theta}{\cos^2\theta}$

ADVANCED PLACEMENT CALCULUS BC EXAM VI

SECTION II

Time: 1 hour and 30 minutes
6 questions†

DIRECTIONS: Show all your work. Grading is based on the methods used to solve the problems as well as the accuracy of your final answers. Please make sure all procedures are clearly shown.

NOTES:

1. $\ln x$ denotes the natural logarithm of x (that is, logarithm to the base e).

2. Unless otherwise specified, the domain of function f is assumed to be the set of all real numbers x for which $f(x)$ is a real number.

† The practice tests in this book incorporate Section II free-response solutions that approximate the content breakdown you will encounter on the AP exam. The overall timing and formatting of the practice tests mirror the actual test; examinees should note, however, that this section is split into two parts on the AP exam. Furthermore, prospective examinees should pay attention to restrictions on calculator use. For details, consult current official College Board materials in print or on the Web.

1. A particle moves along the x-axis so that, at any time $t \geq 0$, its acceleration is given by $a(t) = 6t - 8$. At any time $t = 0$, the velocity of the particle is 5, and its position is –2.

(a) Find $v(t)$, the velocity of the particle at any time $t \geq 0$.

(b) For what values of $t \geq 0$ is the particle moving to the right?

(c) Find $x(t)$, the position of the particle at any time $t \geq 0$.

(d) Find the position(s) where the particle is at rest.

2. Let f be the function defined by $f(x) = \left(x^2 + 2x + 5\right)e^{\frac{x}{2}}$

(a) Find all the critical points of f.

(b) Find all the inflection points of f.

(c) Use your results from parts (a) and (b) to describe where the graph of f is increasing, where it is decreasing, where it is concave upward, and where it is concave downward.

(d) Use your results from parts (a), (b), and (c) to sketch the graph of f.

$$\left[e^{-\frac{1}{2}} \approx 0.6065\right]$$

Label all intercepts, critical points, and inflection points.

3. Population growth in a certain bacteria colony is best described by the equation $y = t^2 e^{3t^2 t\sqrt{t}}$.

(a) Find the rate of growth at $t = 1$.

(b) Find the lowest rate for $t > 0$.

(c) Find the highest rate for $t > 0$.

4. (a) Use the Method of Integration By Parts to derive the formula:

$$\int_c^d f^{-1}(y)dy = bd - ac - \int_a^b f(x)dx$$

where f^{-1} is the inverse of the function f, $c = f(a)$, and $d = f(b)$.

(b) Apply this formula to evaluate $\int_0^1 \arctan y\, dy$.

5. For each of the following, determine the set of all x for which the series converges:

(a) $\sum_{n=1}^{\infty} \left(1 - \frac{x}{n}\right)^n$

(b) $\sum_{n=2}^{\infty} \frac{n^x}{\ln^n}$

(c) $\sum_{n=1}^{\infty} \frac{1}{x^n + \sin n}$

6. Let $f_1(\theta) = 1 + 2\cos\theta$
and $f_2(\theta) = 3 - 2\cos\theta$
Let C_1 be the polar graph of $r = f_1(\theta)$ and C_2 the polar graph of $r = f_2(\theta)$.

(a) Sketch C_1 and C_2 together :

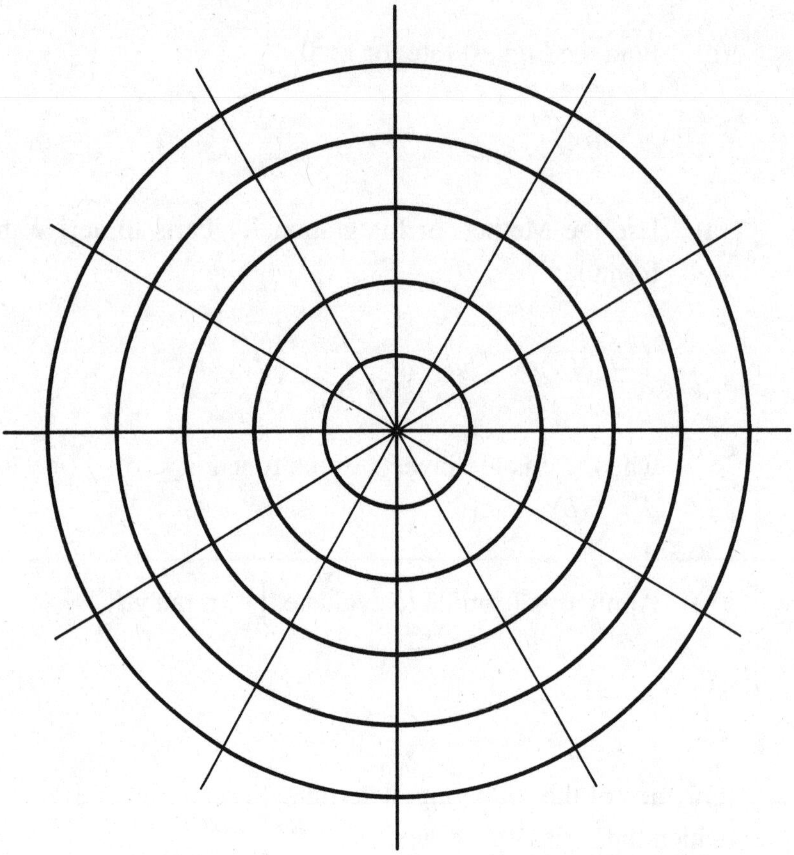

(b) Find the total area of the region inside C_1 and outside C_2.

ADVANCED PLACEMENT CALCULUS BC EXAM VI

ANSWER KEY

SECTION I

1.	B	21.	C
2.	B	22.	A
3.	A	23.	B
4.	A	24.	E
5.	C	25.	C
6.	B	26.	E
7.	E	27.	A
8.	E	28.	D
9.	B	29.	D
10.	B	30.	B
11.	B	31.	A
12.	C	32.	B
13.	E	33.	B
14.	E	34.	A
15.	C	35.	C
16.	B	36.	E
17.	A	37.	A
18.	D	38.	A
19.	D	39.	B
20.	C	40.	C

SECTION II

See Detailed Explanations of Answers.

ADVANCED PLACEMENT CALCULUS BC EXAM VI

SECTION I

DETAILED EXPLANATIONS OF ANSWERS

1. (B)

The area is the integral :

$$A = \int_0^1 (8x - 8x^3)dx$$

Use the Fundamental Theorem of Calculus :

$$A = \int_0^1 (8x - 8x^3)dx$$

$$= 4x^2 - 2x^4 \Big|_0^1$$

$$= \left[4(1)^2 - 2(1)^4\right] - \left[4(0)^2 - 2(0)^4\right]$$

$$= [4 - 2] - [0 - 0]$$

$$= 2$$

2. (B)

The relative maximum occurs at a critical point. Since the function is a polynomial, its critical points are those points where its derivative is zero.

The derivative is :

$f'(x) = 20x^4 + 60x^3 + 60x^2 + 20x$

Factor : $f'(x) = 20x(x^3 + 3x^2 + 3x + 1)$

$= 20x(x + 1)^3$

This is zero at: $x = 0$ and $x = -1$

Use the First Derivative Test to see which of these is a relative maximum. Check $f'(x)$ at sample points in each of the intervals bounded by the critical points :

-2 is in $(-\infty, -1) : f'(-2) = 40 > 0$,

so $f(x)$ is increasing on $(-\infty, -1)$;

$-\frac{1}{2}$ is in $(-1, 0) : f'\left(-\frac{1}{2}\right) = -\frac{5}{4} < 0$,

so $f(x)$ is decreasing on $(-1, 0)$;

1 is in $(0, \infty) : f'(1) = 160 > 0$

so $f(x)$ is increasing on $(0, \infty)$.

Thus f has a relative maximum at $x = -1$ because $f(x)$ is increasing on $(-\infty, -1)$ and decreasing on $(-1, 0)$.

3. (A)

Let $u = x^2 - x + 4$.

Then $du = 2x\,dx - dx = (2x - 1)dx$

so the integrand is :

$$\frac{2x - 1}{x^2 - x + 4}dx = \frac{du}{u}$$

Also, if $x = 1$ then $u = (1)^2 - (1) + 4 = 4$

and if $x = 3$ then $u = (3)^2 - (3) + 4 = 10$.

Substituting and integrating :

$$\int_1^3 \frac{2x - 1}{x^2 - x + 4} dx = \int_4^{10} \frac{du}{u}$$

$$= \ln|u| \Big|_4^{10}$$

$$= \ln 10 - \ln 4$$

$$= \ln \frac{10}{4}$$

$$= \ln \frac{5}{2} = 0.916$$

4. (A)

The acceleration vector is

$$a = \left(\frac{d^2x}{dt^2}, \frac{d^2y}{dt^2} \right).$$

Derive the derivatives :

$$x = t^3 + t$$

$$\frac{dx}{dt} = 3t^2 + 1$$

$$\frac{d^2x}{dt^2} = 6t$$

$$y = t^5 - 2t^2$$

$$\frac{dy}{dt} = 5t^4 - 4t$$

$$\frac{d^2y}{dt^2} = 20t^3 - 4$$

Evaluate $\frac{d^2x}{dt^2}$ and $\frac{d^2y}{dt^2}$ at $t = 2$:

$$\left.\frac{d^2x}{dt^2}\right|_{t=2} = 6(2) = 12$$

$$\left.\frac{d^2y}{dt^2}\right|_{t=2} = 20(2)^3 - 4 = 156$$

Thus : $a = (12, 156)$

5. (C)

For $0 \le x \le \pi$ $\sin 2x \le 2\sin x$
(because $\sin 2x = 2\sin x \cos x$)
fo the area is given by :

$$A = \int_0^\pi (2\sin x - \sin 2x)dx$$

$$= \left(-2\cos x + \frac{1}{2}\cos 2x\right)\Big|_0^\pi$$

$$= \left(-2(-1) + \frac{1}{2}(1)\right) - \left(-2(1) + \frac{1}{2}(1)\right)$$

$$= \left(2 + \frac{1}{2}\right) - \left(-2 + \frac{1}{2}\right)$$

$$= 4$$

6. (B)

Since the denominater is a power, convert the quotient to a product and use the Product Rule :

$$f(x) = \frac{\sin x}{x^2} = x^{-2}\sin x$$

$$f'(x) = \frac{d}{dx}(x^{-2} \cdot \sin x)$$

$$= x^{-2} \cdot \frac{d}{dx}(\sin x) + \sin x \cdot \frac{d}{dx}(x^{-2})$$

$$= x^{-2} \cdot \cos x + \sin x \cdot (-2x^{-3})$$

Substitute before simplifying :

$$f'(\pi) = (\pi)^{-2} \cdot \cos(\pi) + \sin(\pi) \cdot \left(-2(\pi)^{-3}\right)$$

$$= (\pi)^{-2} \cdot (-1) + (0) \cdot \left(-2(\pi)^{-3}\right)$$

$$= \frac{1}{\pi^2} \cdot (-1) + 0$$

$$= -\frac{1}{\pi^2} = 0.101$$

7. (E)

The arc length formula is :

$$L = \int_0^{\frac{\pi}{2}} \sqrt{\left(\frac{dx}{dt}\right)^2 + \left(\frac{dy}{dt}\right)^2}\, dt$$

Here :

$$\frac{dx}{dt} = (12\cos^2 t)(-\sin t)$$

$$\frac{dy}{dt} = (12\sin^2 t)(\cos t)$$

so:

$$\left(\frac{dx}{dt}\right)^2 = 144 \sin^2 t \cos^4 t$$

$$\left(\frac{dy}{dt}\right)^2 = 144 \sin^4 t \cos^2 t$$

so :

$$\left(\frac{dx}{dt}\right)^2 + \left(\frac{dy}{dt}\right)^2 = 144 \sin^2 \cos^4 t + 144 \sin^4 t \cos^2 t$$

$$= (144 \sin^2 \cos^2 t)(\cos^2 t + \sin^2 t)$$
$$= (144 \sin^2 t \cos^2 t)(1)$$

so :

$$\sqrt{\left(\frac{dx}{dt}\right)^2 + \left(\frac{dy}{dt}\right)^2} = 12 \sin t \cos t$$

Thus :

$$L = \int_0^{\frac{\pi}{2}} 12 \sin t \cos t \, dt$$

$$= 6 \sin^2 t \Big|_0^{\frac{\pi}{2}}$$

$$= 6 \cdot (1)^2 - 6 \cdot (0)^2$$
$$= 6$$

8. (E)

The definition of the derivative of f at $x = a$ is :

$$f'(a) = \lim_{x \to a} \frac{f(x) - f(a)}{x - a}$$

Therefore the given information is $f'(2) = 0$.
Thus f is differentiable at $x = 2$, and this guarantees that f is continuous at $x = 2$.

9. (B)

Use implicit differentiation :

$$\frac{d}{dx}(x^2 y^2 + 2xy) = x^2 \cdot \frac{d}{dx}(y^2) + y^2 \cdot \frac{d}{dx}(x^2)$$

$$+ 2x \frac{d}{dx}(y) + y \cdot \frac{d}{dx}(2x)$$

$$= x^2 \cdot 2y \cdot \frac{dy}{dx} + y^2 \cdot 2x + 2x \cdot \frac{dy}{dx} + y \cdot 2$$

$$= 2x^2y \cdot \frac{dy}{dx} + 2xy^2 + 2x \cdot \frac{dy}{dx} + 2y$$

$$\frac{d}{dx}(8) = 0$$

$$x^2y^2 + 2xy = 8$$

$$\frac{d}{dx}(x^2y^2 + 2xy) = \frac{d}{dx}(8)$$

$$2x^2y \cdot \frac{dy}{dx} + 2xy^2 + 2x \cdot \frac{dy}{dx} + 2y = 0$$

Substitute $x = 1$ and $y = 2$:

$$2(1)^2(2) \cdot \frac{dy}{dx} + 2(1) \cdot (2)^2 + 2(1) \cdot \frac{dy}{dx} + 2(2) = 0$$

Solve for $\frac{dy}{dx}$:

$$4\frac{dy}{dx} + 8 + 2\frac{dy}{dx} + 4 = 0$$

$$6\frac{dy}{dx} + 12 = 0$$

$$6\frac{dy}{dx} = -12$$

$$\frac{dy}{dx} = -2$$

10. (B)
Since the series converges absolutely (for all x), $f'(x)$ may be obtained by differentiating term-wise :

$$f'(x) = \frac{d}{dx}\left(\sum_{n=0}^{\infty} \frac{(-1)^n x^{2n+1}}{(2n+1)!}\right)$$

$$= \sum_{n=0}^{\infty} \frac{(-1)^n}{(2n+1)!} \cdot \frac{d}{dx}(x^{2n+1})$$

$$= \sum_{n=0}^{\infty} \frac{(-1)^n}{(2n+1)!} \cdot ((2n+1)x^{2n})$$

$$= \sum_{n=0}^{\infty} \frac{(-1)^n}{(2n)!} x^{2n}$$

This last step follows from the fact that

$$\frac{2n+1}{(2n+1)!} = \frac{2n+1}{(2n+1)\cdot(2n)!} = \frac{1}{(2n)!}$$

For example, if $n = 4$:

$$\frac{2n+1}{(2n+1)!} = \frac{9}{9!} = \frac{9}{9 \cdot 8!} = \frac{1}{8!} = \frac{1}{(2n)!}$$

11. (B)
Since the integrand e^{-t^2} has no antiderivative (expressible in terms of elementary functions), the First Form of the Fundamental Theorem of Calculus cannot be used here. However, the Second Form can. It states that, if f is continuous, then

$$\frac{d}{du}\int_a^u f(t)\,dt = f(u).$$

Combining this with the Chain Rule yields :

$$\frac{d}{dx}\int_a^u f(t)\,dt = f(u) \cdot \frac{du}{dx}.$$

Thus : $\frac{d}{dx}\int_0^{2x} f(t)\,dt = f(2x) \cdot \frac{d(2x)}{dx} = f(2x) \cdot 2$

so : $\frac{d}{dx}\int_0^{2x} e^{-t^2}\,dt = e^{-(2x)^2} \cdot 2$

$= 2e^{-4x^2}$

12. (C)

Integrate by parts :

$$\frac{1}{x-3} - \frac{1}{x+1} = \frac{(x+1)}{(x+1)(x-3)} - \frac{(x-3)}{(x+1)(x-3)}$$

$$= \frac{4}{(x+1)(x-3)}$$

so : $\frac{1}{(x+1)(x-3)} = \frac{1}{4}\left[\frac{1}{x-3} - \frac{1}{x+1}\right]$

Thus : $\int \frac{dx}{(x+1)(x-3)} = \frac{1}{4}\left[\int \frac{dx}{x-3} - \int \frac{dx}{x+1}\right]$

$= \frac{1}{4}[\ln|x-3| - \ln|x+1|]$

$= \frac{1}{4}\ln\left|\frac{x-3}{x+1}\right| + C$

This problem can also be solved by working backwards : differentiate each of the five given solutions to match the integrand $\frac{1}{(x+1)(x-3)}$.

13. (E)

The Mean Value Theorem concludes that

$g'(c) = \dfrac{g(b) - g(a)}{b - a}$ for some number c between b and a. Here, let $g(x) = xf(x)$, $a = 0$, and $b = 1$.

Then : $g'(x) = \dfrac{d}{dx}(x \cdot f(x))$

$= x \cdot \dfrac{d}{dx}(f(x)) + f(x)\dfrac{d}{dx}(x)$

$= x \cdot f'(x) + f(x)$

$g(a) = g(0) = 0 \cdot f(0) = 0$

$g(b) = g(1) = 1 \cdot f(1) = f(1)$

Thus : $g'(c) = c \cdot f'(c) + f(c)$

and $\dfrac{g(b) - g(a)}{b - a} = \dfrac{f(1) - 0}{1 - 0} = f(1)$

Substituting in $g'(c) = \dfrac{g(b) - g(a)}{b - a}$

yields : $c \cdot f'(c) + f(c) = f(1)$.

14. (E)

Series I is a multiple of the Harmonic Series $\sum \frac{1}{n}$ which diverges. Series II converges because it is geometric with common ratio $r = \frac{1}{5} < 1$.

Series III converges because it is alternating and the absolute values of its terms $\frac{1}{5}, \frac{1}{6}, \frac{1}{10}, \frac{1}{11}, \ldots$ tend to zero.

15. (C)

Let: $x = |OA|$

$y = |OB|$

$z = |AB|$

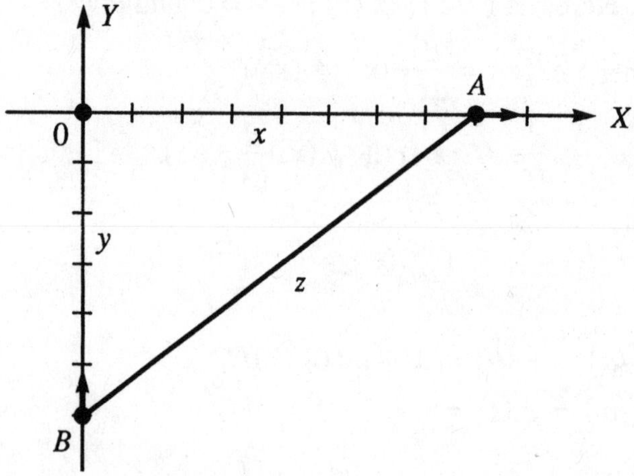

Then x, y, and z are functions of time t, and by the Pythagorean Theorem:

$$x^2 + y^2 = z^2$$

The rates of change of x, y, and z are their derivatives with respect to t:

$$\frac{dx}{dt} = 7$$

$$\frac{dy}{dt} = -2$$

$$\frac{dz}{dt} = ?$$

(Note that $\frac{dy}{dt}$ is negative because the distance $y = |OB|$ is decreasing). To find $\frac{dz}{dt}$, differentiate the Pythagorean equation with respect to t:

$$x^2 + y^2 = z^2$$

$$\frac{d}{dt}(x^2 + y^2) = \frac{d}{dt}(z^2)$$

$$2x \cdot \frac{dx}{dt} + 2y \cdot \frac{dy}{dt} = 2z \cdot \frac{dz}{dt}$$

Substitute :

$$2(8) \cdot (7) + 2(6)(-2) = 2z \cdot \frac{dz}{dt}$$

$$112 - 24 = 2z \frac{dz}{dt}$$

$$2z \frac{dz}{dt} = 88$$

$$z \cdot \frac{dz}{dt} = 44$$

Finally, when $x = 8$ and $y = 6$, $z = 10$ (since $x^2 + y^2 = z^2$). Thus :

$$10 \cdot \frac{dz}{dt} = 44$$

$$\frac{dz}{dt} = \frac{44}{10} = \frac{22}{5}$$

16. (B)

To show that the given statement is false, the function must contradict it. Thus, the function must be continuous for $0 \leq x < \infty$ but have no absolute maximum. By process of elimination :

(A) is not continuous at $x = 1$;

(C) has an absolute maximum (at $x = 0$) ;

(D) has an absolute maximum (at $x = 0$) ;

(E) is not continuous at $x = \frac{\pi}{2}$.

Only (B) is continuous on [0, ∞] and has no absolute maximum.

17. (A)

Use the Quotient Rule and the Chain rule :

$$f'(x) = \frac{d}{dx}\left(\frac{\ln(1+x^4)}{x}\right)$$

$$= \frac{x \cdot \frac{d}{dx}\left(\ln(1+x^4)\right) - \ln(1+x^4) \cdot \frac{d}{dx}(x)}{x^2}$$

$$= \frac{x \cdot \left(\frac{1}{1+x^4}\right)\frac{d}{dx}(1+x^4) - \ln(1+x^4) \cdot 1}{x^2}$$

$$= \frac{x \cdot \left(\frac{1}{1+x^4}\right) \cdot (4x^3) - \ln(1+x^4)}{x^2}$$

Substitute :

$$f'(1) = \frac{(1) \cdot \left(\frac{1}{1+(1)^4}\right)\left(4 \cdot (1)^3\right) - \ln\left(1+(1)^4\right)}{(1)^2}$$

$$= \frac{1 \cdot \left(\frac{1}{2}\right)(4) - \ln 2}{1}$$

$$= 2 - \ln 2 = 1.307$$

18. (D)

For $0 \le x \le \pi$:

$$\sin^2 x \le \sin x \le 2\sin x \le 1 + \sin x$$

so : $(E) \le (A) \le (C) \le (D)$

And $\int_0^{\pi} \sin 2x\, dx = 0$, $\int_0^{\pi} (1 + \sin x)dx = \pi + 2$

so (D) is the largest.

19. (D)

Apply the Chain Rule :

$$y = f(\sqrt{x})$$

$$\frac{dy}{dx} = \frac{d}{dx} f(\sqrt{x})$$

$$= f'(\sqrt{x}) \cdot \frac{d}{dx}(\sqrt{x})$$

$$= f'(\sqrt{x}) \cdot \frac{1}{2\sqrt{x}}$$

$$= \frac{1}{2}x^{-\frac{1}{2}} \cdot f'(\sqrt{x})$$

$$\frac{d^2y}{dx^2} = \frac{d}{dx}\left(\frac{dy}{dx}\right)$$

$$= \frac{d}{dx}\left(\frac{1}{2}x^{-\frac{1}{2}} \cdot f'(\sqrt{x})\right)$$

$$= \left(\frac{1}{2}x^{-\frac{1}{2}}\right) \cdot \frac{d}{dx} f'(\sqrt{x}) + f'(\sqrt{x}) \cdot \frac{d}{dx}\left(\frac{1}{2}x^{-\frac{1}{2}}\right)$$

$$= \frac{1}{2\sqrt{x}} \cdot f''(\sqrt{x}) \cdot \frac{d}{dx}\sqrt{x} + f'(\sqrt{x}) \cdot \left(-\frac{1}{4}x^{-\frac{3}{2}}\right)$$

$$= \frac{1}{2\sqrt{x}} f''(\sqrt{x})\left(\frac{1}{2\sqrt{x}}\right) + f'(\sqrt{x})\left(-\frac{1}{4\sqrt{x}^3}\right)$$

Substitute : $\left.\frac{d^2y}{dx^2}\right|_{x=4} = \frac{1}{2\sqrt{4}} f''(\sqrt{4}) \frac{1}{2\sqrt{4}}$

$$+ f'(\sqrt{4})\left(-\frac{1}{4\sqrt{4}^3}\right)$$

$$= \frac{1}{4} f''(2) \cdot \frac{1}{4} + f'(2)\left(-\frac{1}{32}\right)$$

$$= \frac{1}{16} f''(2) - \frac{1}{32} f'(2)$$

20. (C)

The first derivative is positive where the graph is increasing The second derivative is positive where the graph is concave upward (i.e. turning to the left). The only point marked where the graph is both increasing and concave upward is point C .

21. (C)

Integrate by parts :

Let : $u = x$

$dv = \cos 2x \ dx$

Then : $du = dx$

$v = \frac{1}{2}\sin 2x$

$$\int x \cos 2x \, dx = \int u \, dv$$

$$= uv - \int v \, du$$

$$= (x)\left(\frac{1}{2}\sin 2x\right) - \int\left(\frac{1}{2}\sin 2x\right)dx$$

$$= \frac{1}{2}x \sin 2x - \frac{1}{2}\int \sin 2x \, dx$$

$$= \frac{1}{2}x \sin 2x + \frac{1}{4}\cos 2x + C$$

Note : This problem can also be solved by working backwards : differentiate each of the five given solutions to match the integrand $x \cos 2x$.

22. (A)

$$f(x) = |\sin x| = \begin{cases} \sin x & \text{for } 0 \le x \le \pi \\ -\sin x & \text{for } \pi \le x \le 2\pi \end{cases}$$

so :

$$f'(x) = \begin{cases} \cos x & \text{for } 0 < x < \pi \\ -\cos x & \text{for } \pi < x < 2\pi \end{cases}$$

Only graph (A) agrees with this.

23. (B)

The actual ball within the ice is irrelevant to the problem; the solution would be the same if the entire sphere were solid ice.

The volume of the sphere is

$$V = \frac{4\pi}{3}r^3$$

Both the volume V and radius r are functions of time t. Their rates of change are their derivatives with respect to t. To relate these derivatives, differentiate the equation with respect to t :

$$V = \frac{4\pi}{3}r^3$$

$$\frac{d}{dt}(V) = \frac{d}{dt}\left(\frac{4\pi}{3}r^3\right)$$

$$\frac{dV}{dt} = 4\pi r^2 \cdot \frac{dr}{dt}$$

When the ice is 6 cm thick, the sphere has a radius of 64 cm + 6 cm = 70 cm.
Substitute 70 for r and -2 for $\frac{dV}{dt}$,

and solve for $\frac{dr}{dt}$:

$$\frac{dV}{dt} = 4\pi r^2 \cdot \frac{dr}{dt}$$

$$(-2) = 4\pi(70)^2 \cdot \frac{dr}{dt}$$

$$\frac{dr}{dt} = \frac{-2}{4\pi(70)^2}$$

$$= \frac{-1}{9800\,\pi}$$

The rate of change of the radius is $\frac{-1}{9800\,\pi}$, so the radius is decreasing at the rate $\frac{-1}{9800\,\pi}$ cm/min.
Since the steel ball is assumed to be unchanging, it follows

that the thickness of the ice must also be decreasing at

$\frac{1}{9800}$ cm/min. = 0.00003

24. (E)

Use the Chain Rule :

$$\frac{dy}{dx} = \frac{d}{dx} f(\sin x)$$

$$= f'(\sin x) \cdot \frac{d}{dx}(\sin x)$$

$$= f'(\sin x) \cdot \cos x$$

Substitute :

$$f'(\sin x) = (\sin x)\sqrt{1-(\sin x)^2}$$

$$= \sin x \sqrt{1-\sin^2 x}$$

$$= \sin x \sqrt{\cos^2 x}$$

$$= \sin x \,|\cos x|$$

$$= \sin x \cdot \cos x \quad \text{for } 0 \le x \le \frac{\pi}{2}$$

Thus :

$$\frac{dy}{dx} = f'(\sin x) \cdot \cos x$$

$$= (\sin x \cos x) \cdot \cos x$$

$$= \sin x \cos^2 x$$

25. (C)

(I) need not be true ; some continuous functions (like $|x|$) need not be differentiable. (II) need not be true, as the function $x^2 + 1$ shows. (III) is the Extreme Value Theorem.

26. (E)

The slope of the graph is given by the derivative :

$$\frac{dy}{dx} = 3x^2 + 6x + 5$$

The critical points of this function are those points where its first derivative is zero :

$$0 = \frac{d}{dx}(3x^2 + 6x + 5)$$

$$= 6x + 6$$

$$= x = -1$$

The second derivative of function $f(x) = 3x^2 + 6x + 5$

is $\frac{d^2f}{dx^2} = 6.$

$\frac{d^2f}{dx^2} > 0$ for any x. Thus above function achieves its

minimal value at $x = -1$.

Its minimal value is : $3(-1)^2 + 6(-1) + 5 = 2$

27. (A)

This is a direct calculator problem. For example, *fnInt* ((sin x cos $2x$)^2, x, 0, 2) can easily give the answer 0.715 .

28. (D)

The Mean Value Theorem is the most likely way to obtain an inequality relating a function and its derivative. Its conclusion is that

$$f'(c) = \frac{f(b) - f(a)}{b - a}$$

for some c between a and b. Whatever this c is, the given inequality may be applied with $x = c$:

$$0 < f'(c) < \frac{f(b) - f(a)}{2}$$

Substituting: $0 < \dfrac{f(b) - f(a)}{b - a} < \dfrac{f(b) - f(a)}{2}$

Since $f(b) - f(a) > 0$ and $b - a > 0$,

this yields: $\dfrac{1}{b - a} < \dfrac{1}{2}$

and: $2 < b - a$

so: $a + 2 < b$

29. (D)

Draw the graph of $f'(x)$.

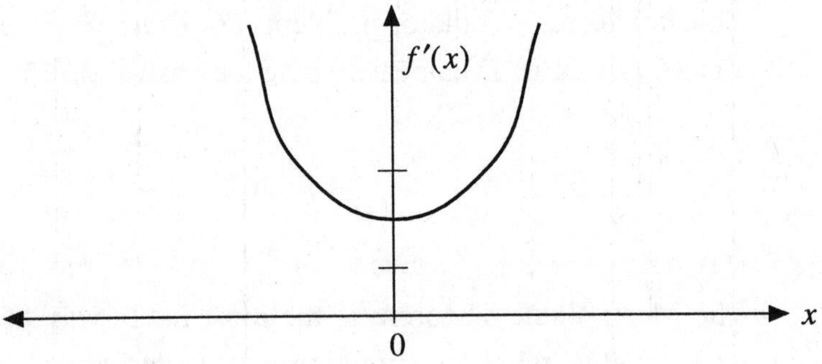

Obviously, a minimum exists at $x = 0$. By tracing on the graph to $x = 0$, you can find $f'_{\min}(x) = 2$.

30. (B)
The distance from a point P(x, y) to the origin (0, 0) is given by : $D = \sqrt{x^2 + y^2}$

This is minimal where $u = D^2 = x^2 + y^2$ is minimal. If P(x,y) is on the given line, then its coordinates x and y satisfy the equation $y = 2x + 7$. Substituting, we have:

$$u = x^2 + y^2$$
$$= x^2 + (2x + 7)^2$$

This function is minimal where its derivative is zero :

$$0 = \frac{du}{dx} = 2x + 2(2x + 7) \cdot 2$$
$$= 10x + 28$$

i.e. $x = -\frac{28}{10} = -\frac{14}{5}$

and $y = 2x + 7 = 2\left(-\frac{14}{5}\right) + 7 = \frac{7}{5}$

Here: $D = \sqrt{u} = \sqrt{x^2 + y^2}$

$$= \sqrt{\left(-\frac{14}{5}\right)^2 + \left(\frac{7}{5}\right)^2}$$

$$= \frac{7}{5}\sqrt{5}$$

31. (A)

Draw graphs of $s(t)$ and $s'(t)$.

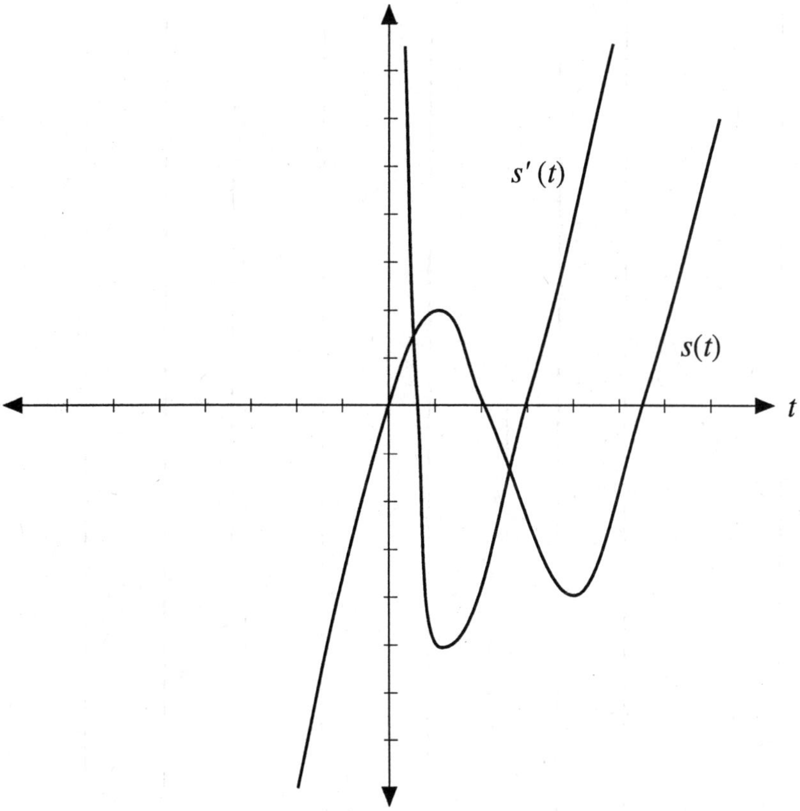

By tracing down the most negative $s'(t)$, you can get –5.4 at $t = 1.27$.

32. (B)

Let $y=\sqrt{1+x^2}$ and $u=\dfrac{x}{1+x^2}$

Then $\dfrac{dy}{dx}=\dfrac{d}{dx}\sqrt{1+x^2}=\dfrac{1}{2\sqrt{1+x^2}}\cdot\dfrac{d}{dx}\left(1+x^2\right)$

$$=\frac{1}{2\sqrt{1+x^2}}(2x)=\frac{x}{\sqrt{1+x^2}}$$

and $\dfrac{du}{dx}=\dfrac{d}{dx}\left(\dfrac{x}{1+x^2}\right)=\dfrac{\left(1+x^2\right)\cdot(1)-(x)(2x)}{\left(1+x^2\right)^2}$

$$=\frac{1+x^2-2x^2}{\left(1+x^2\right)^2}=\frac{1-x^2}{\left(1+x^2\right)^2}$$

Then $\dfrac{dy}{du}=\dfrac{dy/dx}{du/dx}$

$$=\frac{\left(\dfrac{x}{\sqrt{1+x^2}}\right)}{\left(\dfrac{1-x^2}{\left(1+x^2\right)^2}\right)}$$

$$=\frac{x}{1-x^2}\cdot\frac{\left(1+x^2\right)^2}{\sqrt{1+x}}$$

$$=\frac{x\cdot\left(1+x^2\right)^{\frac{3}{2}}}{1-x^2}$$

33. (B)

Use the calculator to solve the problem directly. For example,

fnInt (X^x, *x*, 0, 2), pressing ENTER gives 2.83 .

34. (A)

The definition of the integral is :

$$\int_a^b f(x)\,dx = \lim_{n\to\infty} \sum_{k=1}^{n} f(x_k)\Delta x$$

where the x_k may be chosen arbitrarily in the interval I_k :

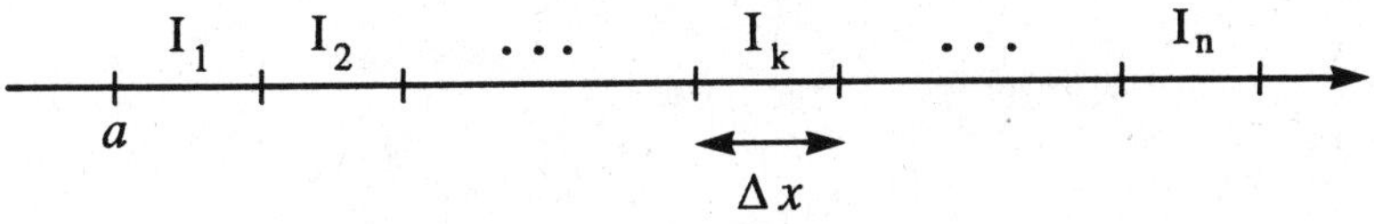

and $\Delta x = \dfrac{b-a}{n}$. This form fits the integral (A), where :

$a = 0$

$b = 1$

$$\Delta x = \frac{b-a}{n} = \frac{1-0}{n} = \frac{1}{n}$$

$$x_k = \frac{k}{n}$$

$$f(x) = \frac{1}{x^2}$$

$$f(x_k) = \frac{1}{\left(\frac{k}{n}\right)^2} = \left(\frac{n}{k}\right)^2$$

so :

$$\sum_{k=1}^{n} f(xu)\Delta x = \sum_{k=1}^{n} \left(\left(\frac{n}{k}\right)^2\right)\left(\frac{1}{n}\right) = \frac{1}{n}\sum_{k=1}^{n} \left(\frac{n}{k}\right)^2$$

$$= \frac{1}{n}\left[\left(\frac{n}{1}\right)^2 + \left(\frac{n}{2}\right)^2 + \ldots + \left(\frac{n}{n}\right)^2\right]$$

35. (C)

Draw graphs $f(x)$ and $f'(x)$.

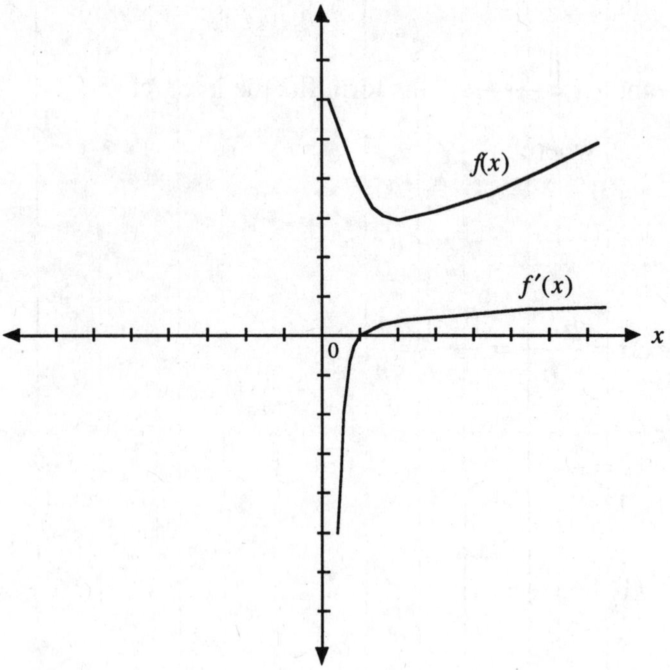

Resetting the viewing window to [0,2] · [–1,1], you can easily find that $c = 1$.

36. (E)

The point 0 is in the interval [–1,1] and the function $\frac{4}{x^2}$ is undefined at this point.

Also, $\int_0^2 \frac{4}{x^2} dx = \int_{-2}^0 \frac{4}{x^2} dx = -\frac{4}{x}\Big|_0^2 = +\infty$

thus, $\int_{-2}^2 \frac{4}{x^2} dx$ does not exist.

37. (A)

This is a first-order linear differential equation

$y' + p(x)y = q(x)$

where $p(x) = -1$

and $q(x) = -xe^{-x}$

Its general solution is

$$y = \frac{1}{u(x)}\left[\int u(x)q(x)dx + C\right]$$

where $u(x)$ is the integrating factor :

$$u(x) = \exp\int p(x)dx$$

$$= \exp\int(-1)\,dx$$

$$= e^{-x}$$

Thus :

$$y = \frac{1}{e^{-x}}\left[\int (e^{-x})(-xe^{x})\,dx + C\right]$$

$$= e^{x}\left[\int(-x)\,dx + C\right]$$

$$= e^{x}\left[\left(-\frac{1}{2}x^2\right) + C\right]$$

$$= \left(C - \frac{1}{2}x^2\right)e^{x}$$

Note : This problem can also be solved by working backwards : evaluate $\frac{dy}{dx} - y$ for each of the five given functions y to match $-xe^x$.

38. (A)

The expression obtains the indeterminant form $\infty - \infty$ as $n \to \infty$.

Use the identity

$$a - b = \frac{a^3 - b^3}{a^2 + ab + b^2}$$

with

$a = \sqrt[3]{n^3 + 5n^2}$

$b = n$

$$\sqrt[3]{n^3 + 5n^2} - n =$$

$$\frac{\left(\sqrt[3]{n^3 + 5n^2}\right)^3 - (n)^3}{\left(\sqrt[3]{n^3 + 5n^2}\right)^2 + \left(\sqrt[3]{n^3 + 5n^2}\right)(n) + (n)^2}$$

$$= \frac{(n^3 + 5n^2) - (n^3)}{\left(\sqrt[3]{(n+5)(n^2)}\right)^2 + \left(\sqrt[3]{(n+5)(n^2)}\right)n + n^2}$$

$$= \frac{5n^2}{\left(\sqrt[3]{n+5}\right)^2 (n^{4/3}) + \sqrt[3]{n+5}\,(n^{5/3}) + n^2}$$

$$= \frac{5n^{2/3}}{\left(\sqrt[3]{n+5}\right)^2 + \sqrt[3]{n+5}\,(n^{1/3}) + n^{2/3}}$$

Now take the limit as $n \to 0$:

$$\frac{5(0)^{2/3}}{(\sqrt[3]{0+5})^2 + \sqrt[3]{0+5}(0) + 0} = \frac{0}{(\sqrt[3]{5})^2 + 0 + 0}$$

$= 0$

39. (B)

The area of each semicircular cross-section is

$A_x = \frac{1}{2} = (\pi y^2 =) = \frac{\pi}{2} y^2$

where x is the point on the x - axis locating the cross-section and y is the radius of the cross-section :

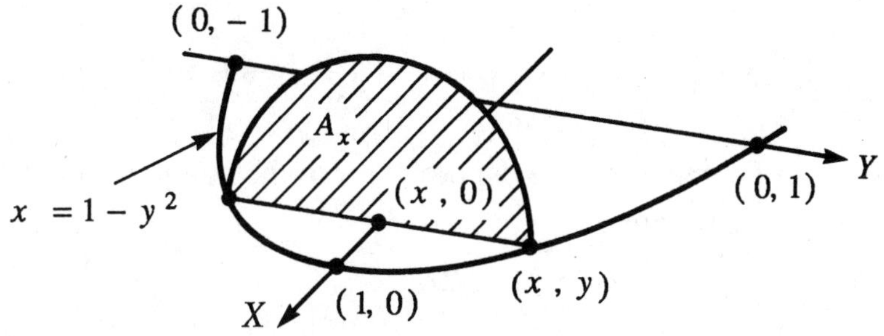

Then the total volume is

$$V = \int_0^1 A_x \, dx$$

$$= \int_0^1 \frac{\pi}{2} y^2 dx$$

$$= \int_0^1 \frac{\pi}{2} (1 - x) dx \text{ , since } y^2 = 1 - x$$

$$= \frac{\pi}{2} \left[x - \frac{1}{2} x^2 \right]_0^1$$

$$= \frac{\pi}{2}\left[\left((1) - \frac{1}{2}(1)^2\right) - \left((0) - \frac{1}{2}(0)^2\right)\right]$$

$$= \frac{\pi}{2}\left[\frac{1}{2}\right]$$

$$= \frac{\pi}{4}$$

40. (C)

If $x - 1 = \sin\theta$, (so $\theta = \arcsin(x - 1)$)
then $dx = \cos\theta\, d\theta$,
and $x = 1 \Rightarrow \sin\theta = x - 1 = 0 \Rightarrow \theta = 0$,

and $x = 2 \Rightarrow \sin\theta = x - 1 = 1 \Rightarrow \theta = \frac{\pi}{2}$.

To transform the denominator of the integrand, complete the square :

$x^2 - 2x = x^2 - 2x + 1 - 1$

$= (x - 1)^2 - 1$
$= (\sin\theta)^2 - 1$
$= (1 - \cos^2\theta) - 1$
$= -\cos^2\theta$

Then :

$$\int_1^2 \frac{dx}{x^2 - 2x} = \int_0^{\frac{\pi}{2}} \frac{\cos\theta\, d\theta}{-\cos^2\theta}$$

$$= -\int_0^{\frac{\pi}{2}} \frac{d\theta}{\cos\theta}$$

ADVANCED PLACEMENT CALCULUS BC EXAM VI

SECTION II

DETAILED EXPLANATIONS OF ANSWERS

1. (a)

The velocity is the antiderivative of the acceleration :

$v(t) = \int a(t)\,dt$

$= \int (6t - 8)\,dt$

$= 3t^2 - 8t + v_0$

Here $v_0 = v(0)$ is the initial velocity, which is given to be $v_0 = 5$.

Thus : $v(t) = 3t^2 - 8t + 5$

(b)

The particle moves to the right whenever $v(t) > 0$:

$3t^2 - 8t + 5 > 0$

Factor the quadratic :
$(3t - 5)(t - 1) > 0$
Either $3t - 5 > 0$ and $t - 1 > 0$, or $3t - 5 < 0$

and $t - 1 < 0$; i.e. either $t > \frac{5}{3}$ and $t > 1$,

or $t < \frac{5}{3}$ and $t < 1$.

Thus : either $t > \frac{5}{3}$ or $t < 1$.

(c)
The position is the antiderivative of the velocity :

$$x(t) = \int v(t)\,dt$$

$$= \int (3t^2 - 8t + 5)\,dt$$

$$= t^3 - 4t^2 + 5t + x_0$$

Here $x_0 = x(0)$ is the initial position, which is given to be $x_0 = -2$.
Thus :
$x(t) = t^3 - 4t^2 + 5t - 2$

(d)
The particle is at rest when its velocity is zero :
$v(t) = 0$
$(3t - 5)(t - 1) = 0$

$$t = \frac{5}{3}, 1$$

$$x\left(\frac{5}{3}\right) = \left(\frac{5}{3}\right)^3 - 4\left(\frac{5}{3}\right)^2 + 5\left(\frac{5}{3}\right) - 2 = -\frac{4}{27}$$

$$x(1) = (1)^3 - 4(1)^2 + 5(1) - 2 = 0$$

Thus the particle rests at $x = 0, -\frac{4}{27}$

2. (a)

$$f'(x) = \frac{d}{dx}(x^2 + 2x + 5)e^{-\frac{x}{2}}$$

$$= (x^2 + 2x + 5) \cdot \frac{d}{dx}\left(e^{-\frac{x}{2}}\right) + e^{\frac{-x}{2}}\frac{d}{dx}(x^2 + 2x + 5)$$

$$= (x^2 + 2x + 5) \cdot \left(e^{-\frac{x}{2}}\right) \cdot \left(-\frac{1}{2}\right) + \left(e^{-\frac{x}{2}}\right)(2x + 2)$$

$$= \left(-\frac{1}{2}x^2 - x - \frac{5}{2}\right)e^{-\frac{x}{2}} + (2x + 2)\, e^{-\frac{x}{2}}$$

$$= \left(-\frac{1}{2}x^2 + x - \frac{1}{2}\right)e^{-\frac{x}{2}}$$

Since this function exists for all x, the critical points are where $f'(x) = 0$:

$$\left(-\frac{1}{2}x^2 + x - \frac{1}{2}\right)e^{-\frac{x}{2}} = 0$$

$$-\frac{1}{2}x^2 + x - \frac{1}{2} = 0$$

$$x^2 - 2x + 1 = 0$$

$$(x - 1)^2 = 0$$

$$x = 1$$

$$y = f(x) = f(1) = \left((1)^2 + 2(1) + 5\right)e^{-\frac{1}{2}} = 8e^{-\frac{1}{2}}$$

Thus the only critical point is $\left(1, 8e^{-\frac{1}{2}}\right)$

(b)

$$f''(x) = \frac{d}{dx}f'(x)$$

$$= \frac{d}{dx}\left(-\frac{1}{2}x^2 + x - \frac{1}{2}\right) \cdot \left(e^{-\frac{x}{2}}\right)$$

$$= \left(-\frac{1}{2}x^2 + x - \frac{1}{2}\right) \cdot \frac{d}{dx}\left(e^{-\frac{x}{2}}\right) + e^{-\frac{x}{2}} \cdot$$

$$\frac{d}{dx}\left(-\frac{1}{2}x^2 + x - \frac{1}{2}\right)$$

$$= \left(-\frac{1}{2}x^2 + x - \frac{1}{2}\right)\left(e^{-\frac{x}{2}}\right)\left(-\frac{1}{2}\right) + \left(e^{-\frac{x}{2}}\right)(-x + 1)$$

$$= \left(\frac{1}{4}x^2 - \frac{1}{2}x + \frac{1}{4}\right)e^{-\frac{x}{2}} + (-x + 1)e^{-\frac{x}{2}}$$

$$= \left(\frac{1}{4}x^2 - \frac{3}{2}x + \frac{5}{4}\right)e^{-\frac{x}{2}}$$

The inflection points are where $f''(x) = 0$:

$$\left(\frac{1}{4}x^2 - \frac{3}{2}x + \frac{5}{4}\right)e^{-\frac{x}{2}} = 0$$

$$\frac{1}{4}x^2 - \frac{3}{2}x + \frac{5}{4} = 0$$

$$x^2 - 6x + 5 = 0$$

$$(x - 1)(x - 5) = 0$$

$$x = 1, 5$$

$$f(1) = 8e^{-\frac{1}{2}}$$

$$f(5) = \left((5)^2 + 2(5) + 5\right)e^{-\frac{5}{2}} = 40e^{-\frac{5}{2}}$$

Thus, the two inflection points are $\left(1, 8e^{-\frac{1}{2}}\right)$ and $\left(5, 40e^{-\frac{5}{2}}\right)$.

(c)

This analysis is best summarized by a table :

x	$f(x)$	$f'(x)$	$f''(x)$	conclusions
$x < 1$		$-$	$+$	decreasing c.c. up
$x = 1$	$8e^{-\frac{1}{2}}$	0	0	
$1 < x < 5$		$-$	$-$	decreasing c.c. down
$x = 5$	$40e^{-\frac{5}{2}}$	$-$	0	
$x > 5$		$-$	$+$	decreasing c.c. up

The signs of $f'(x)$ and $f''(x)$ are determined from the following factored forms :

$$f'(x) = -\frac{1}{2}(x-1)^2 e^{-\frac{x}{2}}$$

$$f''(x) = \frac{1}{4}(x-1)(x-5)e^{-\frac{x}{2}}$$

(d)

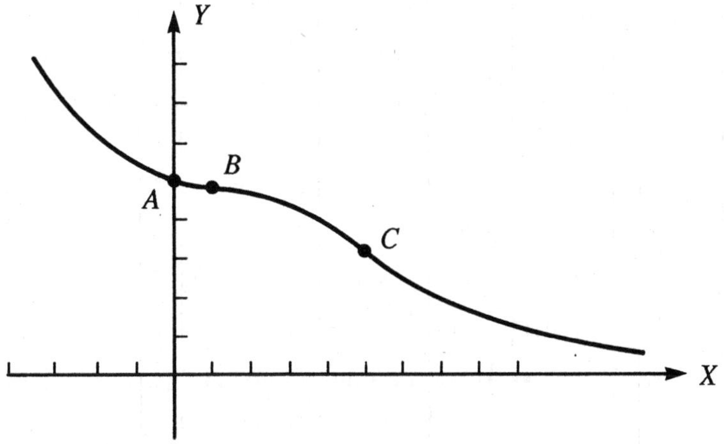

$(A) = (0, 5)$

$$(B) = \left(1, 8e^{-\frac{1}{2}}\right)$$

$$(C) = \left(5, 40e^{-\frac{5}{2}}\right)$$

The only intercept is A. The only critical point is B. The two inflection points are B and C.

3. (a) Use the calculator directly,

$der\,1\left(t\wedge 2e\wedge(3t\wedge 2+\sqrt{t}),\ x,\ 1\right)$ gives 464.1 .

(b) Draw the graph of y.

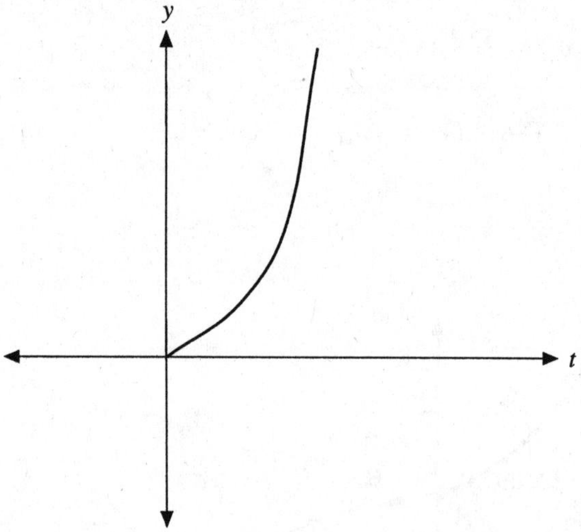

The lowest is obviously at $t = 0$; when $t = 0.001$, $y' = 0.002$. Thus, it can be seen from the graph as $t \to 0$, $y' \to 0$. So, the lowest rate is 0.

(c) Obviously, as $t \to \infty$, $y' \to \infty$.

4. (a)

Let $y = f(x)$ so that $x = f^{-1}(y)$; then

$$\int_c^d f^{-1}(y)\,dy = \int_c^d x\,dy.$$

Integrating by parts :

$$\int x\,dy = xy - \int y\,dx$$

$$= x\,f(x) - \int f(x)\,dx$$

so :

$$\int_c^d x\,dy = x\,f(x)\Big|_{y=c}^{y=d} - \int_{y=c}^{y=d} f(x)\,dx$$

$$= x\,f(x)\Big|_{x=a}^{x=b} - \int_{x=a}^{x=b} f(x)\,dx$$

$$= b\,f(b) - a\,f(a) - \int_a^b f(x)\,dx$$

$$= bd - ac - \int_a^b f(x)\,dx$$

(b)

If $f^{-1}(y)$ arctan, y then $f(x) = \tan x$.
Also $y = 0 \Rightarrow x = 0$ and

$y = 1 \Rightarrow x = \frac{\pi}{4}$.

Thus :

$$\int_0^1 \arctan y\,dy = \int_c^d f^{-1}(y)\,dy$$

$$= bd - ac - \int_a^c f(x)\,dx$$

$$= \left(\frac{\pi}{4}\right)(1) - (0)(0) - \int_0^{\frac{\pi}{4}} \tan x\,dx$$

$$= \frac{\pi}{4} + \ln|\sec x|\Big|_0^{\frac{\pi}{4}}$$

$$= \frac{\pi}{4} + \ln 2 - \ln 1$$

$$= \frac{\pi}{2} + \ln 2$$

5. (a)

$$a_n = \left(1 - \frac{x}{n}\right)^n$$

$$\lim_{n \to \infty} a_n = \lim_{n \to \infty}\left(1 - \frac{x}{n}\right)^n = e^{-x}$$

Since $e^{-x} > 0$ for all x, the series converges for no x (by the "Nth Term Test").

(b)

$$a_n = \frac{n^x}{\ln n}$$

$$x_{n+1} = \frac{(n+1)^x}{\ln(n+1)}$$

$$\frac{x_{n+1}}{a_n} = \frac{(n+1)^x}{n^x} \cdot \frac{\ln n}{\ln(n+1)} = \left(\frac{n+1}{n}\right)^x \frac{\ln n}{\ln(n+1)}$$

$$= \left(1 + \frac{1}{n}\right)^x \frac{\ln n}{\ln(n+1)}$$

By L' Hôpital's Rule,

$$\lim_{n \to \infty} \frac{\ln n}{\ln(n+1)} = \lim_{n \to \infty} \frac{\left(\frac{1}{n}\right)}{\left(\frac{1}{n+1}\right)}$$

$$= \lim_{n \to \infty} \frac{n+1}{n} = 1$$

Thus :

$$\lim_{n \to \infty} \frac{a_{n+1}}{a_n} = \lim_{n \to \infty} \left(1 + \frac{1}{n}\right)^x \cdot \lim_{n \to \infty} \frac{\ln n}{\ln(n+1)}$$

$$= e^x \cdot 1$$

$$= e^x$$

Thus, by the "Ratio Test", the series converges if

$e^x < 1$

i.e. $x < 0$

If $x = 0$, the series is $\sum_{n=2}^{\infty} \frac{1}{\ln}$, which diverges, because it dominates the harmonic series $\sum_{n=2}^{\infty} 1$ (since $\frac{1}{\ln n} > \frac{1}{n}$).

Thus, the given series converges for all $x < 0$.

(c)

$$a_n = \frac{1}{x^n + \sin n}$$

The series diverges for $|x| \le 1$ because, in this case, $\lim_{n \to \infty} a_n \neq 0$ $\lim_{n \to \infty} x^n = 0$ and $\lim_{n \to \infty} \sin n$ does not exist).

Assume $|x| > 1$. Then a_n is comparable to:

$$b_n = \frac{1}{x^n} = x^{-n}$$

Indeed :

$$\lim_{n \to \infty} \frac{b_n}{a_n} = \lim_{n \to \infty} \frac{x^n + \sin n}{x^n}$$

$$= \lim_{n \to \infty} \left(1 + \frac{\sin n}{x^n}\right)$$

$$= 1$$

(since $\lim_{n \to \infty} \frac{\sin n}{x^n} = 0$).

And the series $\sum_{n=1}^{\infty} b_n = \sum_{n=1}^{\infty} x^{-n}$ converges for $|x| > 1$

since it is geometric with ratio x^{-1}.

Thus, by the "Limit Comparison Test," $\sum_{n=1}^{\infty} a_n$

converges. Thus the given series converges for $|x| > 1$

i.e. if $x < -1$ or $x > 1$.

6. (a)

The rectangular graphs of f_1 and f_2 are :

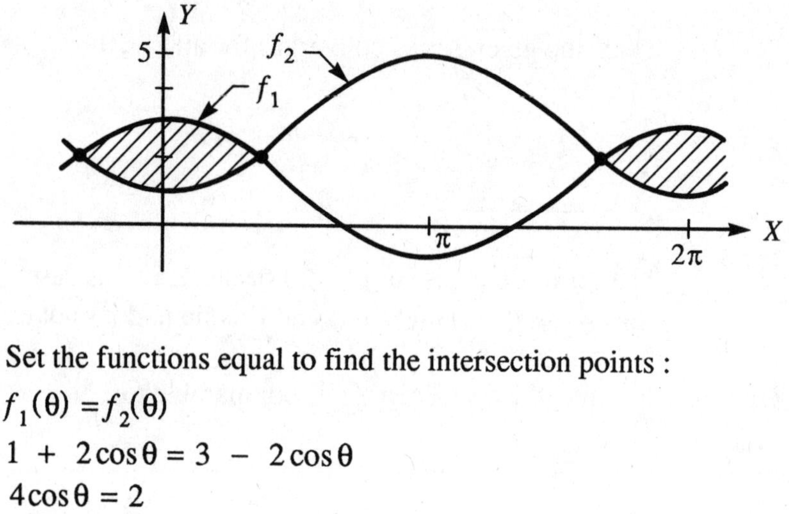

Set the functions equal to find the intersection points :

$f_1(\theta) = f_2(\theta)$

$1 + 2\cos\theta = 3 - 2\cos\theta$

$4\cos\theta = 2$

$\cos\theta = \frac{1}{2}$

$\theta = -\frac{\pi}{3}, \frac{\pi}{3}, \frac{5\pi}{3}, \ldots$

The intersection points are :

$A = \left(2, -\frac{\pi}{3}\right)$

$B = \left(2, \frac{\pi}{3}\right)$

(b)

The area formula for polar graphs is:

$$A = \frac{1}{2}\int_{\alpha}^{\beta} r^2 \, d\theta$$

By symmetry, the total area (shaded) is twice the area of the region where

$$0 \le \theta \le \frac{\pi}{3}.$$

Thus:

$$A = 2\left(\frac{1}{2}\int_0^{\frac{\pi}{3}}\left[f_1(\theta)^2 - f_2(\theta)^2\right]\right)d\theta$$

$$= \int_0^{\frac{\pi}{3}}\left[(1+2\cos\theta)^2 - (3-2\cos\theta)^2\right]d\theta$$

$$= \int_0^{\frac{\pi}{3}}\left[(1+4\cos\theta+4\cos^2\theta)-(9-12\cos\theta+4\cos^2\theta)\right]d\theta$$

$$= \int_0^{\frac{\pi}{3}}\left[-8+16\cos\theta\right]d\theta$$

$$= -8\theta + 16\sin\theta \Big|_0^{\frac{\pi}{3}}$$

$$= -8\left(\frac{\pi}{3}\right) + 16\left(\frac{\sqrt{3}}{2}\right)$$

$$= 8\sqrt{3} - \frac{8\pi}{3}$$

THE ADVANCED PLACEMENT EXAMINATION IN

CALCULUS BC

ANSWER SHEETS

ADVANCED PLACEMENT EXAMINATION

CALCULUS BC

ANSWER SHEET
TEST 1

1.	(A)	(B)	(C)	(D)	(E)	21.	(A)	(B)	(C)	(D)	(E)
2.	(A)	(B)	(C)	(D)	(E)	22.	(A)	(B)	(C)	(D)	(E)
3.	(A)	(B)	(C)	(D)	(E)	23.	(A)	(B)	(C)	(D)	(E)
4.	(A)	(B)	(C)	(D)	(E)	24.	(A)	(B)	(C)	(D)	(E)
5.	(A)	(B)	(C)	(D)	(E)	25.	(A)	(B)	(C)	(D)	(E)
6.	(A)	(B)	(C)	(D)	(E)	26.	(A)	(B)	(C)	(D)	(E)
7.	(A)	(B)	(C)	(D)	(E)	27.	(A)	(B)	(C)	(D)	(E)
8.	(A)	(B)	(C)	(D)	(E)	28.	(A)	(B)	(C)	(D)	(E)
9.	(A)	(B)	(C)	(D)	(E)	29.	(A)	(B)	(C)	(D)	(E)
10.	(A)	(B)	(C)	(D)	(E)	30.	(A)	(B)	(C)	(D)	(E)
11.	(A)	(B)	(C)	(D)	(E)	31.	(A)	(B)	(C)	(D)	(E)
12.	(A)	(B)	(C)	(D)	(E)	32.	(A)	(B)	(C)	(D)	(E)
13.	(A)	(B)	(C)	(D)	(E)	33.	(A)	(B)	(C)	(D)	(E)
14.	(A)	(B)	(C)	(D)	(E)	34.	(A)	(B)	(C)	(D)	(E)
15.	(A)	(B)	(C)	(D)	(E)	35.	(A)	(B)	(C)	(D)	(E)
16.	(A)	(B)	(C)	(D)	(E)	36.	(A)	(B)	(C)	(D)	(E)
17.	(A)	(B)	(C)	(D)	(E)	37.	(A)	(B)	(C)	(D)	(E)
18.	(A)	(B)	(C)	(D)	(E)	38.	(A)	(B)	(C)	(D)	(E)
19.	(A)	(B)	(C)	(D)	(E)	39.	(A)	(B)	(C)	(D)	(E)
20.	(A)	(B)	(C)	(D)	(E)	40.	(A)	(B)	(C)	(D)	(E)

ADVANCED PLACEMENT EXAMINATION

CALCULUS BC

ANSWER SHEET
TEST 2

1.	(A)	(B)	(C)	(D)	(E)	21.	(A)	(B)	(C)	(D)	(E)
2.	(A)	(B)	(C)	(D)	(E)	22.	(A)	(B)	(C)	(D)	(E)
3.	(A)	(B)	(C)	(D)	(E)	23.	(A)	(B)	(C)	(D)	(E)
4.	(A)	(B)	(C)	(D)	(E)	24.	(A)	(B)	(C)	(D)	(E)
5.	(A)	(B)	(C)	(D)	(E)	25.	(A)	(B)	(C)	(D)	(E)
6.	(A)	(B)	(C)	(D)	(E)	26.	(A)	(B)	(C)	(D)	(E)
7.	(A)	(B)	(C)	(D)	(E)	27.	(A)	(B)	(C)	(D)	(E)
8.	(A)	(B)	(C)	(D)	(E)	28.	(A)	(B)	(C)	(D)	(E)
9.	(A)	(B)	(C)	(D)	(E)	29.	(A)	(B)	(C)	(D)	(E)
10.	(A)	(B)	(C)	(D)	(E)	30.	(A)	(B)	(C)	(D)	(E)
11.	(A)	(B)	(C)	(D)	(E)	31.	(A)	(B)	(C)	(D)	(E)
12.	(A)	(B)	(C)	(D)	(E)	32.	(A)	(B)	(C)	(D)	(E)
13.	(A)	(B)	(C)	(D)	(E)	33.	(A)	(B)	(C)	(D)	(E)
14.	(A)	(B)	(C)	(D)	(E)	34.	(A)	(B)	(C)	(D)	(E)
15.	(A)	(B)	(C)	(D)	(E)	35.	(A)	(B)	(C)	(D)	(E)
16.	(A)	(B)	(C)	(D)	(E)	36.	(A)	(B)	(C)	(D)	(E)
17.	(A)	(B)	(C)	(D)	(E)	37.	(A)	(B)	(C)	(D)	(E)
18.	(A)	(B)	(C)	(D)	(E)	38.	(A)	(B)	(C)	(D)	(E)
19.	(A)	(B)	(C)	(D)	(E)	39.	(A)	(B)	(C)	(D)	(E)
20.	(A)	(B)	(C)	(D)	(E)	40.	(A)	(B)	(C)	(D)	(E)

ADVANCED PLACEMENT EXAMINATION

CALCULUS BC

ANSWER SHEET
TEST 3

1.	(A)	(B)	(C)	(D)	(E)	21.	(A)	(B)	(C)	(D)	(E)
2.	(A)	(B)	(C)	(D)	(E)	22.	(A)	(B)	(C)	(D)	(E)
3.	(A)	(B)	(C)	(D)	(E)	23.	(A)	(B)	(C)	(D)	(E)
4.	(A)	(B)	(C)	(D)	(E)	24.	(A)	(B)	(C)	(D)	(E)
5.	(A)	(B)	(C)	(D)	(E)	25.	(A)	(B)	(C)	(D)	(E)
6.	(A)	(B)	(C)	(D)	(E)	26.	(A)	(B)	(C)	(D)	(E)
7.	(A)	(B)	(C)	(D)	(E)	27.	(A)	(B)	(C)	(D)	(E)
8.	(A)	(B)	(C)	(D)	(E)	28.	(A)	(B)	(C)	(D)	(E)
9.	(A)	(B)	(C)	(D)	(E)	29.	(A)	(B)	(C)	(D)	(E)
10.	(A)	(B)	(C)	(D)	(E)	30.	(A)	(B)	(C)	(D)	(E)
11.	(A)	(B)	(C)	(D)	(E)	31.	(A)	(B)	(C)	(D)	(E)
12.	(A)	(B)	(C)	(D)	(E)	32.	(A)	(B)	(C)	(D)	(E)
13.	(A)	(B)	(C)	(D)	(E)	33.	(A)	(B)	(C)	(D)	(E)
14.	(A)	(B)	(C)	(D)	(E)	34.	(A)	(B)	(C)	(D)	(E)
15.	(A)	(B)	(C)	(D)	(E)	35.	(A)	(B)	(C)	(D)	(E)
16.	(A)	(B)	(C)	(D)	(E)	36.	(A)	(B)	(C)	(D)	(E)
17.	(A)	(B)	(C)	(D)	(E)	37.	(A)	(B)	(C)	(D)	(E)
18.	(A)	(B)	(C)	(D)	(E)	38.	(A)	(B)	(C)	(D)	(E)
19.	(A)	(B)	(C)	(D)	(E)	39.	(A)	(B)	(C)	(D)	(E)
20.	(A)	(B)	(C)	(D)	(E)	40.	(A)	(B)	(C)	(D)	(E)

ADVANCED PLACEMENT EXAMINATION

CALCULUS BC

ANSWER SHEET
TEST 4

1.	Ⓐ	Ⓑ	Ⓒ	Ⓓ	Ⓔ
2.	Ⓐ	Ⓑ	Ⓒ	Ⓓ	Ⓔ
3.	Ⓐ	Ⓑ	Ⓒ	Ⓓ	Ⓔ
4.	Ⓐ	Ⓑ	Ⓒ	Ⓓ	Ⓔ
5.	Ⓐ	Ⓑ	Ⓒ	Ⓓ	Ⓔ
6.	Ⓐ	Ⓑ	Ⓒ	Ⓓ	Ⓔ
7.	Ⓐ	Ⓑ	Ⓒ	Ⓓ	Ⓔ
8.	Ⓐ	Ⓑ	Ⓒ	Ⓓ	Ⓔ
9.	Ⓐ	Ⓑ	Ⓒ	Ⓓ	Ⓔ
10.	Ⓐ	Ⓑ	Ⓒ	Ⓓ	Ⓔ
11.	Ⓐ	Ⓑ	Ⓒ	Ⓓ	Ⓔ
12.	Ⓐ	Ⓑ	Ⓒ	Ⓓ	Ⓔ
13.	Ⓐ	Ⓑ	Ⓒ	Ⓓ	Ⓔ
14.	Ⓐ	Ⓑ	Ⓒ	Ⓓ	Ⓔ
15.	Ⓐ	Ⓑ	Ⓒ	Ⓓ	Ⓔ
16.	Ⓐ	Ⓑ	Ⓒ	Ⓓ	Ⓔ
17.	Ⓐ	Ⓑ	Ⓒ	Ⓓ	Ⓔ
18.	Ⓐ	Ⓑ	Ⓒ	Ⓓ	Ⓔ
19.	Ⓐ	Ⓑ	Ⓒ	Ⓓ	Ⓔ
20.	Ⓐ	Ⓑ	Ⓒ	Ⓓ	Ⓔ
21.	Ⓐ	Ⓑ	Ⓒ	Ⓓ	Ⓔ
22.	Ⓐ	Ⓑ	Ⓒ	Ⓓ	Ⓔ
23.	Ⓐ	Ⓑ	Ⓒ	Ⓓ	Ⓔ
24.	Ⓐ	Ⓑ	Ⓒ	Ⓓ	Ⓔ
25.	Ⓐ	Ⓑ	Ⓒ	Ⓓ	Ⓔ
26.	Ⓐ	Ⓑ	Ⓒ	Ⓓ	Ⓔ
27.	Ⓐ	Ⓑ	Ⓒ	Ⓓ	Ⓔ
28.	Ⓐ	Ⓑ	Ⓒ	Ⓓ	Ⓔ
29.	Ⓐ	Ⓑ	Ⓒ	Ⓓ	Ⓔ
30.	Ⓐ	Ⓑ	Ⓒ	Ⓓ	Ⓔ
31.	Ⓐ	Ⓑ	Ⓒ	Ⓓ	Ⓔ
32.	Ⓐ	Ⓑ	Ⓒ	Ⓓ	Ⓔ
33.	Ⓐ	Ⓑ	Ⓒ	Ⓓ	Ⓔ
34.	Ⓐ	Ⓑ	Ⓒ	Ⓓ	Ⓔ
35.	Ⓐ	Ⓑ	Ⓒ	Ⓓ	Ⓔ
36.	Ⓐ	Ⓑ	Ⓒ	Ⓓ	Ⓔ
37.	Ⓐ	Ⓑ	Ⓒ	Ⓓ	Ⓔ
38.	Ⓐ	Ⓑ	Ⓒ	Ⓓ	Ⓔ
39.	Ⓐ	Ⓑ	Ⓒ	Ⓓ	Ⓔ
40.	Ⓐ	Ⓑ	Ⓒ	Ⓓ	Ⓔ

ADVANCED PLACEMENT EXAMINATION

CALCULUS BC

ANSWER SHEET

TEST 5

1.	(A)	(B)	(C)	(D)	(E)	21.	(A)	(B)	(C)	(D)	(E)
2.	(A)	(B)	(C)	(D)	(E)	22.	(A)	(B)	(C)	(D)	(E)
3.	(A)	(B)	(C)	(D)	(E)	23.	(A)	(B)	(C)	(D)	(E)
4.	(A)	(B)	(C)	(D)	(E)	24.	(A)	(B)	(C)	(D)	(E)
5.	(A)	(B)	(C)	(D)	(E)	25.	(A)	(B)	(C)	(D)	(E)
6.	(A)	(B)	(C)	(D)	(E)	26.	(A)	(B)	(C)	(D)	(E)
7.	(A)	(B)	(C)	(D)	(E)	27.	(A)	(B)	(C)	(D)	(E)
8.	(A)	(B)	(C)	(D)	(E)	28.	(A)	(B)	(C)	(D)	(E)
9.	(A)	(B)	(C)	(D)	(E)	29.	(A)	(B)	(C)	(D)	(E)
10.	(A)	(B)	(C)	(D)	(E)	30.	(A)	(B)	(C)	(D)	(E)
11.	(A)	(B)	(C)	(D)	(E)	31.	(A)	(B)	(C)	(D)	(E)
12.	(A)	(B)	(C)	(D)	(E)	32.	(A)	(B)	(C)	(D)	(E)
13.	(A)	(B)	(C)	(D)	(E)	33.	(A)	(B)	(C)	(D)	(E)
14.	(A)	(B)	(C)	(D)	(E)	34.	(A)	(B)	(C)	(D)	(E)
15.	(A)	(B)	(C)	(D)	(E)	35.	(A)	(B)	(C)	(D)	(E)
16.	(A)	(B)	(C)	(D)	(E)	36.	(A)	(B)	(C)	(D)	(E)
17.	(A)	(B)	(C)	(D)	(E)	37.	(A)	(B)	(C)	(D)	(E)
18.	(A)	(B)	(C)	(D)	(E)	38.	(A)	(B)	(C)	(D)	(E)
19.	(A)	(B)	(C)	(D)	(E)	39.	(A)	(B)	(C)	(D)	(E)
20.	(A)	(B)	(C)	(D)	(E)	40.	(A)	(B)	(C)	(D)	(E)

ADVANCED PLACEMENT EXAMINATION

CALCULUS BC

ANSWER SHEET
TEST 6

1.	(A)	(B)	(C)	(D)	(E)	21.	(A)	(B)	(C)	(D)	(E)
2.	(A)	(B)	(C)	(D)	(E)	22.	(A)	(B)	(C)	(D)	(E)
3.	(A)	(B)	(C)	(D)	(E)	23.	(A)	(B)	(C)	(D)	(E)
4.	(A)	(B)	(C)	(D)	(E)	24.	(A)	(B)	(C)	(D)	(E)
5.	(A)	(B)	(C)	(D)	(E)	25.	(A)	(B)	(C)	(D)	(E)
6.	(A)	(B)	(C)	(D)	(E)	26.	(A)	(B)	(C)	(D)	(E)
7.	(A)	(B)	(C)	(D)	(E)	27.	(A)	(B)	(C)	(D)	(E)
8.	(A)	(B)	(C)	(D)	(E)	28.	(A)	(B)	(C)	(D)	(E)
9.	(A)	(B)	(C)	(D)	(E)	29.	(A)	(B)	(C)	(D)	(E)
10.	(A)	(B)	(C)	(D)	(E)	30.	(A)	(B)	(C)	(D)	(E)
11.	(A)	(B)	(C)	(D)	(E)	31.	(A)	(B)	(C)	(D)	(E)
12.	(A)	(B)	(C)	(D)	(E)	32.	(A)	(B)	(C)	(D)	(E)
13.	(A)	(B)	(C)	(D)	(E)	33.	(A)	(B)	(C)	(D)	(E)
14.	(A)	(B)	(C)	(D)	(E)	34.	(A)	(B)	(C)	(D)	(E)
15.	(A)	(B)	(C)	(D)	(E)	35.	(A)	(B)	(C)	(D)	(E)
16.	(A)	(B)	(C)	(D)	(E)	36.	(A)	(B)	(C)	(D)	(E)
17.	(A)	(B)	(C)	(D)	(E)	37.	(A)	(B)	(C)	(D)	(E)
18.	(A)	(B)	(C)	(D)	(E)	38.	(A)	(B)	(C)	(D)	(E)
19.	(A)	(B)	(C)	(D)	(E)	39.	(A)	(B)	(C)	(D)	(E)
20.	(A)	(B)	(C)	(D)	(E)	40.	(A)	(B)	(C)	(D)	(E)

ADVANCED PLACEMENT EXAMINATION

CALCULUS BC

ANSWER SHEET
TEST __

1.	Ⓐ	Ⓑ	Ⓒ	Ⓓ	Ⓔ	21.	Ⓐ	Ⓑ	Ⓒ	Ⓓ	Ⓔ
2.	Ⓐ	Ⓑ	Ⓒ	Ⓓ	Ⓔ	22.	Ⓐ	Ⓑ	Ⓒ	Ⓓ	Ⓔ
3.	Ⓐ	Ⓑ	Ⓒ	Ⓓ	Ⓔ	23.	Ⓐ	Ⓑ	Ⓒ	Ⓓ	Ⓔ
4.	Ⓐ	Ⓑ	Ⓒ	Ⓓ	Ⓔ	24.	Ⓐ	Ⓑ	Ⓒ	Ⓓ	Ⓔ
5.	Ⓐ	Ⓑ	Ⓒ	Ⓓ	Ⓔ	25.	Ⓐ	Ⓑ	Ⓒ	Ⓓ	Ⓔ
6.	Ⓐ	Ⓑ	Ⓒ	Ⓓ	Ⓔ	26.	Ⓐ	Ⓑ	Ⓒ	Ⓓ	Ⓔ
7.	Ⓐ	Ⓑ	Ⓒ	Ⓓ	Ⓔ	27.	Ⓐ	Ⓑ	Ⓒ	Ⓓ	Ⓔ
8.	Ⓐ	Ⓑ	Ⓒ	Ⓓ	Ⓔ	28.	Ⓐ	Ⓑ	Ⓒ	Ⓓ	Ⓔ
9.	Ⓐ	Ⓑ	Ⓒ	Ⓓ	Ⓔ	29.	Ⓐ	Ⓑ	Ⓒ	Ⓓ	Ⓔ
10.	Ⓐ	Ⓑ	Ⓒ	Ⓓ	Ⓔ	30.	Ⓐ	Ⓑ	Ⓒ	Ⓓ	Ⓔ
11.	Ⓐ	Ⓑ	Ⓒ	Ⓓ	Ⓔ	31.	Ⓐ	Ⓑ	Ⓒ	Ⓓ	Ⓔ
12.	Ⓐ	Ⓑ	Ⓒ	Ⓓ	Ⓔ	32.	Ⓐ	Ⓑ	Ⓒ	Ⓓ	Ⓔ
13.	Ⓐ	Ⓑ	Ⓒ	Ⓓ	Ⓔ	33.	Ⓐ	Ⓑ	Ⓒ	Ⓓ	Ⓔ
14.	Ⓐ	Ⓑ	Ⓒ	Ⓓ	Ⓔ	34.	Ⓐ	Ⓑ	Ⓒ	Ⓓ	Ⓔ
15.	Ⓐ	Ⓑ	Ⓒ	Ⓓ	Ⓔ	35.	Ⓐ	Ⓑ	Ⓒ	Ⓓ	Ⓔ
16.	Ⓐ	Ⓑ	Ⓒ	Ⓓ	Ⓔ	36.	Ⓐ	Ⓑ	Ⓒ	Ⓓ	Ⓔ
17.	Ⓐ	Ⓑ	Ⓒ	Ⓓ	Ⓔ	37.	Ⓐ	Ⓑ	Ⓒ	Ⓓ	Ⓔ
18.	Ⓐ	Ⓑ	Ⓒ	Ⓓ	Ⓔ	38.	Ⓐ	Ⓑ	Ⓒ	Ⓓ	Ⓔ
19.	Ⓐ	Ⓑ	Ⓒ	Ⓓ	Ⓔ	39.	Ⓐ	Ⓑ	Ⓒ	Ⓓ	Ⓔ
20.	Ⓐ	Ⓑ	Ⓒ	Ⓓ	Ⓔ	40.	Ⓐ	Ⓑ	Ⓒ	Ⓓ	Ⓔ

ADVANCED PLACEMENT EXAMINATION

CALCULUS BC

ANSWER SHEET
TEST ___

1.	(A)	(B)	(C)	(D)	(E)
2.	(A)	(B)	(C)	(D)	(E)
3.	(A)	(B)	(C)	(D)	(E)
4.	(A)	(B)	(C)	(D)	(E)
5.	(A)	(B)	(C)	(D)	(E)
6.	(A)	(B)	(C)	(D)	(E)
7.	(A)	(B)	(C)	(D)	(E)
8.	(A)	(B)	(C)	(D)	(E)
9.	(A)	(B)	(C)	(D)	(E)
10.	(A)	(B)	(C)	(D)	(E)
11.	(A)	(B)	(C)	(D)	(E)
12.	(A)	(B)	(C)	(D)	(E)
13.	(A)	(B)	(C)	(D)	(E)
14.	(A)	(B)	(C)	(D)	(E)
15.	(A)	(B)	(C)	(D)	(E)
16.	(A)	(B)	(C)	(D)	(E)
17.	(A)	(B)	(C)	(D)	(E)
18.	(A)	(B)	(C)	(D)	(E)
19.	(A)	(B)	(C)	(D)	(E)
20.	(A)	(B)	(C)	(D)	(E)
21.	(A)	(B)	(C)	(D)	(E)
22.	(A)	(B)	(C)	(D)	(E)
23.	(A)	(B)	(C)	(D)	(E)
24.	(A)	(B)	(C)	(D)	(E)
25.	(A)	(B)	(C)	(D)	(E)
26.	(A)	(B)	(C)	(D)	(E)
27.	(A)	(B)	(C)	(D)	(E)
28.	(A)	(B)	(C)	(D)	(E)
29.	(A)	(B)	(C)	(D)	(E)
30.	(A)	(B)	(C)	(D)	(E)
31.	(A)	(B)	(C)	(D)	(E)
32.	(A)	(B)	(C)	(D)	(E)
33.	(A)	(B)	(C)	(D)	(E)
34.	(A)	(B)	(C)	(D)	(E)
35.	(A)	(B)	(C)	(D)	(E)
36.	(A)	(B)	(C)	(D)	(E)
37.	(A)	(B)	(C)	(D)	(E)
38.	(A)	(B)	(C)	(D)	(E)
39.	(A)	(B)	(C)	(D)	(E)
40.	(A)	(B)	(C)	(D)	(E)

ABOUT RESEARCH & EDUCATION ASSOCIATION

Founded in 1959, Research & Education Association (REA) is dedicated to publishing the finest and most effective educational materials—including software, study guides, and test preps—for students in middle school, high school, college, graduate school, and beyond.

REA's test preparation series includes books and software for all academic levels in almost all disciplines. REA publishes test preps for students who have not yet entered high school, as well as high school students preparing to enter college. Students from countries around the world seeking to attend college in the United States will find the assistance they need in REA's publications. For college students seeking advanced degrees, REA publishes test preps for many major graduate school admission examinations in a wide variety of disciplines, including engineering, law, and medicine. Students at every level, in every field, with every ambition can find what they are looking for among REA's publications.

REA's series presents tests that accurately depict the official exams in both degree of difficulty and types of questions. REA's practice tests are always based upon the most recently administered exams, and include every type of question that can be expected on the actual exams.

REA's publications and educational materials are highly regarded and continually receive an unprecedented amount of praise from professionals, instructors, librarians, parents, and students. Our authors are as diverse as the subject matter represented in the books we publish. They are well known in their respective disciplines and serve on the faculties of prestigious colleges and universities throughout the United States and Canada.

We invite you to visit us at *www.rea.com* to find out how "REA is making the world smarter."

ACKNOWLEDGMENTS

In addition to our authors, we would like to thank Larry B. Kling, Vice President, Editorial, for supervising production of this revised edition; Pam Weston, Vice President, Publishing, for setting the quality standards for production integrity and managing the publication to completion; and Anne Winthrop Esposito, Senior Editor, for coordinating revisions.

(more on back page)

REA's Test Prep Books Are The Best!

(a sample of the hundreds of letters REA receives each year)

"I am writing to congratulate you on preparing an exceptional study guide. In five years of teaching this course I have never encountered a more thorough, comprehensive, concise and realistic preparation for this examination."
Teacher, Davie, FL

"I have found your publications, *The Best Test Preparation...*, to be exactly that."
Teacher, Aptos, CA

"I used your *CLEP Introductory Sociology* book and rank it 99% — thank you!"
Student, Jerusalem, Israel

"Your *GMAT* book greatly helped me on the test. Thank you."
Student, Oxford, OH

"I recently got the French *SAT II* Exam book from REA. I congratulate you on first-rate French practice tests."
Instructor, Los Angeles, CA

"Your *AP English Literature and Composition* book is most impressive."
Student, Montgomery, AL

"The REA *LSAT* Test Preparation guide is a winner!"
Instructor, Spartanburg, SC

(more on previous page)